TREASURE HUNTER'S DIGEST

By Jack Lewis

Digest Books, Inc., Northfield, Illinois

EDITORIAL DIRECTOR
Bob Springer

ASSOCIATE EDITOR
Mark Thiffault

PHOTO EDITOR
Chuck Tyler

ART DIRECTOR
Michele Barber

PRODUCTION COORDINATOR
Wendy Lee Wisehart

PRODUCTION ASSISTANTS
Diane E. Bir
Mary Sams

ASSOCIATE PUBLISHER
Sheldon Factor

ISBN 0-695-80523-1   Library of Congress Catalog Card No. 74-25253

contents

about the author

JACK LEWIS, first editor of TREASURE Magazine — one of the oldest in the field — and editor and publisher of GUN WORLD Magazine for nearly sixteen years, has pursued a wide and varied career, ranging from ranch hand and farm worker to Hollywood stuntman. He temporarily deserted the last calling after suffering a broken back; the author of a number of novels, many of them dealing with the Marine Corps, he has been laborer, pea picker, structural steel worker, newspaper reporter, private detective, process server, horse wrangler and screen and television writer.

A veteran of World War II and Korean actions, he is a major in the Marine Corps Reserve and was on active duty in 1970 to pursue a special study in Vietnam. He also is publisher of BOW & ARROW and HORSE and HORSEMAN Magazines.

Chapter 1

WHAT IS TREASURE?

THERE ARE COUNTLESS treasures across the world and equally numberless ways of hunting them. For the neophyte who never has hunted treasure, this — a world all its own — may seem romantic and the source of endless wealth. Most of us have been brought up on tales of the Lost Loot of Lima, the Oak Island treasure and a host of other legends having to do with fabulous caches of gold and jewels that could make even a Rockefeller raise an eyebrow.

But for the average individual, many of these treasures are beyond their financial means when it comes to searching far from home. However, there are profitable treasures that can be located almost in the backyard of your home. Knowing what to look for and where to look are the two prime requisites.

The first thing the beginner, no matter what he seeks, should learn is patience and to move slowly. There are plenty of legends — some of them even true — concerning the fabled riches of the lone bachelor miser who lived at the edge of town; the train robbers who were caught and killed, but not until they hid their ill-gained loot and even the

stories of sunken wrecks on the bottom of not only oceans, but lakes and rivers. The last might produce artifacts worth money to collectors even if there is no money aboard.

Bill Mahan, one of the best known treasure hunters in the business, takes many of these legends with more than the normal amount of salt. He suggests caution, when you run into such tales.

"I have known of the teller stating that he could go right to the spot, but he did not have the time to go pick up the million dollars and could not afford the cost of getting there and taking the time to dig it up," he says.

Such characters often are found around bars and similar establishments; usually they are looking for transportation loot to get them to the site of the treasure. If you'll foot the bill, they'll split with you. Actually, they simply split, themselves never to be seen on the local premises again.

There are almost as many con games as there are treasures, some of them showing newness and imagination, others being old hat but still successful when perpetrated upon the unknowing. One of the greatest tools of the con

While there are still fabulous treasures to be found, most are more modest than this version at Disneyland's famed Treasure Room.

Basically, It Is Anything You Find That Is Worth Money And The Possibilities Are Endless!

man is human greed and there are those, normally cautious in their day-to-day dealings, who tend to get carried away when promised riches beyond their normal range of dreams.

Today's West still is scattered with old mining camps and ghost towns, but with the increased interest in treasure hunting in recent years, most of these have been picked over to a great degree. However, there still are treasures to be found, when one knows what it is he is seeking and thinks of unlikely areas in which to find it.

For example, one treasure hunter, Bill Luther of Inglewood, California, all but made a career of digging old outhouse pits in ghost towns of his home state. After fifty

or more years, the contents of human excrement had become as much a part of the soil as the rest of the area, making it an easy and not unpleasant task. But out of the areas beneath the old two-holers, Luther took countless old firearms, coins and other artifacts of a frontier culture. Some were simply lost through the holes in the seat, while this often was considered a prime place in which to ditch a handgun, if its owner was in danger of being searched or had other reason for wanting to get rid of the weapon.

In some areas, Civil War relics are the thing. Again, the battlefields have been picked over in the more than a century, but armament and equipment still can be found.

A.M. Van Fossen of Houston, Texas, shows samples from an abandoned silver mine, which he located with the aid of a metal detector combined with great patience.

Most treasure hunters dream of discovering a cache such as this. Wells Fargo strongbox was recovered in the Oklahoma hills, allegedly part of Dalton gang's loot.

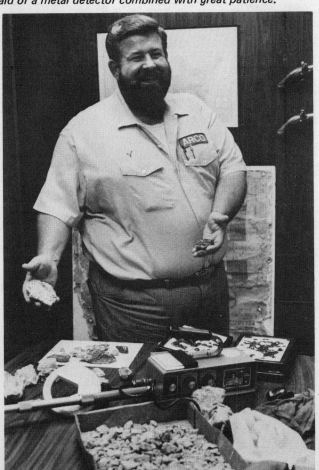

Civil War relics were recovered from river at Selma, Alabama. They were jettisoned in depths to prevent capture by Federal troops. The .58 Minie ball has an odd, triangular mark in its nose. Cannister shot is of cast iron. Both are from the collection of Ralph T. Walker.

In Civil War days, Selma, Alabama, was the home of a Confederate arsenal. On the night of April 1, 1865, all of the ammunition and anything that could be of practical use was dumped into the local river.

Ralph Walker, a local gunsmith, and several others spent several weeks a few years back in attempting to recover some of the cannon that were said to have been sent to the bottom that night.

"There were no cannon," Walker says, "but we did recover some odds and ends."

More recently, a scuba diver asked Walker to show him the location of the supposed horde. In making several dives, he found some of the aged ammunition and tools. A dam had been built downstream earlier and silt is beginning to back up, covering the river's soapstone bottom, thus hiding forever the Civil War relics.

In some of the recesses of the soapstone, however, the diver did find more relics, including Confederate cannister shot that was fashioned of cast iron, along with bullets of the period.

Inasmuch as these items had lain on the bottom of the river one month short of 110 years, they were considered of historical value by collectors.

"Because of the silt that is continuing to back up against the downstream dam, covering the river bottom, the rest of these items undoubtedly are lost to us for all time, unless someone wished to go to the expense of a dredging operation at a later date," Walker says.

There are any number of families across the nation who have turned treasure hunting into a group recreation project, building it into a hobby that provides an opportunity for all members of the family to get into the open, investigating the nooks and crannies of nature, often finding interesting items and relics that can be built into an interesting and even valuable collection.

The simplest things may be of value to someone, which brings to mind the story of Walter Craig, a dealer in surplus and antique arms out of Alabama.

Craig had purchased hundreds of Spanish rifles that had been assembled for use in the Spanish-American War of 1898 and had sold most of them. The wooden packing cases had been burned behind his office, but the longer he

Bill Adams of Atlanta, Georgia, displays a small part of the collection of Civil War relics he has found.

stared at the pile of ashes, the more he wondered about the residue.

Finally, he hired some youngsters to sift the ashes through a mesh, salvaging all of the Spanish hand-wrought nails. He put these in a pail in his store and offered them for sale at twenty-five cents each as genuine relics of the Spanish-American War. Within a week, several thousand of them had been purchased by collectors!

This is an extreme case, of course, and some of today's valued heirlooms are being covered over by civilization or, if you prefer, modernization.

Coin collecting also can be interesting as well as lucrative. There are any number of areas in which to search, but many treasure hunters prefer the yards of old country churches. Many of these churches, in early times, had dirt floors or, if of wood, there were wide cracks between the hand-hewn boards. Many a coin — valuable on today's market — rolled through the cracks in the floor during the weekly collection or simply was dropped and lost in the dirt.

Old homesites also can offer good territory for searching. The experts suggest using a metal detector under shade trees in the yards, since lying on the grass on a summer evening was almost a ritual for many years before television. Often, coins fell from men's pockets as they lay there.

Near the kitchen door is another likely area, for housewives often threw their dirty dishwater out the door and one sometimes can locate silverware of heirloom nature.

Old bottles have become valuable and there are any number of clubs that specialize in such collections. In fact, these bottles don't even have to be of ancient vintage; just unusual. For example, a number of liquor firms have put up

This Christmas Coke bottle has the date, December 25, 1923, cast into its surface, making it valuable item.

It takes an expert to tell the old bottles that are worth money, but this collection contains numerous examples dear to the collectors.

Early soda bottles are sought by the collecting fraternity. One on left is Delaware Punch bottle, dated March 4, 1924. Other was for a brand of soda known as Frosty. (Above) Bob Marcentelli uses Yukon Model 99B Compass metal/mineral detector in Santa Ana Mountains.

their products in especially formed bottles, making a limited run. Even empty, some of these bottles are preferred collector items.

The Avon firm, makers of perfumes and toiletries, has followed a similar policy of offering their odorous concoctions in unusual bottles. Anyone who has a complete collection of Avon bottles also has a small fortune at hand!

In years gone by, for example, early Mason jars often were discarded, but some of them now are worth $10 or more, depending upon whether collectors consider them as examples of fine glasswork of that specific period.

In finding old bottles, however, one can use a metal detector, since the glass containers and empty tin cans usually went into the same garbage pit. Once the detector has located the pit, zeroing in on the metal cans, the search for bottles beneath the covered-over surface can begin.

Oddly enough, some of those old cans and bottles may be even more valuable than one would think, as many early settlers had little use for banks and similar savings institu-

tions. Instead, they tended to stuff Mason jars or tight-lidded cans with cash and bury it against a rainy day that didn't come. Many a family has died out without ever tapping these hidden resources and the money still is there for the finding. However, these caches are not found in garbage pits, but usually within viewing distance of a prominent window, often in a flower garden or similar area.

There are those individuals — fiction aside — who make a profitable livelihood doing recovery jobs for insurance companies. This does not mean that one need be a deep-sea diver complete with rubber suit and globe-shaped headpiece. It can be a good deal simpler.

Each weekend, thousands of items — some of them of great value — are lost at beaches and other vacation spots. Along the seashores of Southern California, for instance, countless beachcombers keep themselves in beans by sifting the sands for lost wristwatches, rings and similar items. The item found may be difficult to sell, if it can be identified, but there are many instances of such individuals finding

Above: Isabel Marcentelli hangs old bottles in the sun. If glass turns purple, it was manufactured between 1880 and 1914. Turning amber dates manufacture in 1914-1930 era. (Left) Rough surface of this glass bottle is from whittle marks in wooden mould used in casting it. (Below) The embossed lettering on bottles indicates they are of 1860-1900 vintage.

diamond rings worth several thousand dollars and receiving a minimum of ten percent of the value for returning it to the insurance company that covers the item.

Many of these beachcombers use simple devices for sifting the sand each week after the crowds have departed. If nothing else, as one of them puts it, he can make eating money just in selling the beer and soft drink bottles he recovers and turns in for the deposit refund.

Once in awhile, one of these treasure seekers may strike a real bonanza in the beach sands. As a result of hurricanes and similar storms at sea, the treasures from wrecks sometimes are washed ashore to be buried in the sands. All too often, of course, the grinding action of sand reduces the value of such old coins, but if of gold, they still can be most valuable — especially at the prices of gold in this age!

There also are any number of stories of individuals literally giving away treasures, not knowing what they are. For example, there was a Rhode Island woman who found some old silver — tarnished and badly dented — in her attic.

To get rid of it, she donated it to a rummage sale. Much later — and somewhat sadder — she learned that she had given away several pieces actually made by Paul Revere!

In a Pennsylvania antique shop, another man spotted a painting and paid only $40. It later turned out to be a genuine Rubens, which was worth several thousand dollars. A New Jersey hobbyist found an old chest in an antique shop. To make it match its surroundings in his home, he sanded it down and painted it, thus destroying the value of a Sheraton sideboard that today would be worth an estimated $3500!

One of the big problems with this sort of treasure finding is the fact that one almost has to be an expert in each specific field. For example, a man in Pennsylvania found an old brass button in his garden a few years ago and sold it for $150. Button collectors are as rabid as any other kind of collector and willing to pay the price for something new to add to their array of goodies.

Among the old items in your attic there can be what

amounts to a gold mine, if it hasn't already been picked over by someone who knows what he is doing. That old set of glass goblets, that old chair or even those old books may be worth a good deal of money to someone.

One way of checking out the value is to find a reputable antique dealer, but be certain to check his references before you get involved. Chances are, if any dealer offers to buy something from you, it is worth up to a hundred percent more than he will offer, as the mark-up on such items is high.

Look for old letters, stamps, books, as all can have high value under the right circumstance. For example, a book fancier in England bought a bushel basket full of old books for what amounted to a few cents. In going through them, he found an old Flemish hymn book that turned out to be worth $80,000 after being authenticated by experts.

All too often, we tend to think of treasure as something that has been lost for centuries beneath the sea, as the Lost Dutchman mine or the supposed loot from Jesse James' train robberies. But treasure surrounds us even now. For example, the so-called Punch Jones diamond, weighing thirty-four carats, was found in a vacant lot in West Virginia. There are diamonds, some of them good only for industrial use, a few of gem quality, to be found in any number of locations in the United States, with Arkansas considered the current leader in finds.

While everyone is looking for the Lost Lode or whatever, there are plenty of coin collectors who have discovered minor bonanzas literally in their backyards — or as close as the nearest parking meter.

A gent named Gene Silvernail has built a sizeable coin collection simply by going into areas which have been equipped with parking meters for a number of years, searching the grass and topsoil surrounding each meter. Over a period of several years, there is no telling how many coins can be dropped and lost in such areas.

A metal detector can help, but all too often this detects coins beneath the surface and you can get a ticket for de-

Proving that treasure is where you find it, this 1909 working Southern Pacific Railroad lantern was picked up at a Southern California swap meet for less than $1.

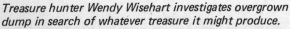

Treasure hunter Wendy Wisehart investigates overgrown dump in search of whatever treasure it might produce.

Result of Ms. Wisehart's search was this old Mason jar bearing patent numbers dating back to November, 1868.

facing public property by digging up the parkway between the curb and the sidewalk.

Silvernail makes the point that there are many relatively modern coins — some of them found in such situations as the one described above — that can be of far greater value than some that are a thousand or so years old. For example, a 1950D Jefferson nickel will bring up to seven times as much as many coins that are ten centuries old. A 1909S VDB Lincoln penny in good condition is worth $135. It's minuscule by comparison to the Lost Dutchman Mine, of course, but you can find plenty of coins that have increased in value. At the other extreme, fortunes have been spent in finding the mine in the Superstition Mountains and more fortunes undoubtedly will be spent. It's still waiting to be located.

If you look through some of your old drawers, you may find there's a small fortune tucked away in the form of novel or unlikely buttons. Odd as it may seem, there is a lively trade for these among collectors.

To the average beginner in this facet of treasure hunting, old buttons containing pictures would appear to be the most valuable, but this is not necessarily true. For example, one of the most common seems the most complicated and is called the Pony Express button, showing a horse at full gallop. There are numerous imitations of this particular button and the Post Office Department even used the figure on a postage stamp in 1940. While some collectors say that picture buttons have been in existence only for four hundred years or so, others insist they date back to biblical times.

In the period of the Civil War and after, buttons were popular as decorations as well as for the more practical use of keeping clothed. During this period in history, young girls made a hobby of collecting strings of unusual buttons, the superstition being that, when one had a total of a hundred buttons on the string, she would find a husband. There is little to verify that this was a successful device for marriage, but with some of these strings still around today, they are of value and one often can find extremely rare buttons among the collections.

Buttons have been made of virtually every material

This collection of rings, coins and other relics was found by Ed Milota of Visalia, Calif., with detector.

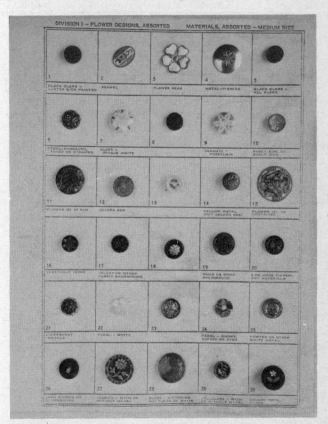

It is difficult to offer hard, fast guides as to the value of a given button. Price is governed by rarity, antiquity, historical significance, workmanship, et al.

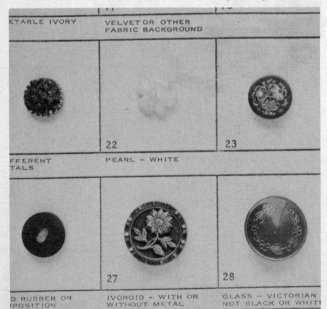

As will be noted by the legend carried in collector's book, button collecting is a highly organized hobby. Some buttons sell for $100 up, depending upon rarity.

known to man down through the ages. Included are ivory, paper, gems, wood, bone, metal, shell, glass, pottery, rubber, ad infinitum.

For the uninitiated, there are several books that can be of help, although some may be out of print at this writing. Included among the volumes touted by collectors to illustrate value are "Button Collectors' History" by Grace Horney Ford; "Button Classics" by Maple and Couse; and "The Button Collector's Second Journal" by Lillian Smith Albert.

For what it is worth, checking your grandmother's old sewing basket just could bring up a button worth fifty dollars or more — if you know what you are looking for.

Once in a lifetime, one may find a treasure trail as complicated as the one written about by Edgar Allan Poe in his "Gold Bug," in which one had to sight along certain lines, drop plumb bobs through the eyes of skeletons and pace off exact distances.

For the most part, however, such plans are dreamed up in the minds of fiction writers. Western prospectors, stagecoach bandits and even the Spanish Main pirates were too lacking in imagination for such hocus pocus. They may have marked the sites of their treasures or mines so they could find them again — so that others to follow might find them — but in the main, the marking systems were pretty primitive and to the point.

Men's minds work pretty much alike in many respects, according to psychiatrists; it has been shown that this was largely true in the creation of treasure signs the world over.

Shown here are some of the more common symbols utilized in marking the locations of treasure and lost mines. Some, of course, have been individually conceived, but the meaning remains much the same. For example, an arrow marked in a horizontal position normally means for the searcher to keep going in the direction indicated; that he is

still on the trail. Pointing down to the ground, it can mean little else but that this is the place to dig. An X, as always, "marks the spot," as might a carved replica of the sun with radiation rays. From the time of the early tribes, these simple markings have indicated wealth or treasure in one form or another.

In the American West, most of the signs pointing to treasure of Indian or Spanish origin, seem to hold many parallels, as will be noted from the collection of old treasure signs accompanying this article.

When burying wealth in a wild territory, there often was no time to go into elaborate plans of hiding. Often, piles of stones or trees blazed at the three corners of a triangle served to mark the treasure site.

Many of the old Spanish treasures, both the wealth derived from conquest and that collected by the church, were hurriedly buried as the soldiers or priests were forced to flee before hostile Indians, floods or even pestilence. It often was the practice to mark the hiding place of the hoards with symbols representing things used in everyday life. For example, a U-shaped mark often represented the mark of a horse's hoof and meant that one was to travel in the direction of the imaginary animal. A rock or tree marked with a crude carving of a box or chest usually indicated the spot where the treasure could be located.

It was necessary to use such simple signs, as it was realized that others may be sent later to recover the wealth; it would simplify their finding it. Often, of course, these gatherers of wealth were killed or died before having a chance to pass on the information. The treasures are still there.

Veteran treasure hunters point out, however, that the marks and signs are becoming increasingly difficult to locate. All too often, time and weather have taken their toll. Trees have died or been cut down, the telltale mark on its bark being turned into lumber or firewood. Etchings in rocks often are eliminated by wind and water. As civilization has closed in, often the marks have been destroyed as buildings have been erected or land cleared.

With the sweep of civilization, these old signs may soon vanish entirely. The only possibility of these thousands of hidden treasures ever being discovered when this happens are remote. However, there are those who argue that with the constant improvements in electronics, metal detectors will be perfected to the point that they will eventually be discovered no matter where they lie.

Right: These are some of the signs that one might find along a treasure trail, many of them of Indian origin. (Below) This old miner's shack was built from dynamite boxes. Today, even the boxes would have collector's value.

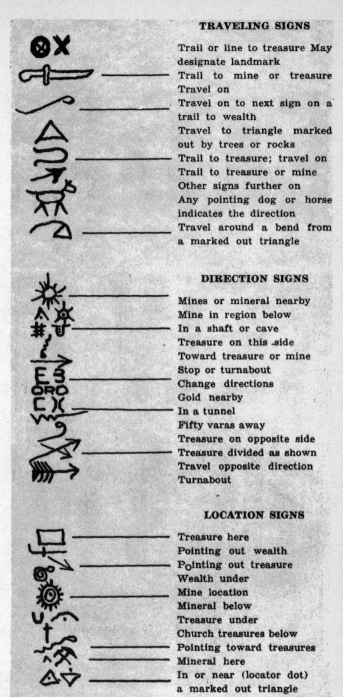

TRAVELING SIGNS

Trail or line to treasure May designate landmark
Trail to mine or treasure
Travel on
Travel on to next sign on a trail to wealth
Travel to triangle marked out by trees or rocks
Trail to treasure; travel on
Trail to treasure or mine
Other signs further on
Any pointing dog or horse indicates the direction
Travel around a bend from a marked out triangle

DIRECTION SIGNS

Mines or mineral nearby
Mine in region below
In a shaft or cave
Treasure on this side
Toward treasure or mine
Stop or turnabout
Change directions
Gold nearby
In a tunnel
Fifty varas away
Treasure on opposite side
Treasure divided as shown
Travel opposite direction
Turnabout

LOCATION SIGNS

Treasure here
Pointing out wealth
Pointing out treasure
Wealth under
Mine location
Mineral below
Treasure under
Church treasures below
Pointing toward treasures
Mineral here
In or near (locator dot)
a marked out triangle

THE DESERT MYSTERIES

Chapter 2

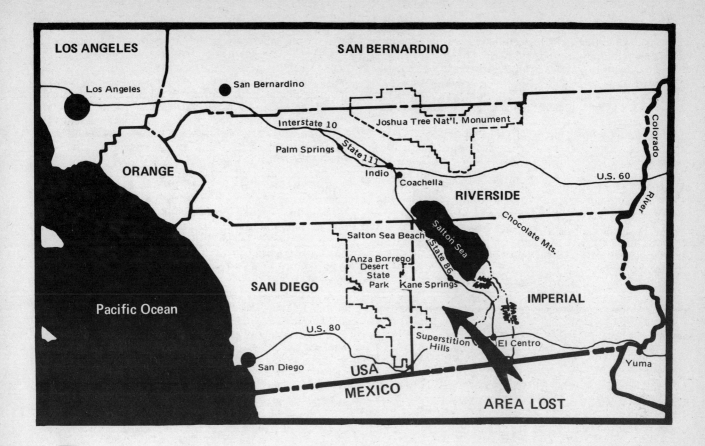

PERHAPS THE MOST unusual story of treasure to come out of the broad expanses of the American desert has to do with an ancient Spanish galleon that lies somewhere amid the sand dunes of Southern California's rugged Imperial Valley.

The vessel, supposedly loaded with pearls, has been the subject of searches for more than three centuries. Several times it has been found, then lost, when the shifting desert sands seemingly covered it. If fact — mixed with growing legend — can be believed, the so-called Ship In The Desert is still there, waiting for its hoard of wealth to be taken.

The first question to enter the mind of anyone of dubious nature is: What would a ship be doing in the desert, more than two hundred miles from the Gulf of California?

While location of the bleached bones of the ship is uncertain, reports over the years — coupled with old Spanish documents — suggest that it is somewhere south of the Salton Sea, east of Anza Borrego Desert State Park and north of the treacherous Superstition Hills, which flank the Mexican border southwest of El Centro. Unlikely as it may seem, the Superstitions are spotted with quicksand which provide a natural trap for the unwary searcher.

The Salton Sea, itself, is a huge body of salt water some thirty miles long and more than twenty miles wide, lying in the desert sands of the valley, its surface more than two hundred feet below sea level.

Apparently, this once was a part of the Gulf of California, which would tie in logically with the treasure ship being lost in the sands, but it actually came into being in 1905, when the Colorado River to the east overflowed and covered the Imperial Valley. This desert depression, first mentioned by Professor W.P. Blake, a government geologist, in 1853, became the collection basin for the overflow. For a number of years, its level dropped because of evaporation, but with great parts of the Imperial Valley now under cultivation, the depth seems to have been more or less stabilized by runoff from irrigation ditches. At least, several major real estate companies have felt safe in developing recreational-oriented communities on its shores.

Kane Springs, to the west of the Salton Sea, is the oldest known watering hole in this California desert and long was the campground for desert prospectors as well as for passing bands of Indians.

A look at a map will show that the area described as the resting place for the Spanish vessel is a great mass of shifting sand, much of which has yet to be surveyed.

The Wastelands
Of This Nation Hold
Untold Millions In Lost — And
Still Undiscovered — Wealth!

Separating legend from fact probably is impossible. After all, writers and story tellers have been embellishing the tale for three centuries, but as nearly as can be determined, the series of events began in 1610, when a Spanish captain, Alvarez de Cordone, received a royal commission from King Philip III of Spain to search Mexican waters for pearls for the crown and to make explorations of the coastal waters.

Cordone was directed to build three vessels and to recruit two more sea captains to command them. The captains chosen were Pedro de Rosales and Juan de Iturbe.

At that time, Acapulco was the chief seaport on the Mexican Pacific Coast and it was here that the three galleons were built. Meantime, Cordone arranged for some 150 African slaves — all experienced pearl divers — to be imported and assigned to the three vessels. According to record, the divers ranged in age from teen-age boys to men in their seventies, but all had proved their qualifications for this type of work.

The technique used by these divers was crude and

Artist's impression from old print shows the gear and technique used by African pearl divers, who carried 50-pound stones as a means of getting to bottom of the sea.

dangerous. They worked in pairs, one taking a line down with him, while a huge stone, weighing up to fifty pounds, was attached to his arm or leg. When he slipped into the water, the weight of the stone would carry him to the bottom. The line running to the surface was used to signal the assistant and to recover the diver. The divers could remain below for as much as a minute and a half before signalling to be pulled up. Each of the divers carried with him a net bag into which were put the live oysters collected on the bottom. When the diver was brought up, the shell-filled bag came with him.

The expedition captain found that a diver could make an average of thirty trips to the bottom a day, gathering a dozen oysters each time. With half of the 150 divers performing, that meant nearly 27,000 shells a day could be brought up from the oyster beds. Every oyster, of course, did not contain a pearl. In fact, the odds were against it, but with the number of shells being brought to the ship decks and opened, the success had to be good in spite of the odds.

It was well known even then that the waters off Mexico's Pacific Coast where the pearl-laden mollusks thrived, were yielding the sought-after black varieties. Others were found in a wide variety of colors, ranging from rose and bronze to blue, yellow and even purple.

The expedition finally sailed from Acapulco in July, 1612, beginning to search the waters along the coast, launching divers into the depths whenever an oyster bed was spotted in the clear waters.

Along the shores, the Spaniards spotted bands of Indians and even saw some of them diving for oysters. From the deck of his command ship, Captain Cordone could see that many sections of the beach were littered with oyster shells, where the Indians had stripped them of their meat, leaving the tough, hard protector to the elements. It occurred to him that the Indians also should be finding pearls in those shells.

At one Indian village, the three vessels dropped anchor offshore and the Spaniards went ashore, where they were greeted in friendly fashion. Somewhat covertly, the seamen inspected the oyster shells, but found no pearls. A bit of careful questioning revealed that the Indians recognized the beauty of the baubles, if not the value, and had saved them. The chief showed them several reed-woven baskets filled with fine pearls.

The Spanish captain managed to explain to the chief that he wanted the pearls and agreed to trade food and clothing for them. The pearls were taken aboard the vessel commanded by Juan de Iturbe and several bundles of clothing and tins of biscuits were brought ashore as exchange. These were deposited on the shore and the Spanish hurried to return to their ships, aware that they had allowed greed to overcome honesty in their dealings.

The Indians discovered almost immediately that the clothing was worn out and constituted nothing more than a collection of rags. The food was wormy. As the Spaniards rowed for their ships, the Indians on shore began shooting at them with arrows. Cordone was caught in the chest by an arrow and nearly fell overboard before he collapsed instead in the bottom of the small boat.

The expedition's surgeon diagnosed the captain's wound as serious and that he required more attention than could be rendered at sea. His galleon was ordered back to Acapulco, the wounded captain aboard.

The vessels commanded by Iturbe and Rosales continued the search for pearls, the coffers growing more full with each passing day. Then came the morning that the watch reported to Captain Iturbe that there was land on the port side. Checking his crude maps made by earlier explorers, Iturbe found that he was entering the Gulf of California.

Near a landmark now known as Isla Angel de la Guarda, Captain Rosales' ship struck an underwater reef, which tore a gaping hole in her hull. As the ship was sinking, the pearls, crew and divers were hurriedly transferred to the one remaining ship; the one commanded by Iturbe.

The two sea captains considered the advisability of returning to Acapulco with their combined store of wealth, but they had just finished working over an oyster bed near what now is La Paz. It had yielded the largest, most valuable pearls yet taken. It stood to reason that even better pearls might lie farther to the north, as that seemed to be the pattern.

When the last remaining boat reached the mouth of what now is the Colorado River, Iturbe decided to explore the waterway for a few days. After all, the expedition had been commissioned to explore the area as well as take its wealth.

Over the reaches of history, the Colorado River has changed course several times. Iturbe apparently sailed northward along the stream of that time, coming finally to a great inland sea, which may have been what now is the Salton Sea. Fed by the Colorado River, it may even have been fresh water at that time, the salt having been added by mineral deposits in the soil. Iturbe sailed northward until the waters were too shallow for safety, then dispatched Captain Rosales ashore in a small boat to investigate the terrain. Two days later, the captain returned to declare that there was nothing but sand and dried salt beds, with sparse vegetation that had to be much the same as that found today, mostly grassweed, sagebrush and creosote.

During Rosales' absence, a happening had gone virtually unnoticed, but now it was apparent. The level of the water was falling. There are theories that there was an earthquake at this time, which disrupted the entire area's topography. The truth probably never will be known as to exactly what did create this sudden phenomenon.

Whatever the reason, the seamen set out for the south under full sail only to discover that the narrow neck of fresh water that had connected this inland sea with the Gulf of California no longer existed. It was simply gone.

Panic did not begin immediately. Instead, the Spanish captain sailed his ship around the edges of the enclosed sea, while the water level continued to drop. Finally, the vessel ran aground in the shallows. Before measures could be taken to float her again, the water had dropped to the point that the vessel was sitting fully exposed in the sandy muck, the surface steaming, as it began to dry.

There are varying stories as to what actually happened thereafter. Some report that Iturbe was able to make the Gulf of California with the few of his party who survived the desert. Others say that he died along the route. But it is reckoned that they failed to carry away the pearls, taking food and water only, in hopes of defeating the desert.

Whatever the sea captain's personal fate, the legend persisted, but it was not until 1890 that an old prospector led his burro into the oasis at Kane Springs to state he had found the ship. It was nearby in the desert, he insisted, half buried in sand.

He asked for volunteers to dig out the treasure, agreeing to share the pearls. He suddenly was surrounded by help, but when they went back into the desert, the old man was unable to locate the exact spot.

As early as 1870, there had been searches for the old

On the bottom of the oyster-growing lagoon, the pearl diver was held in place by the rock, as he sought the pearl-bearing shells for Spanish.

sailing vessel and several accounts were reported in West Coast newspapers. For example, the Sacramento Union, in its edition of October 6, 1870, reported that "an advance party of four, from San Bernardino, have left to visit the famous wrecked ship in the California desert. The ship, which must have lain a wreck for over 250 years, is built of teakwood and is perfectly sound. The bow and stern are plainly visible, and she is 240 miles from the Gulf of California."

Exactly one week later, the same newspaper reported: "The ship-hunting party in the California desert has returned to San Bernardino." Then, in its edition of November 16, 1870, the Union stated that "another search is being made for the fossil ship in the California desert by the men who went for it before but did not find the prize."

The Inyo Independent, on September 27, 1873, reported: "This ship-in-the-desert story, which has heretofore been attributed to a writer's lively imagination, is verified by the James expedition explorers. In the California desert, over 200 miles from the Gulf of California, they found the mast of a vessel."

An article also had appeared earlier in a San Bernardino paper, outlining the search for the ship by a party led by one Charlie Clusker. The writer of this particular account had embellished it with an item of his own.

"It was less than a year ago," he wrote, "while on a periodic tour of the California desert, that I had the good fortune to make camp with an old habitue of the wasteland. Inevitably the conversation turned to the subject of lost mines, of buried treasure, and finally to the desert ship.

" 'I think I know where the old hulk lies,' he said, in a confidential tone.

" 'Would you betray a vital secret if you told me?' I asked.

" 'Well, maybe not. You know the southeast corner of this country is covered with sand hills. Every time a big wind hits them they move — sometimes a foot or two, sometimes a rod or more. I got it figured out that those dunes have covered up the old ship. They'll keep on moving, of course, and someday the old pocket will be uncovered. The man who finds it will make the biggest strike in history and don't you forget it.' "

If one hangs around the barrooms of Brawley, California, he sooner or later will hear another account of discovery. This one seems to involve a young Indian, who

In addition to the pearls found in Mexican waters, the Spanish learned that the local Indians had gathered thousands of them in taking oysters.

staggered into town, more dead than alive, sometime in the 1920s. Half-crazed by thirst, he insisted he had found the ship in the desert.

Recovered, he had returned to attempt to find the vessel again, but was unsuccessful. Ultimately, he committed suicide. This account, I suspect, is of local manufacture and probably fiction, as I can find no written account in local newspapers of the era.

However, in January, 1870, an article appeared in the New York Galaxy wherein one Albert S. Evans claims to have seen the old ship in 1860, south of the road leading from San Bernardino.

According to Evans' account, "Southward to the very horizon stretched a great plain of snowy salt, the white ghost of a dead sea which once covered all of this accursed land, but has passed away forever.

"Across this white plain, as across the waters of a placid lake, the moon threw a track of shimmering light, so bright as almost to dazzle the eye of the beholder. Right in this burning pathway of light far out in the center of the ghost-ly sea, where foot of man has never trod, lay what appeared in the distance to be the wreck of a gallant ship, which might have gone down there centuries ago, when the bold Spanish adventurers, bearing the cross and sword in either hand, were pushing their way to the northwest in search of the fountain of youth, the famed Kingdom of Cibola."

In writing of the vision of the ship, however, Evans made no mention of the treasure supposedly aboard her. It is possible he had not heard the legend before and did see the ship, not being aware of the potential wealth almost within his grasp.

As mentioned earlier, it has become virtually impossible to separate truth from legend at this late date, but the fact remains that there was an expedition from which one of the ships returned to Acapulco with its wounded leader; another of the ships did sink and there was a fortune in pearls involved. Old records attest to the fact that Iturbe did leave his ship marooned in the desert.

The ship is waiting today to be discovered beneath the endless millions of tons of sand!

In the Twenties, a Mexican youth is supposed to have found the treasure ship, while searching the desert area.

The Desert
Mysteries: Part B

SAGA
OF THE
LOST
DUTCHMAN

Actually, There Are Eight Lost Mines In Arizona's Superstition Mountains, But This One Gets The Publicity!

NO BOOK ON treasure hunting would be complete without mention of the so-called Lost Dutchman Mine. Over the years, this legend — based upon truth, but diluted by writer's and storyteller's fancies — has become as much a part of Americana as Washington throwing the silver dollar across the Delaware.

That does not mean there is not a Lost Dutchman Mine; there probably is, but the facts have been so clouded over the decades by fancy that it is difficult for even professional treasure hunters, historians and researchers to determine where truth leaves off and fiction begins. The result is a matter of legend that makes searching difficult.

But whatever the rumors, the legends, the fact remains that, to date, more than forty people have died in Arizona's rugged Superstition Mountains, while looking for the lost mine. There have been numerous causes of death, including thirst, snake bite and even sunstroke, but more than half of the deaths have been of an even more violent nature.

As late as 1961, one Jay Clapp — a veteran of more than a decade of professional treasure hunting — went into the Superstitions in search of the Lost Dutchman. His body was discovered three years later — actually, his skeleton — deep in the accursed mountains.

In June, 1931, a retired civil service worker, **Adolph** Ruth, went into the mountain range, carrying a map, **which** his son, Dr. Erwin Ruth, had received in 1913, from **a man** named Peralta.

Adolph Ruth, the record shows, stopped over at **a ranch,** where he discussed his hopes of finding the long-lost **mine.** He showed the map to several individuals and finally **talked** to well-known local prospectors into guiding him to **Willow** Springs in the Superstition's West Boulder Canyon, **where** he set up camp. The pair of prospectors returned to **civiliza-** tion, after telling Ruth that they would return in ten **days** with fresh supplies.

But when this pair returned to the campsite, they **found** nothing but the treasure hunter's boots and his bedroll. **At** first, they thought he might be out hunting for the **lost** mine, but when he failed to return, they began to **wonder** why he had taken off sans footwear. The situation **was** reported to lawmen in the area and a two-county hunt **was** instituted. Six months later Adolph Ruth's skeleton **was** discovered in a nearby canyon — minus his head.

The buried skull was uncovered by dogs many **yards** from the body, two bullet holes having shattered the **fragile** bone.

Adolph Ruth stopped at a ranch on his way into the Superstitions. He showed his map, discussing hopes of locating the Lost Dutchman Mine.

The searchers also found a memo book with notes in Ruth's handwriting. He had written:

It lies within an imaginary circle whose diameter is not more than five miles and whose center is marked by the Weaver's Needle.

On the same page was written:

Veni, vidi, vice — about 200 feet across the canyon.

Weaver's Needle is a prominent landmark that has figured in many stories regarding the Lost Dutchman Mine. Incidentally, in spite of an extensive search, there was no sign of the treasure map that Ruth had displayed earlier and which he was known to have taken into the wilds with him.

Sixteen years later, the body of one James L. Craven, another treasure hunter, was discovered — sans head. Again, it was found some distance away...two bullet holes in the skull.

Craven is supposed to have had a map indicating the location of the Lost Dutchman and in June, 1947, had set up a base camp in La Barge Canyon. When he was not heard of after a month, a search party found his camp, with about two days' food supply gone. But it was not until eight months later that they found his decapitated body. From the evidence, he had left camp with his pick, shovel, canteen and rifle. None of these were found with the headless corpse. And as before, the skull finally, when found, was buried some distance from the rest of the skeleton.

Over the years, searchers have found signs that led them on, each new find lending some sort of credence to the legends that have grown up around the so-called Lost Dutchman Mine. They have found ancient mule trails, suggesting that there may have been a regular run out of the mountains; there is a spring deep in the mountains that has been boxed in with masonry and one searcher found parts of a suit of ancient Spanish armor; another discovered three hundred pairs of Mexican straw sandals hidden in a crevice in the rocks. But what is the reasoning behind all of these signs?

To even begin to understand the significance, one first has to know something of the legends. There are many versions, of course, and one can take his pick. But after sorting them out, trying to sluff off fiction in favor of truth, there are facts that seem to stand out. For instance, there may not be one lost mine, but actually as many as

Ruth set up his camp near Willow Springs in the wildest area of the Superstitions. He never was seen alive again. His decapitated body, head were found, after long searches, in separate locations.

Weaver's Needle is a landmark in the Superstition Mountains that is mentioned frequently in regard to the location of the Peralta mines.

eighteen! And The Lost Dutchman, while the best publicized, probably is not the richest lost mine in the Superstitions.

But the entire mystery began in 1748, when Don Miguel Peralta was granted some 3750 square miles of Arizona desert for services to the Spanish crown. The land remained in the Peralta family for exactly one century, when in 1848, the treaty of Guadalupe Hidalgo made it a part of the United States territories.

The Peraltas had mined silver in Sonora for years and given little attention to their holdings in what now is the State of Arizona. However, by the 1840s, the silver was disappearing and the family was looking for new mineral deposits for the Peralta coffers.

According to old Peralta family records, there were at least eighteen silver and gold mines operated by the

dynasty's peons in the Superstitions. But when the United States took over the area at the end of the Mexican War, apparently there was uncertainty as to the legal title to the land. The result was that Don Peralta — a descendant of the original Don Miguel Peralta — doubled his work force in the mines, hoping to extract as much gold as possible before the family lost legal title to the land and its wealth.

Headed by Pedro Peralta, the oldest son, gold was mined as rapidly as possible, the ore being hauled to a site on the Salt River, where it was milled to partially strip the rose quartz from the gold. Then a train of mules was brought in to haul out the take.

Most of the gold is alleged to have been hauled out of the Superstitions by these trains, as the Apaches grew progressively more threatening, stirred up by all of the activity in their sacred mountains.

Two of the younger Peralta brothers took the hint and left, but Pedro, either through greed or what he considered duty to the family since he was the oldest, outfitted the largest pack train of all, taking with him more than sixty peons and twenty pack mules. According to legend, before he left, he drew a map for each of his brothers. Neither had been to the mines proper, but had been stationed at the Salt River camp, overseeing the milling operations. The theory was that Pedro Peralta knew the dangers he faced and wanted his brothers to know the sources of the family wealth.

As he and his miners moved out into the Superstitions for their last effort in the mines, Pedro Peralta devised a series of markers that he already had included in the maps he had drawn. At least, that is the way the legend tells it. Actually, it is more likely that the markers were erected earlier so that the map could be drawn to conform. Whichever came first — and if the maps ever did actually exist — a number of unlikely markers have been found.

It should be pointed out, however, that there have been literally hundreds of Peralta maps over the years, most of them drawn out of imagination and sold to the unwary. However, some of these maps have led their owners to their deaths in the Superstitions.

Many of the markers have been changed in appearance by vandals over the years and others were dismantled by the Apaches. However, one set of three stone tablets was discovered in 1949 and resulted in a search of well over a decade by the man who came to possess them.

Pedro Peralta continued to operate the mines for nearly a year, taking as much gold out of the ground as possible in what he knew could be the final period of possession by his family. There was increasing Apache hostility, but Peralta maintained a strong guard and apparently tended to underestimate the Indians.

When his milling operation at Salt River finally was attacked in September, 1848, the senior Peralta son ordered the mules loaded with the high grade gold ore. On the way out of the hills, the Apaches attacked and it became a running battle, the Mexican workers being cut down one at a time.

With disaster overtaking them, the Mexicans rebelled to the point that they released the gold-loaded mules, although some already had been killed in the fighting. The meat from the animals had been taken by the Indians, along with the rawhide bags holding the gold, the fine, yellow powder being thrown to the winds. This part of the legend, incidentally, was the basis for the classic story, "Treasure Of The Sierra Madre."

The rest of the mules, escaping into the mountains, ultimately were hunted down by the Indians and slaughtered for food. In some cases, the gold-filled packs were stripped from them and left lying and it is possible that the Mexicans may have unloaded some of the mules before release, trying to hide the gold before the animals were released.

Some of these isolated packs — gold pouring from the rotted rawhide pouches — were found later. As late as

When the milling operation at Salt River was attacked by the Apaches in 1848, it marked the beginning of the end of mining activities in the Superstitions for the following two decades.

1914, a pair of Norwegian miners found gold worth $18,000 on an old lava flow where there couldn't possibly have been gold ore anywhere close to the surface.

Following this disaster in which most of the Mexicans were killed by the Apaches, the Indians held power in the Superstitions for two decades. In fact, it wasn't until 1865, during the period that famed frontiersman Kit Carson was the Indian agent at Fort McDowell, that the Peralta legend gained renewed interest.

This came about as the result of the work of a Dr. Abraham Thorne, a friend of Carson's, who was a contract surgeon for the army, also using his medical talents on behalf of the Apaches near the fort.

It was in September, 1865, that one of the Apaches told the surgeon that he would be shown the location of a great store of gold. He was told he would be gone only one night.

Thorne met with the Apaches, was blindfolded and his horse was led by one of the Indians. According to his later recollections, they crossed what had to be the Salt River, then rode upward for about twenty miles.

At dawn, they halted and the doctor was allowed to remove his blindfold. What he saw in the face of the canyon where they had stopped was a vein of quartz that — reflecting the rising sun — appeared to be almost pure gold!

While the Apache braves waited, Dr. Thorne was allowed to fill a sack with all the gold he could carry. Remounted, he was blindfolded again for the return trip. However, while loading his sack with the rich ore, he glanced about for landmarks and saw what he later identified as the upper tip of Weaver's Needle, the major rise in the Superstitions. It was several miles to the south.

During the return trip, Thorne said later, his blindfold slipped at one point. He again was able to see Weaver's Needle, as well as the ruins of an old building where two canyons joined. Back at the fort, he arranged for transport of his sack of ore to the mint in San Francisco, where it brought him $6,000!

Not wanting to betray the trust the Apaches had shown in him, Thorne told only a few friends and relatives of his experience. It was not until 1883 that he led a party, including his brother, back along the treasure route. He did find the remains of the old building he had seen, but long, hard searches for the vein of gold proved fruitless.

Jacob Walz — the legendary Dutchman, known by some

In their final effort to get the milled gold out of the Superstitions, the Mexican workers were forced to engage in a running battle with the Apaches. Most of them were killed, the gold-carrying mules scattered.

as Waltz and even Walzer — entered the scene in 1871, when he turned up in Phoenix with his partner, Jacob Weiser. Both are alleged to have been German immigrants. They had purchased a map from the Peralta family with permission to mine some of the remaining property. This was supposed to have been in partial payment for helping Don Peralta remove more gold from one of the Peralta mines. It would appear, however, that the Mexican land-holder had not told them that there was more than one mine in the Superstitions.

Walz and Weiser used their map to locate the mine they had been given permission to work, but as they neared it, they found two men in the excavation. Without getting closer, the two Germans shot them. Upon approaching, however, they discovered the two suntanned men were not Apaches. Instead, they were Peralta employees, who seemingly had been taking gold from the mine on their own.

According to later accounts by Walz, himself, the two men worked the mine long hours, accumulating a supply of high grade gold ore that they stored in three different sites. The theory was that if claim jumpers or raiders moved in, they would be able to show them one of the two smaller caches, keeping the major part of their ore in a third hiding place.

Running low on provisions, Walz returned to Phoenix for several days. When he returned, he found the campsite

In finding the gold, the Indians placed more value on the rawhide bags than in the yellow contents.

destroyed and most of their equipment gone — along with his partner, Jacob Weiser.

Walz took the gold from one of the smaller caches and moved out of the Superstitions, blaming himself for his partner's death, although there were those who felt he had slain Weiser for the gold. There also were those who said there was no gold mine and that Walz had gained his wealth by highgrading the Vulture Mine at Wickenburg.

The Dutchman bought a chicken ranch near Phoenix and lived there in his last years, while the stories about him and his exploits blossomed into legend.

Walz did have one friend in Phoenix in whom he confided, telling the entire story. This was a Mrs. Thelma Thomas, who ran a bakery. He also loaned her $1400 in gold, explaining that this was only a small part of the gold available. The large cache collected by Weiser and himself was untouched and the mine, itself, was far from worked out.

By that time, the last renegade Apaches were being rounded up and held behind barbed wire as prisoners of war, so the danger was reduced. Mrs. Thomas, with her stepson, talked Walz into a return trip into the Superstitions in 1891, but his health was failing. Before the plan could be put into effect, Walz died. That was in October, 1891. Supposedly, the secret died with him, but that is not necessarily the case.

Walz was buried without ever knowing that his partner, Jacob Weiser, had not been killed at the site of the mine. Instead, a man who identified himself as Weiser was brought to Dr. John D. Walker by a group of Pima Indians. He had a bad arrow wound in his shoulder, which the frontier physician treated.

He told of mining the Superstitions with his partner, who had gone for more supplies. He had been attacked by Apaches and, wounded, had escaped, to be found by the Pimas. He was certain that Walz had been killed by the Apaches.

Before Weiser died of pneumonia, he gave Dr. Walker a map drawn on a piece of rawhide. He identified it as the Peralta map, which he and Walz had owned jointly. The physician took all this for the ravings of an ill man, but later allowed Thomas F. Weedin, a newspaper man, to make a copy.

Jacob Walz returned to Phoenix for several days for the purpose of restocking provisions. He was away, as a result, when his partner was attacked by Apaches.

Some years later, Weedin told Sims Ely of the map, but when the former searched his files, he could not find the copy he had been allowed to make.

Ely and Jim Bark, both successful Arizonans, spent years searching for the Lost Dutchman Mine as a hobby rather than an infatuation. Bark had bought a ranch in 1890, which encompassed all of the Superstitions. He had met Jacob Walz through Thelma Thomas. It was Bark who later dubbed it the Lost Dutchman Mine.

Sims Ely was a latecomer to Arizona, arriving three years after Walz' death, and there is no record as to how he and Bark came to join forces in the search. They failed to find the mine, but did compile a great deal of information that has been used by more recent searchers.

As late as 1912, the answer to why the Lost Dutchman — and the rest of the Peralta mines — never have been discovered may have been revealed by an old Indian known as Apache Jack.

The Indian explained to one treasure hunter, George Scholey, that he had been one of thirty squaws and youngsters who had been sent into the mountains after the massacre of 1848 to fill the mine shafts. The pilings, tools and all other evidence were thrown into the shafts, which then were filled and covered with ironwood logs. These were smeared with caliche, which hardens into a plastic-like coating, then dirt was added and bushes planted over the entrances.

The Apaches had long ago placed a death sentence on the head of any tribesman who betrayed the secret, but Apache Jack finally was persuaded to lead Scholey into the area. Apparently, the old tribal law had its effect, for the Indian abruptly refused to go beyond the top of Black Mountain, one of the Superstition peaks. Instead, he returned to his tribal grounds — and was found dead a short time later, supposedly poisoned.

Today, the legends of the Apaches themselves are dying as the white man's way of life takes over. Robert Geronimo, grandson of the famed Apache leader of the last century, decries the fact that most of the children of the Mescalero Apache tribe no longer learn their native tongue.

It may well be that the location of the Peralta mines — the Lost Dutchman among them — has died with the passing of some of the old warriors.

But whatever the answer, there seems to be fact that there is a Lost Dutchman Mine, but how rich it might be is open to question. Just as there are another seventeen mines operated by the Peralta family — and none of them have been found.

In 1912, Apache Jack agreed to lead a party into the Superstitions to the location of the long lost mine. He died soon after, apparently poisoned by his tribe.

Jim Bark spent years, with his partner, seeking the location of the Lost Dutchman Mine. The records they collected have done much to establish credibility.

The Desert
Mysteries:
Part C

Somewhere In Mexico's Deserts And Mountains Rests The Revolutionary's Stolen Wealth!

THE TALES OF Pancho Villa, perhaps best known of the bandit revolutionaries of Latin America, are legion and truth has grown into legend in spite of the fact that he has been dead less than fifty-five years.

Among the legends which have grown around Villa are those of the hidden wealth which he supposedly buried before putting down his arms and ultimately meeting his death in 1923, when he was killed by a shotgun blast while driving through the streets in a Model-T Ford.

Two of the stories of Villa's buried treasures seem to have some basis in fact, however. One of his treasures probably is lost to mankind forever. The second may someday be discovered.

During his reign of terror prior to putting down his arms and being granted amnesty in 1920, Villa and his followers appeared with the richly loaded packtrain into the mountains near Tepehuanes, Durango, while the rest of the rebel army waited.

Several days later, Pancho Villa reappeared — alone. It always has been assumed that he buried the riches in the mountain wilderness, then killed those who had helped him in order to keep them from digging up the treasure on their own or telling of its whereabouts.

Following his surrender in 1920, Villa was granted a ranch and a pension near the village of Parral. Before his death three years later at the hands of one of his former lieutenants, he would disappear periodically into the mountains, returning days — sometimes weeks — later with his saddlebags weighted down with gold and silver.

The Hidden Hoard Of Pancho Villa

raided the Minero Bank of Chihuahua. They not only cleaned out the vaults of the bank but drilled into one of the bank's metal pillars, where more than half a million in gold coins had been hidden against such a raid, and carted off the entire take.

During this same period, Villa and his band of cutthroats had pre-dated the gangsters of the Thirties by going in for wholesale kidnapping of wealthy and influential families. The ransom from these endeavors is said to have amounted to millions.

According to information contained in old newspaper accounts, Villa carried the loot about for several months in a pack train, following a "pay-as-you-go" plan of supporting his troops.

One night, however, Villa and several of his band dis-

When he was assassinated, he apparently died too rapidly to tell the whereabouts of his cache.

There are those, of course, who doubt the existence of this treasure at all, discounting it as a part of the Villa legend. Wherever it may be, if it does exist at all, it is not likely that it ever will be found unless some person is lucky enough simply to stumble across it. Even this is not likely, for the vast mountain wilderness of Mexico covers hundreds of thousands of square miles; the treasure may be hidden away in any canyon or creek bed.

Another legend of Villa's hidden wealth, however, is certain to intrigue treasure hunters — amateur and professional.

In 1916, Villa and his band of rebel bandits were hiding out in the mountains east of the village of Dolores in

While Villa's army was considered an armed rabble, it was equipped with cannon and other then modern devices of warfare.

31

Villa's revolutionaries man a gun emplacement in the mountains above the desert, where the treasure of their leader may still be hidden.

Above: Villa's men begin attack on city of Jaurez. (Right) Well hidden revolutionary fires from cliffside.

Chihuahua. He had been systematically looting mines in the area, including the ore-rich Dolores Mine in the Sierra Madre range. The mine was American owned and Villa's outlaws are reported to have slain all of the Americans, leading to the expedition of American cavalry under General John J. Pershing into Mexican territory after him.

Villa is supposed to have accumulated more than $7,000,000 gold and smelted it in his own hidden smelter in the mountains near Temosachic, then hiding it nearby.

With both the Mexican and United States governments after his scalp, Villa apparently decided to consolidate his loot and ordered one of his lieutenants, Jesus Gonzales, to bring all of the gold from its hiding places to Temosachic.

Near his destination, a train of gold-ladened oxcarts behind him, Gonzales received word that Mexican Federal troops were hot on his trail. Acting in desperation, the bandit lieutenant turned due east and paced off 515 meters, marking a spot where he then ordered a hole dug. The gold, smelted into heavy bars, was buried on this spot.

No sooner had the burial place of the loot been camou-

Trains were a favorite target of revolutionaries. Capture of them disrupted Federale communications, afforded the rebels transportation and sometimes also carried gold.

flaged than the Federal troops swooped down upon the bandits. All except Gonzales and an Indian guerrilla were killed in the battle. These two escaped and made their way through the mountains to Villa's hideout, where they told of what had happened.

Pancho Villa, according to reports, had the Indian shot, leaving only himself and Gonzales with knowledge of the hiding place of the gold.

Villa, of course, died in the manner described earlier, but the government had failed to offer Jesus Gonzales any kind of immunity. He headed up Villa's former followers and continued raiding and pillaging until one of the band shot him.

Gonzales, seriously wounded, was taken to Dolores, where an American doctor treated him, telling the outlaw that he had only a few days to live. Gonzales is said to have told the surgeon of the location of the treasure, but this is doubtful, since the medical man never made an attempt to find it. In fact, to date, there has been no report that this $7,000,000 hoard ever has been found.

One is likely to note similarities between the two stories reaccounted here of Villa's hidden treasure. Both may be true; they may be different versions of the same incident. The fact remains that Pancho Villa had collected millions in stolen wealth and that it disappeared.

It is officially recorded that the band of rebels transporting the gold near the village of Temosachic was slain by the Federales; their bodies were burned beside the road by the troops who did not want to take the time to bury them. This is supposed to have taken place approximately a mile from the village. If the gold still is there and was not dug up by Villa before his death, electronic detectors should be able to locate it.

Half of any loot found, of course, will be claimed by the Mexican government, but it might well be worth a try.

Only a few years ago, news of Villa's treasure, nearly forgotten, leaped into the headlines, when an 80-year-old Mexican woman told of it on her deathbed in Brawley, California. She claimed to have been a nurse with Villa's troops and to have been present at the time Gonzales was being treated for his wounds by the American doctor.

She, too, said the millions of dollars in gold still lay in the ground, probably turned black with age.

During meeting to explore a truce, Villa (center) poses with Generals Alvaro Obregon, John J. Pershing. The latter pursued him in Mexico.

THE LITTLE LEGENDS

THE WEST IS literally rife with other legends of lost treasure, most of them with some basis in fact. For example, there is the missing three hundred pounds in gold bullion that was taken from a stagecoach bound for Nevada Territory's Carson City Mint in 1871.

The gold was being transported from Virginia City and would have to pass through such mining communities as Gold Hill, Silver City and Spring Valley, all of which were known for their populations of road agents. These villages, however, were negotiated without incident.

It was when the stagecoach, topped by a driver and shotgun guard, neared the town of Empire that four masked men leaped in front of the four-horse team, sixguns pointed at the shotgun guard. The latter allowed discretion to replace valor and dropped his weapon. Without a word from the four men, the driver and guard dropped the strongbox after lifting it out of the coach's boot. One of the holdup experts fired a shot in the air in signal for the driver to whip his horses into a run toward Carson City.

The local sheriff formed a posse immediately and began to follow the trail of the bandits, using a local Piute Indian tracker. As it turned out, the four men were on foot, having left their horses some distance away. They had split up the loot and were packing it on their backs, this making for slow going. One of the reasons for leaving their horses so far away was to confuse trackers, but the Indian was better than they had expected.

The posse overtook the four holdup men as they claimed their horses near the banks of the Carson River and there was a gunfight. When it was over, only one of the four, Manuel Gonzales, survived...but there was no gold!

Gonzales was taken to Carson City, where he stood trial, admitting only that they had buried the gold, intending to return for it with the horses. Gonzales was sentenced to twenty years in the Nevada Territorial Prison at Carson City, where he insisted he could see the site of the buried gold from his cell window.

Wells Fargo agents — not to mention hundreds of independent searchers — combed the area for weeks, but failed to find the gold. The one disturbing consideration was that, if the Piute tracker was able to follow the boot prints of the four walking men, why had he not been able to spot the freshly dug area where the gold allegedly was buried?

Whatever the answer, Gonzales contracted tuberculosis in 1877. The officials of Wells Fargo, realizing he had only a short time, arranged for an immediate pardon. The theory was that he would return to his gold cache immediately and agents would be right in his wake to recover the stolen loot.

However, Gonzales simply wandered about Carson City, picking up a few odd jobs, not even bothering to leave the town limits. One local citizen — perhaps motivated more by greed than charity — took Gonzales into his home. During the last days of his life, this individual reported, the

Manuel Gonzales insisted he was able to see the hiding place of the Wells Fargo robbery loot from his jail cell, but when released, he apparently ignored it.

Of The Hundreds Of Stories Of Lost Wealth, Here Are Some Of The Lesser Known!

Mexican bandit discussed his early life as an outlaw and said that someday he would dig up the gold. But he never revealed its location, the citizen contended.

Wells Fargo detectives continued to cover Gonzales until he died. At that time, the search was abandoned by the stage firm. Over the years, however, there have been countless efforts to find the three hundred pounds of gold bullion. The loot supposedly is located east of Carson City in an area south of the old stage route and north of the Carson River.

On the assumption that the Piute tracker did not actually find the location and return later to claim it or the kindly citizen didn't learn the location prior to Manuel Gonzales' death, the gold still is waiting to be discovered.

At the turn of the century, a Spanish sheepherder was summering a flock in an area known as Squaw Meadows, just north of McCall, Idaho. To pass the time, he would wander the area around his woolly charges, collecting what he considered to be pretty rocks.

When Winter came on, the Spaniard quit his job and returned to Spain. It was not until the following Spring that the owner of the sheep visited the abandoned summer camp, where he discovered a pile of red-colored rocks that intrigued him. Apparently the Spanish sheepherder had seen the rock on a ledge in the area and had cut off some of the protrusions, bringing them back to his camp.

The sheepman, intrigued by the color of the rocks, broke one of them open with a hatchet and discovered wire gold running through it. The others proved equally rich in gold. The sheepman immediately began searching the area for a ledge that would match the samples. Meantime, he sent a letter to Spain, contacting his former employee, but when the Spaniard replied, he refused to divulge exactly where he had found the gold-bearing rocks.

This legend has been the cause for countless searches through the area for the red rock outcropping, but to date there is no record of it ever having been located.

In the middle of the last century, an engineer named John M. Gunn arrived in New Mexico Territory and began living with the Indians at the Laguna pueblo, an Indian village that today still is seen just off U.S. Route 66 west of Albuquerque. It was Gunn who compiled a history of the local Laguna and Acoma tribes and revealed the story of the Acoma silver strike.

According to Gunn's account, in 1862, the local Indian agent, identified as one Thomas Griner, discovered an old

Spanish manuscript that told of the location of a silver mine near the Acoma pueblo. The pueblo, incidentally, dates back to 1598, when the first Spanish colony was established in New Mexico. Both the Acoma and Laguna pueblos are located on the first trail blazed through New Mexico by the gold-seeking Spanish.

Griner retained the manuscript, but considered it just another bit of memorabilia left over from the Indian revolt of 1680 when the Spanish were driven out of the area temporarily.

But word of the treasure came to light again in 1889. At that time, the Atlantic & Pacific Railroad had been built through the territory and one of the timekeepers on the job was an Irish immigrant named Matt Daly. On one of his trips along the right-of-way, legend has it, Daly fell into conversation with an old Indian at McCarty's Station. This was an old railroad stop — long since abandoned — located at the edge of today's Laguna pueblo.

The Indian gave Daly a piece of silver ore, indicating that the mine was nearby, between Rio Puerco and Bluewater. Intrigued, but not knowing what to do with his knowledge, Daly took the piece of ore to William Brockman, a track foreman for the railroad. The latter took the ore to Denver, where an assayer stated the silver ore would run more than $800 to the ton. Doubting this indication of wealth, Brockman had the findings double-checked by assayers in San Francisco and Socorro, New Mexico. The reports matched.

Envisioning riches, Brockman immediately took steps to gain mining rights on the Indian reservation. He even went to Washington, D.C., where he enlisted the aid of an Ohio congressman. The two began to work their way through the endless red tape that would be required to invade the reservation for prospecting and mining. Apparently, it became too much for them, for the entire project was abandoned.

Investigation shows that there are now digging scars in the area indicated as the site of the mine. If the old Indian was telling the truth about the location of the silver lode, the tribes inhabiting that section of Valencia County, New Mexico, today own countless wealth — it only has to be found.

At McCall, Idaho, a Spanish sheepherder allegedly discovered a ledge of almost pure gold, but later refused to divulge the exact location of his find.

The silver-laden mules were driven into a lake where the wealth was dropped into the water. But following the Indian attack, those sent to recover it, found the silver had sunk in the quicksand. It has not been recovered.

Today, the community of Spanish Fort, Texas, is a virtual ghost town, although once it was a more or less thriving spot on the Chisholm Trail.

The town goes back beyond the Texas cattle drives, however, for it first was settled by Louisiana French in 1718, a fort being built at the edge of a lake. The lake since has been drained and the fort site and lake bed now are part of an agricultural field. At one time, there was an Indian settlement, too, on the banks of Village Creek which runs through the area, adjoining the historic Red River. Based upon archeological findings, it would appear that upward of 10,000 Indians once lived in this settlement.

The French located several rich silver deposits in the area and they have continued to be worked on a limited basis down through the decades. A smelter was located on a nearby farm and local historians insist it was in use for a good length of time, for cinders from coal and charcoal cover at least a quarter of an acre, being spread there when burned out.

The local Indians were of the Taovaya tribe and were constantly at war against the marauding Comanches. The French, too, had their problems, but continued to move out the smelted silver bricks by packtrain. According to

local legend, one of these trains — with twenty or more mules burdened with silver — was attacked by Indians. The mule skinners ran the pack animals into the lake, quickly stripping the silver and sinking it into the murky waters. As soon as this was done, they ran for the fort, some of them making its gates.

Several days later, when the danger had passed and the Comanches had moved on, the French drovers returned to the lake, seeking the sunken silver, but it had disappeared beneath the quicksand that bottomed a portion of the lake.

To date, two parties of searchers have used modern scientific means to search for the silver in what now is a dry lake bed. In each case, according to reports, it was a dowsing rod that led both to the same spot.

In one of the searches, a twelve-inch pipe about twenty feet in length was sunk at the site, the sand being removed from inside the pipe as it was sunk into the ground.

Almost at its full depth, it was stopped by what tests showed to be a rotting tree trunk. But there was no silver.

In 1758, the Spanish Army attacked the fort to find it manned by French and friendly Indians. The battle was short and the Spanish fled. However, in recent years, a number of bronze cannon balls and numerous muzzleloader bullets have been found at the battle site. To date, no one has recovered the silver from the dry lake bed — if it ever was there.

Today, Barstow, California is a sprawling desert community on the main route from Los Angeles to Las Vegas and is the home of one of the Marine Corps' largest repair and supply facilities.

But only a scant few years ago, it was little more than a spot on a map and a stopping-over watering place for desert prospectors. From this past has sprung a legend of a gold brick worth an alleged quarter-million dollars that was stolen, buried — and lost to the world.

The story is well known by old-timers of the desert community, although some admit they feel it is legend rather than fact. However, at the basis of most legends there is a kernel of fact. This may well be the situation in this case.

According to the local story, a shipment of gold bullion in brick form was transferred at the railroad station in Barstow and was stored in a building. During the time it awaited shipment on another train, one of the bricks disappeared and local law enforcement officials scoured the area to no avail.

A couple of decades later, two desert dwellers were sharing a campfire near the ghost town of Calico — now resurrected as a tourist attraction — when one claimed he had stolen the gold brick. His companion turned him in as soon as possible, but when a sheriff's posse arrived at the Calico camp, the supposed thief was gone. He never was found.

Out of the jumble of rumor has come a map which has been reproduced in Southern California newspapers any number of times, but the terrain has changed considerably over the years. Originally, there were the tracks of the Sante Fe railroad, the railway station, the Mojave River, a bridge, a grove of trees and a rock corral, all supposedly keys to the location of the gold brick. The corral is gone, of course, and freeways have cut through the area to change the look of the terrain.

Another problem is the obvious fact that a gold brick worth $250,000 would have weighed in the vicinity of a thousand pounds — based upon turn-of-the-century gold prices — and could hardly have been moved by one man. It also is unlikely that it would have been smelted in so large a mass, although silver was made in heavy bars in the area to discourage theft.

Bricks weighing a hundred pounds were more logical in that era and still would have been worth $25,000. If there ever was such a missing piece of gold, the legend may well have increased the value ten-fold over the years.

Found in Texas, this is a part of robbers' loot valued at over $140,000 in Mexican pesos taken in a 1914 robbery.

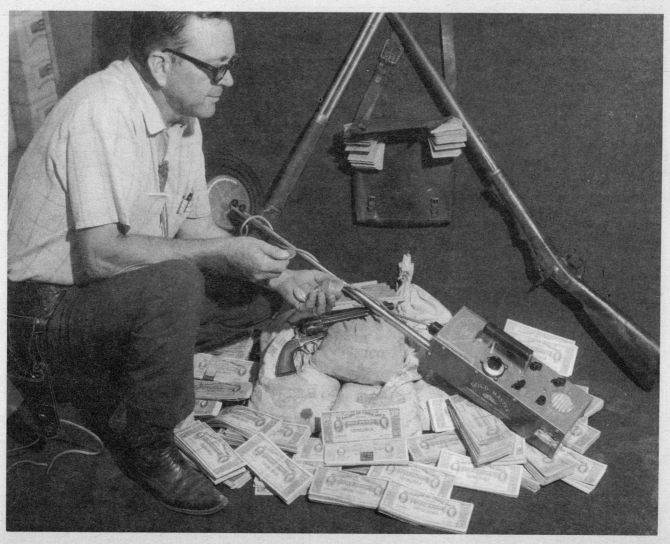

Chapter 3

The Deep Six

The Caribbean Is Rife With Sunken Treasures; Some Of Them Have Even Been Discovered!

THE CARIBBEAN SEA, that expanse of water extending south of Florida and to the areas of South and Central America, long has been considered one of the most lucrative treasure areas of the world.

There are several reasons for this. First, it was through this area that most of the Spanish, Dutch and English treasure ships sailed after their varied rapes of South and Central America. Too, the stormy seas with frequent hurricanes resulted in numerous wrecks and sinkings, the fortunes in jewels, gold and silver going to the bottom in most cases. The waters are treacherous with shoals, sandbars and coral reefs coming up from the supposed deeps to rip the hulls of passing vessels.

And it was in this area that the pirates of old operated for the most part. In taking a ship by act of piracy, more than one treasure ship went to the bottom before the pirates could board her and remove the wealth.

A great number of finds have been made in these waters, but there still is great wealth to be discovered by those willing to take the time, do the research and — in most cases — spend the money required for such expeditions.

A case of Florida treasure never recovered has to do with an old fisherman who operated out of the Florida Keys during the 1930s. According to local legend, the old man went to sleep one day while fishing. When he awoke, the wind had carried him aground on a small sandbar.

The fisherman stepped over the side of his small boat to push it off the sand. At that moment, he noted that the bottom seemed to be scattered with bars of metal. According to his later recounting, the bars were scattered over an area of about three hundred feet in diameter, perfectly visible in the clear waters.

Not all pirate attacks were successes and many a treasure went to the sea's bottom before it could be captured.

The fisherman took them for pig iron ballast from a freighter, but tossed several of them into his own boat, figuring he could find a use for them back at his home port.

When he returned to the dock, he unloaded the bars and stacked them on the pier. They lay there for several days before someone noticed that, beneath the barnacles and other encrusting material, the bars appeared to be a dull gray color.

The fisherman, now curious, took one of these ingots to a local jeweler, who announced that it was of pure silver!

Then sadness enters the tale. The fisherman could not find the source of his wealth. He died ultimately, still looking for the sandbar where he had been sent aground by wind and tide, but until now the wealth never has been rediscovered.

But there have been happier episodes, too. In July, 1965, one Robert M. Weller rose to the surface beside his search vessel, pushed back his scuba mask and extended his hand toward his partners.

He held a fistful of 1732 pillar dollars. After nearly 232 years, he had discovered the treasure of the "El Sueco do Arozon." This Spanish packet had been caught in a hurricane in 1733 along with other treasure ships of the Spanish Armada, the famed treasure convoy that left for Spain each July from the New World. In that gigantic storm, ten vessels of the fleet were sunk.

Weller and his partners had made an extensive study of the incident and finally had begun searching offshore from Duck Key in the Florida Keys. All was legal and planned, as they were operating under a lease granted by the State of Florida.

In the clear water, it had been comparatively easy to find the sunken ship's ballast rocks. But in the years between, all debris from the wreckage had been carried

39

Delores Fisher, a better than average diver, holds aloft what is left of a pewter platter taken from Spanish wreck.

away by tide and weather. One problem, too, was that the area had been worked over by other treasure hunters.

Out of funds, Weller joined with three others: Ray Maneiri, Pat Patterson and Bradley Patten, all of whom were intrigued with the fact that this specific pile of ballast rocks seemed to be in only eight feet of water and only forty yards offshore.

Judging from the size of the mound of stones, the treasure hunters felt this had been a fairly small ship but, at that point, they didn't even know its true identity. The ballast rock was scattered over a radius of nearly a hundred yards, but the greatest concentration seemed to be a pile about three feet deep and twenty feet in length.

Closer investigation revealed that coral had literally cemented the stones together, but inside, there were signs of metal, mostly nails and bolts of hand manufacture. A bit at a time, the three men began to remove the solidified mass, swinging heavy hammers against chisels in the effort-slowing water. It became a mammoth task, stretching into weeks.

Meantime, there was a new problem. One of the divers noted that a small boat with three men was lying off the

The same Delores Fisher examines a gold disk as well as a number of gold coins during a pause in firm's offices. The salvage firm actually operates from its own boat.

island, the occupants watching them with binoculars. This continued for some days. In addition, sharks began to show up in the area, one of them a twenty-foot, man-eating hammerhead.

Weller's dog jumped overboard at one point and was promptly swallowed by the hammerhead. On another day, Weller was literally trapped on the bottom, according to his later reports, trying to avoid a shark. Then the divers discovered that someone — presumed to be the three observers — was moving over the wreck during the night, dropping raw horsemeat in the immediate area for the purpose of drawing sharks!

That made the divers even more certain they were onto something big. This became even more evident when one of them rose to the surface with the rusted, encrusted remains of a Spanish flintlock rifle. As it was pulled from the rocks, the weapon literally was broken in two because of its deteriorated state. Soon, though, the searchers began to come up with cannon balls, canister shot and other weaponry, as well as buttons, ivory relics and even a pair of jeweled cufflinks. Needless to say, as the relics became more numerous, excitement increased. All of these items

Above: Divers for Treasure Salvors display gold ingots which were recovered from a 1622 wreck. (Left) This is called a Spanish biscuit and is the shape in which gold was cast for shipment from the New World centuries ago.

This is the treasure hunting vessel owned by Treasure Salvors for use in actual hunting and digging for wealth.

would be of value to collectors, but the real treasure — if there was one — was yet to be found.

Then came the Fourth of July. On that day, Weller and his partners felt as though they were in the midst of a parade, for all sorts of tourists thronged the nearby shore for the holiday. They also found their efforts hindered by the fact that their own boat was surrounded by pleasure boats that had invaded the area. They weren't even certain that the shark feeders weren't among those who came close to see what was happening.

The operation was covered — to a degree, at least — by the statement that "we are teaching scuba diving." That seemed to satisfy the curious.

It was late in the afternoon and most of the crowd had left when Weller spotted something colored among the rocks and sand. He plunged his hand into a crevice, felt the round flatness of coins and scooped up a handful. Clutching them to the chest of his wetsuit, he began to kick his way to the surface.

Aboard the boat, he discovered that he had more than four hundred pillar dollars, each dated 1732. The State of Florida evaluated the find and estimated the artifacts and coins at being worth $30,000.

But that was when more problems set in. It became necessary to pay the state its contractual split of $7500, then there was a company that had the original lease on the site. The firm came in for a cut, too. The partners split what remained, then each of the individuals had to make settlement with the U.S. Treasury Department in the matter of internal revenue.

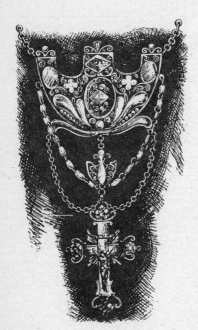

The less experienced treasure hunters dream of finding the crown jewels of a kingdom, but in the Caribbean, such items as these are unlikely. Instead, most of the treasures are in rough minted or cast bars or bagged jewels for shipment.

When it was all over, Weller admitted that he had more satisfaction than money out of the operation. The proceeds, however, have gone into more treasure hunting. At the time of this find, Weller planned to begin looking for another Spanish Armada ship, the "Almiranta," which was alleged to have gone down with some $2,500,000 in gold aboard.

Weller, however, was up against some competition in the person of one Mel Fisher, a professional treasure hunter who operates a firm called Treasure Salvors. In fact, Fisher — in recent years — has come to be called "Mister Treasure" by the pros.

In 1973, Fisher located the wreckage of the "Almiranta," the "La Margarita" and the "Nuestra Senora de Atocha," all parts of the fleet that went down in the hurricane.

Fisher's entire family became involved in the search, since his wife, Delores, is an excellent diver, as are both of his teen-age children, Kim and Dirk. In fact, Fisher contends that either of the youngsters are fully capable of skippering the sixty-five-foot boat, "Southwind," from which hunting operations are conducted.

Fisher earlier had discovered another segment of the Spanish fleet, which had sunk in 1715 and had spent several years in working it. In all, he is reputed to have collected nearly $4,000,000 from it before the riches began to run out and he moved on to new territory.

The Atocha wreck had been the subject of many a search over the past three centuries. In fact, the Spanish of three hundred years ago were the first to search for it, hoping to recover the wealth for the coffers of the king in Madrid.

According to Fisher, who researches all projects carefully before committing his efforts, the manifest for the Atocha wreck ran more than three hundred pages! According to the written records, there were more than nine hundred bars of silver, each weighing more than sixty pounds. There also were some fifteen tons of gold aboard the wreck, as well as jewels.

Fisher also learned that, of some 250 people who were aboard the vessel at the time it sank in the hurricane, there were only five survivors.

Most of the records of the sunken fleet are gathering dust in the Archives of the Indies in Seville, Spain. But with the few records he had been able to assemble, Fisher began to sort out the facts, discard the legends and attempt to determine where in the broad expanse of the Caribbean the wreckage lay.

The records available state that the ships sank in the vicinity of Cabeza de Los Martires. In Spanish, the word, "cabeza" means "head" and all of the Florida Keys were called "martires" by the early Spanish. With the chain of islands extending over many miles, which end of the chain could the term refer to?

The distance from Miami to Key West, covering the entire chain of islands, is some 165 miles. Not knowing whether the term, cabeza, referred to the Key West end of the chain or to that nearest Miami, Fisher decided he would start at the latter end, moving slowly down the Keys to search the entire area.

He began the slow search in 1968, using funds from previous treasure finds to finance his operation. It took him two years to search his way to Key West, but he had

This gold chain was recovered by one of Treasure Salvors' divers from the 1622 wreck located off Florida Keys.

bypassed some sixty miles of small islands and coral reefs. At that time point, Fisher moved the entire Treasure Salvor's operation — office and equipment — to Key West to carry on the continuing search. At this point, he admits, finding the Atocha was verging on an obsession.

In the Summer of 1971, Fisher was working an area inshore of the deep dropoff in the Marquesas. On one pass, he noted that his underwater metal detector was acting strangely. He dropped a buoy in the area, made a parallel pass over the point and found that the needle on the mag hit the peg. He was over something big! According to Fisher, the area of activity seemed to be about 150 feet long and forty feet or so wide; approximately the dimensions of a ship.

"The water was only about twenty-two-feet deep," Fisher recalls, "but because of the wind and rain we had been having for a week, I couldn't see bottom."

The boat was anchored and Fisher went over the side in his diving gear. Fighting a strong current, he swam for the bottom, but all he could see was sand.

"Years of experience had taught us that any wreck that was visible above the sand probably had been worked," Fisher says. "A wreck that was buried completely probably was covered by the same hurricane that had sunk it and the cargo might very well be intact."

The boat was anchored on the site and that evening, the crew went over the additional records they had obtained since beginning their search in 1968. They learned that the La Margarita had sunk near Dry Tortuga and that the Atocha sank within sight of her. Later, a part of the hull of the latter vessel was found washed ashore.

The waters were calmer when the vessel was brought directly over the site of the supposed buried wreck and the blowing equipment lowered to the bottom. The mechanism stirred up the sand, causing it to be carried away on the currents. However, after half a day, they found that the current was filling the hole with new sand as rapidly as the old was being carried away. At the end of the day, they had made virtually no progress. By probing, they had found that the sand was up to a dozen feet deep.

A good deal of consideration was given to the project and finally it was decided that a breakwater was needed. Only a few miles away was a 460-foot freighter that was nearly a hundred years old. No longer seaworthy, it could

This gold bar and the grape shot on top of the oil drum were recovered from the 1622 fleet's wreckage found in the shallows off the Florida Keys.

be purchased for a few dollars. Also, thinking ahead, Fisher and his crew realized that when they sank it to become the breakwater, the main deck still would be above water and could be used for office space and quarters. As something of an omen, the name of the vessel was "Real Gold."

Theory was that the ship would be sunk only temporarily, the valves being opened for the purpose. After it had served its purpose, the valves could be closed by a diver, the ship pumped out and refloated. As it turned out, this was great as an idea, but there were complications. It seems there is a law called the Federal Refuse Act of 1899, which states an object cannot be placed or sunk on the bottom of the ocean without full Congressional approval.

After two months of searching, Fisher and his firm found a pair of tugboats which had much larger propellers. Taken to the site, they soon uncovered the wreck. The diving began and almost daily items began to come off the bottom, such as pewter and silver plates. They didn't expect to find coins, as the Spanish didn't begin to mint gold until 1627 and the date of this wreck was 1622. But there should have been gold and doubt was beginning to show among the crew.

Then two gold bars, each weighing about 2½ pounds, were brought off the bottom. Morale immediately soared. There still was a problem, though. These bars had no official markings to indicate they were property of the crown. Instead, they appeared to be contraband; gold that had been smuggled aboard by a crew member of the sunken ship for his own use. However, there had been enough in the way of artifacts come off the bottom that were included in the ship's manifest to assure that this was indeed the Margarita.

Then, in July, 1973, one of the divers came up with a gold disk that was listed on the Atocha manifest. This led to some mass confusion. After that, in rapid succession came three silver bars, all weighing more than sixty pounds each. One of these, the records showed, also had been aboard the Atocha. Being found in rapid succession were forty-odd pounds of gold pieces-of-eight, a handmade gold chain and a rosary. Oddly, some of the coins were shown to have been minted in Bogota, Colombia, and bore the dates of 1620 and 1621. The fact that coins had been minted this early exploded all previous theories, of course.

The work has continued, with more gold and silver com-

When heavily armed ships went to the bottom, their armament soon became encrusted with coral, other sea life, but if discovered, even the old cannon can prove to be of great value.

ing out of the wreck site at this writing, but there still should be some $15,000,000 in gold and silver in the area. But the task has not been without its dangers. Two men have been killed thus far. One was a diver who simply went down and never returned. The other was a boy who dived off the boat and came up in the turning propeller blades.

The take to date, Fisher says, is something over $4,000,000.

Kip Wagner was considered another of the Florida area's top treasure hunters prior to his death and it was his 1959 discoveries that were largely responsible for locating the treasure from the Spanish Plate Fleet that was destroyed in 1715. The ten galleons making up the fleet had been rotting on the bottom of the sea for almost 250 years, until Wagner's discovery that netted more than $5,000,000 for the Real Eight Company, another treasure-oriented Florida firm.

As with other wrecks, most of the wood had been washed away by storms or had been eaten away by teredo worms. Left on the bottom were the piles of coral-cemented ballast rock.

One of the reasons for the riches at the bottom of the sea is the fact that during the War of Spanish Succession (1701-1713), much of the riches in coin and bullion was held because of a lack of ships. When the war ended, a fleet was dispatched to bring the wealth back to Spain, all of them surrounded by armed galleons. Estimates — based

Above: One of the true deans of professional treasure hunting, Mel Fisher rests between dives. (Below) The same diver comes up from depths with a silver disk.

upon old records — are that some $15,000,000 in gold and silver was included in the fleet that set sail from Havana.

Five days out of the Cuban port, the flotilla was caught in a hurricane in the Bahama Channel. Ten of the eleven ships were sunk, with more than a thousand crewmen lost.

Salvage operations were begun by the Spanish several months later and several million dollars is said to have been recovered.

Gold holds well in salt water, but silver tends to be affected. The Real Eight Company's find shows that the bulk of the treasure found was silver pieces-of-eight. But after more than two centuries in the brine, many of the coins were fused together by action of the sea water. One chest was brought up that, when opened, revealed a lump of silver weighing more than two hundred pounds.

Some of the items salvaged have been auctioned by firms dealing in such materials. Two auctions were held in New York City, the first in 1967, the second in 1972. A third was held in Los Angeles in 1973.

In the last auction, placed on the block were 244 gold coins and 356 coins of silver. Also included were gold and silver jewelry, a cannon, cannon balls, pewter items and even several Chinese porcelain cups that must have been a part of the ship's equipment. Many of the coins, incidentally, had been coined in Peru, Mexico and Colombia. There were numerous examples that previously had been unknown to coin collectors and these became singularly important in value. Total return from that particular auction was in the vicinity of half a million dollars.

Perhaps the highest priced item of the sale, however, was a gold whistle — the emblem of rank of a captain or general. The whistle was suspended on a chain of 2,176 gold links and sold for $50,000. According to Spanish history, had the ship been involved in battle and captured, it would have been traditional for the whistle to be thrown overboard, which is one reason it is considered a great rarity.

Henry Cannon, one of the principals of the Real Eight Company, says he believes "we have only recovered a small portion of the wealth lying on the ocean floor. By auctioning some of our finds we are getting the items out into the hands of the public. Meantime, such sales also help to finance further searching for the balance of the treasure of the Spanish Plate Fleet."

Individual on left is representative of Florida Board of Archives and History, looking on as Delores Fisher and son, Dirk, examine gold chain from the Margarita.

Death of the Andrea Doria

Lifeboats already have been launched from one side of the Andrea Doria, as the proud Italian ship is in early stages of sinking after accident.

This Modern Treasure Ship Lies Waiting For Its $4,000,000 Horde To Be Taken!

The Deep Six: Part B

The bow of the Swedish liner SS Stockholm was badly damaged, after the vessel rammed the SS Andrea Doria in a fog off of Nantucket Island, but this vessel was able to limp into port with the aid of the Coast Guard.

ALTHOUGH HISTORY IS rife with reports of sunken treasure ships, riverboats and lake steamers, one doesn't have to go back all that far to learn of vessels that have gone to the bottom bearing literally millions of dollars. Some of those wrecks, such as the Italian luxury liner Andrea Doria, still are waiting to be searched and the treasure recovered.

It was on the night of July 25, 1956, that the liner sank in 240 feet of water, forty-five miles south of Nantucket, off the Massachusetts coast. The ship went down after being broadsided by the Stockholm in one of the freak sea accidents of the era.

The captain of the Andrea Doria, a gentleman named Calamai, was considered a better than average seaman or the 656-foot vessel out of Genoa, Italy, never would have been placed in his charge. In spite of the fact that his ship was surrounded by heavy fog, he felt that the radar equipment aboard her was more than adequate protection against other ships in the area. Besides, he was trying his best to meet an arrival schedule in New York.

The Stockholm, outfitted at her bow with ice-breaking equipment, was outbound from New York, headed for Europe. According to reconstruction of the circumstances by the U.S. Coast Guard, had both ships held their slated courses, they would have passed each other. But apparently there was misunderstanding between the two captains, who were in contact by radio. The captain of the Andrea Doria hoped to pass starboard-to-starboard of the other ship, so he turned to the left. The captain of the Swedish-flagged vessel was not aware of the turn and, meaning to pass portside-to-portside, turned to the right. At approximately 11 p.m., the Stockholm's ice-breaking equipment smashed into the starboard side of the 29,082-ton luxury liner. The liner suffered a fracture in her hull below the water line and began to list to starboard almost immediately, as water rushed into the holds. In fact, the list was so bad that it became impossible to lower the portside lifeboats!

Frantic calls for assistance brought other vessels steaming through the fog to aid in rescuing survivors and Coast Guard units, alerted immediately, rushed to the scene.

The rescue efforts, hampered by the heavy fog, went on for nearly eleven hours. At approximately 10 a.m. on July 26, the Andrea Doria disappeared beneath the black waters of the Atlantic, leaving only a mass of floating debris to mark her passing.

The bow of the Stockholm was badly damaged, accord-

49

ing to Coast Guard reports, but she was able to make New York escorted by Coast Guard vessels.

The list of valuables that went down with the ship varies greatly, depending upon the report reviewed, but there is no doubt that there is at least $4,000,000 in cash and valuables on the Atlantic floor at the forty-fathom mark, waiting to be claimed.

Not that it hasn't been attempted. It has, but the one known effort was unsuccessful.

A comparison of various reports submitted to insurance companies and other agencies shows that cash and negotiable bonds aboard the vessel amount to more than $2,000,000 alone. There also is a great deal of valuable jewelry still in many of the staterooms, left behind by panicked passengers. Actress Ruth Roman, for example, left all of her jewels behind as she attempted to save her small son. Although there is no way at this time of telling what damage has been done by water over the past two decades, there also are a number of valuable paintings, including several by Rembrandt, in the wreckage. The collection was being brought from Europe to be displayed in New York.

Another item listed was a Chrysler experimental automobile that had been designed for use in the future and was considered to have cost $100,000 just to build. The propellers and anchor also are of great value simply as salvage, as would be the ship's silverware. Added up, this accounts for the projected figure of $4,000,000. In addition, anything brought up from the wreck would find some demand among collectors who concentrate upon such relics.

In July, 1973, a pair of former Navy divers out of San Diego, California, began the first — and thus far, the only — attempt to regain the sunken wealth from the ill-fated ocean liner. The two, heading a team of eighteen divers,

Survivors of the sea accident are taken aboard U.S. Coast Guard bouy tender, after many survivors spent the long, foggy night in lifeboats.

Seamen were unable to launch half of the lifeboats on the Andrea Doria, because the vessel listed so badly that the tackle was badly fouled.

were Donald Rodocker, then 27, and Christopher De Lucchi, then 22. The previous year, De Lucchi had set a world's record for open sea saturation diving, going down 845 feet. At the time, he was a diving instructor for the Navy. Included in the array of divers assembled for the treasure try were technicians, a diving physician and cameramen. The latter, of course, were on hand to get a film that would perhaps help to recoup some of the $300,000 allegedly invested in the search.

The team had purchased the Naragansett, an old fishing boat from which to launch their operations. Loaded aboard this was a five by twelve-foot chamber that would allow Rodocker and De Lucchi to live on the bottom for days, thus eliminating great amounts of decompression time in returning to the surface. This chamber was nicknamed "Mother" by the crew and was equipped with piped-in music, sanitation facilities and bunks. Once the wreck was located, this chamber was secured to the Andrea Doria and a sea elevator was installed, thus allowing those on the surface to lower food, supplies, medicines and necessary search equipment to those below.

A great deal of thought — not to mention modern technology — had gone into the planning phase and the gathering of the necessary equipment.

But in spite of all of the careful pre-planning, there were immediate problems. For example, the underwater chamber developed problems in its electrical circuits. After only two hours beneath the water, it had to be raised from the ocean floor and hauled back to Fairhaven, Massachusetts, for the needed repairs.

This required a week and was considered a temporary setback. However, in their haste to get "Mother" back into operation, the treasure divers began to haul the chamber back to the site at night. The chamber was being towed

Andrea Doria is listing badly to its starboard side. A below the waterline rupture caused the vessel to sink. A Coast Guard vessel stands by at its death

Empty lifeboat, the survivors rescued, floats aimlessly in foreground, as the Italian luxury liner turns on its side in last moments afloat.

behind a boat. A passing freighter, unidentified in the thick night fog, set up a heavy wake that had residual effects. Under the stress, the tow line broke and it required hours of frantic work to rescue the repaired chamber and keep it from sinking on the spot.

Finally, on August 3, this underwater habitat was lowered in the vicinity of the Andrea Doria and tied off to the wreckage. Operating from this underwater home base, the divers moved into the wreckage of the luxury liner and began cutting away metal that blocked their paths, making their way through the vessel's passageways.

According to reports from the crew, although the water was cold and not precisely their habitat, a number of sharks began to cruise the area, observing the progress. On the

third day of the search, a few artifacts were being sent to the surface, but nothing of exceptional value.

Whatever ghosts of the depths had sent the luxury liner to the bottom seemed to plague the crew bent upon salvage.

First, the lines that sent air into the underwater chamber developed trouble and the divers were unable to operate from there until repairs could be made. Also, the lines that fed fuel to the cutting torches began to foul. However, these also were repaired and the search went on.

On August 15, the diving experts cut their way into the office of the ship's purser where most valuables would have been kept. The next morning, they announced they would begin cutting into the vaults located in the office.

The SS Andrea Doria sinks beneath the waters off Nantucket. Some $4,000,000 is still aboard her.

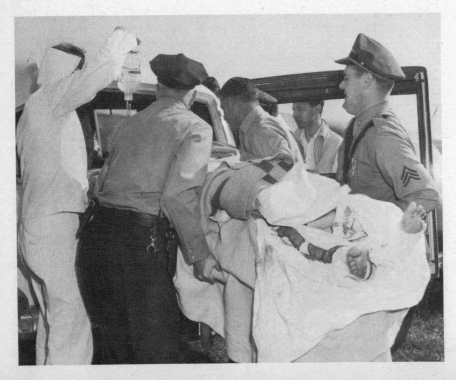

One of the critically injured from the stricken vessel is transferred to ambulance after rescue. Many of passengers left valuables behind.

But whoever may be the patron saint of treasure hunters seemed to have deserted the crew led by the two former Navy divers. That same evening, the sea went wild, huge waves washing over their operations vessel. In spite of the weather, the next day the divers went down again to inspect the wreckage, ready to attack the vaults in the purser's office.

But they soon were on the surface again. They reported that it was impossible to continue operating in the heavy seas. In addition, the bad weather had had its effect below the surface, too. That section of the luxury liner where they had been working had been virtually demolished, the entire purser's area covered by steel cables, bulkheads and wood from the ship's cabins. It had become a death trap.

Perhaps wisely, the divers allowed common sense to take over from ambition and greed.

According to reports, the only item that these divers brought up from the wreckage that might be considered worth money were four silver plates from the ship's main dining room and a bottle of rare perfume.

There are rumors that other divers have gone into the wreckage on a smaller, less ambitious scale, using explosives to clear their way. However, these divers never have been identified and there is no record that any of the take ever has been reported.

So far as can be determined, the Andrea Doria, where five people met death on that foggy night in 1956, still lies rusting on the bottom, waiting for her treasures to be gathered in.

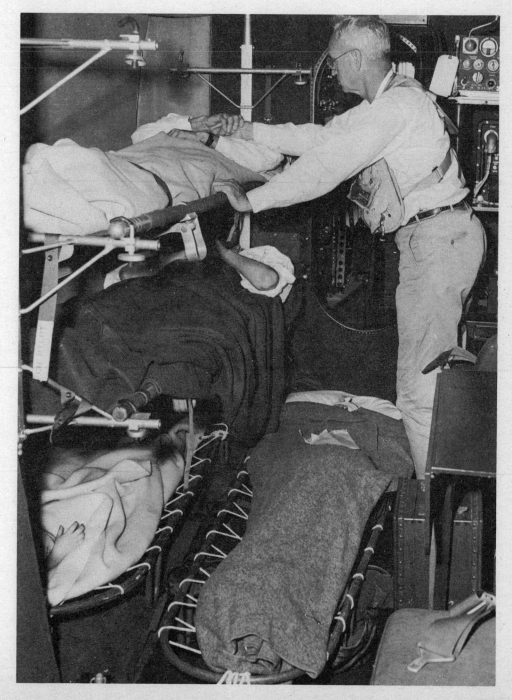

Injured passenger from the sea disaster is treated aboard a Coast Guard amphibian, as it returns to the mainland.

Chapter 4

LEGENDS OF THE LAKES

Not All Of The World's Lost Treasure Is At The Bottom Of The Briny Deep!

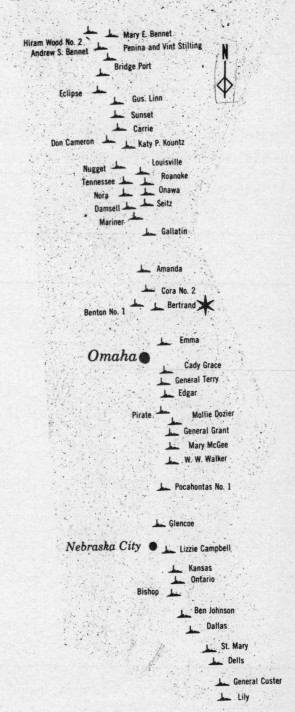

COURTESY OF NEBRASKAland

MOST OF US tend to think of sunken treasure as being the result of pirate attacks on the high seas, wealth lost forever at eighty fathoms, and in similar terms derived largely from old Errol Flynn movies about Captain Blood and Captain Kidd.

But there are countless treasures found in the freshwater bayous of this country, ranging from unsalvaged hordes on the Great Lakes through a lost British payroll somewhere in New York's Hudson River. The Missouri River, a few years ago, yielded the remains of the sternwheeler, Bertrand, which provided more than 200,000 items of historical — and resultingly, monetary — value.

During the last century, the Missouri and Mississippi rivers were major thoroughfares for trade, these waterways being used to handle much of the bulky cargo going North from New Orleans and the farm products coming South for shipment. Both rivers were treacherous, for it required little more than a hard rain for the streams to change course, new sandbars to be created and even log jams to threaten any boat whose captain was unwary. Much of this problem has been discussed by such writers as Mark Twain over the years, who accurately described life on a riverboat in some of his writings.

It was in March, 1865, that the sternwheeler left St. Louis under command of her captain, James Yores. Her destination was to be Fort Benton in Montana Territory, that being that final stretch of water of the Missouri on which so large a vessel could navigate. The river was swollen by spring rains and Captain Yores expected it to take him two months to negotiate its hazards.

According to records, the sternwheeler was heavily loaded, part of her cargo being flasks of liquid mercury needed in the gold fields for separating gold from its ore. The rest of the cargo was listed as general supplies, although there were supposed to be more than twenty tons of the quicksilver aboard. By today's standards, such a recovery would, in itself, be worth a fortune.

The mercury — or quicksilver, as it was popularly called in that era — would be carried overland by wagon and pack train to the frontier mining camps of Virginia City, Nevada, and Deer Lodge and Hellgate, Montana. The last named town now is known as Missoula, incidentally.

On April 1, 1865, the Bertrand hit some kind of snag in the river, sending her bow so high that water began to flow over the rails. She went down in less than ten minutes only a mile or so downstream from what then was the village of DeSoto in Nebraska Territory. This made the 161-foot vessel only one of more than four hundred riverboats allegedly sunk along the Missouri during that era.

Within a week, insurance companies had sent a crew of divers to the river for salvage purposes, but there are no records as to what actually was recovered. Instead, the legends grew with the years, while the Missouri River chang-

Above: Once the remains of the Bertrand, a sternwheeler that sank in the Missouri River in 1865, were found, the excavation work was carried on with great care, until the entire hulk was uncovered and the artifacts found. The river had changed course several times as a result of floods and the wreck was buried beneath tons of silt. (Upper right) Old bitters bottles were formed in shape of log cabins. (Lower right) Boxes were still well preserved.

ed her course no less than four times, eventually burying the riverboat beneath countless tons of silt and mud.

However, late in 1967, a pair of Omaha men, Samuel Corbino and Jesse Pursell, obtained a permit from the Federal Government to search for the Bertrand in what now is the DeSoto National Wildlife Refuge. It was necessary for the two men to sign an agreement in accordance with the Antiquities Act of 1906, whereby any artifacts taken from the wreck would be the property of the United States Government. Any treasure — identified in this case as gold, mercury and whiskey — would be shared, with the hunters receiving sixty percent of the value, the Government retaining forty percent.

The principal instruments in the hands of the treasure hunters were some old charts of the river, which reflected the course at the time of the sinking, and a flux-gate magnetometer, the latter designed to show readings on masses of buried metal.

In late 1967, they found an area that showed high metal readings and in February, 1968, they drilled core samples in the area. The samplings showed that a large object — possibly a boat — was located some thirty feet below the ground's surface. The drillings brought up bits of tin, tallow, wood, leather and even preserved cherries! The neck of

a bottle smelling of whiskey also was recovered through this sampling program, along with a bar of lead.

This was enough to convince the searchers that they needed heavy equipment. With this brought in, carefully they began to remove the silt deposits, but they ran into a problem when they encountered brackish water some ten feet below the surface of the ground.

A series of wells was installed to lower the water level, allowing operations to continue. It wasn't until late October, 1968, however, that the first section of the boat was uncovered. The following month, the workers found a box which was labeled, "Superior Palm Soap." More important, written across it were the words: "Stores — Bertrand." In an area where there were countless wrecks, the searchers had found the one they sought.

Needless to say, the search had become expensive and it was not until July 14, 1969, that four flasks of mercury were located amid the wreckage. These were the first negotiable items the salvagers had found from which they might reclaim a part of their investment. Five more flasks — each holding seventy-six pounds of mercury — were found in the wreckage. There also were signs that most of the mercury had been removed by the divers who had entered the wreck

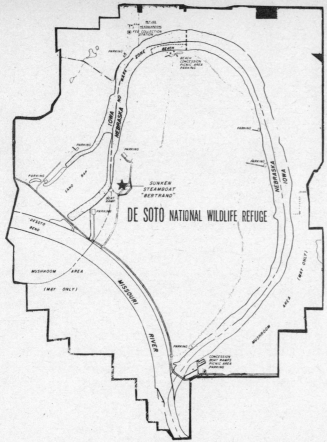

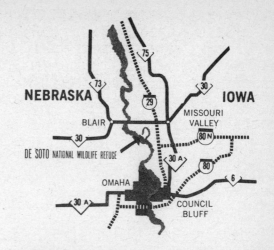

Above: Map shows location of the Bertrand wreckage in the De Soto National Wildlife Refuge. (Upper right) Area of discovery in relationship to landmarks of present day. (Right) This coal oil lamp was among artifacts found.

more than a century before, with these flasks simply being overlooked.

Huge pumps were brought in to lower the water level to the bottom of the wooden hull. The pumping operations continued around the clock and by late Fall, 1969, all of the cargo had been removed from the wreckage. According to James E. Frates, manager of the DeSoto National Wildlife Refuge, charts were made and photographs taken for historical purposes. The cargo all was sprayed down with water, then sealed in polyethylene and removed to a

Hundreds of riverboats plied the inland waters in the last century, with many of them going to a watery death caused by hazards of navigation.

storage room where preservation operations would begin. Once the remains of the vessel had been cleaned out, it was literally returned to its lonely grave. The empty hull was refilled with sand, the pumps halted and the water table allowed to rise once more.

The recovery of the cargo is considered a great historical find and a new building is even being set up on the wildlife refuge to house laboratory equipment and provide storage space during the five years that will be required to clean and preserve the artifacts taken from the wreckage. Actually, there were more than two million items taken from the wreckage, but perhaps only one-tenth are worth preserving.

At this point, there are even plans to develop a visitor center, where the public can view the items that came from the wreckage. Before it was over, not only the Bureau of Sports Fisheries, but several other agencies became involved. It was the General Services Administration that negotiated the contract with Corbino and Pursell. While it is not known how much the two men received in return for their investment, it is estimated that the profits were more than adequate.

The residents along Chicago's Gold Coast, vacationers at Michigan City, Indiana, plus those who frequent the other resort and residential areas flanking the Great Lakes seldom think of treasure. Certainly they realize that this series of lakes — larger than some seas of the world in total surface — constitutes a major water shipping route of the globe, but most don't think beyond that.

However, records show that more than 10,000 vessels have been wrecked or sunk in the waters of these four bodies of connected water: Lake Michigan, Lake Superior, Lake Huron and Lake Erie.

Most of these wrecks are supposed to lie in waters that are easily accessible to scuba divers, yet few of them ever have been researched. Reason for the seeming lack of interest may rest in the fact that legends surrounding the wrecks tend to simply discourage the average diver.

Divers ask, for example, if the locations of these wrecks are known, isn't it likely that most of the valuables have long since been recovered? Also, most of the Great Lakes' wrecks do not abound with gold, silver and jewels, as is the case with pirate vessels in the Caribbean.

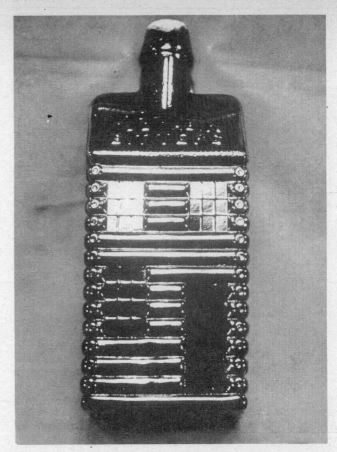

This bottle holding Old Cabin bitters is of interest to historians because of the intricate glasswork. It was among the items discovered in buried Bertrand ruins.

But perhaps, in such thinking, the basics of treasure hunting are being ignored. The professional knows that anything that is of sufficient value to be marketable can be considered a find. There are known wrecks in the Great Lakes loaded with copper ingots. With copper prices today,

Rough-finished bottles cast in wood moulds were used to hold pepper sauce that was being transported to frontier forts on the Missouri River.

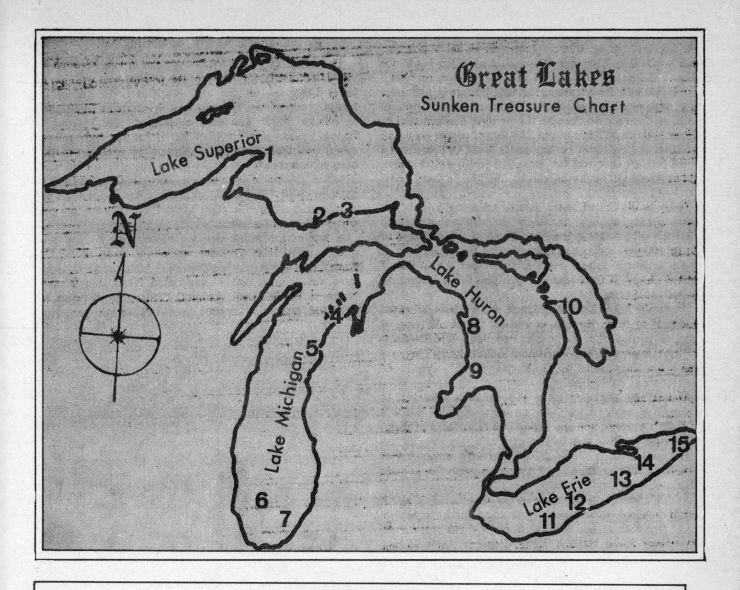

Great Lakes
Sunken Treasure Chart

LEGEND

1. The passenger steamer *Sunbeam,* lost on Sept. 28, 1863, with cargo of barreled whiskey. The passenger's personal effects are still aboard.

2. The steamer *Superior* lost on Oct. 29, 1856, with a cargo of specie and whiskey.

3. The steamer *Smith Mare,* sunk on June 18, 1889, with a cargo of 350 barrels of whiskey and a reported load of silver ore.

4. The *Westmoreland.*

5. The brig *Black Hawk,* foundered in Nov. of 1862 with a cargo of stained glass, worth a fortune to collectors today.

6. The *David Dows,* the only five-masted vessel to sail the Lakes, foundered in 1889. Any relic of her would be saleable to collectors.

7. The steamer *Chicora,* sank on New Year's Day, 1895, with specie and 120 barrels of whiskey.

8. The *Pewabic.*

9. The *Kitty Reeves,* a three-masted schooner, was lost on Nov. 7, 1870, with $250,000 in copper ingots.

10. The *Griffon,* built by Rene Robert Cavalier, de la Salle, the French explorer. The *Griffon* was the first ship to sail Lakes Erie, Michigan, and Huron. In 1679, with a cargo of furs, the vessel was lost, and her bones are believed to lie here.

11. The steamer *Anthony Wayne,* lost on April 28, 1850, between six and eight miles North West of the Vermillion River, with a cargo of specie and 200 barrels of whiskey. The personal effects of the passengers still rest in the hulk.

12. The barge *Cleveco,* lost on Dec. 2, 1942, with a cargo of 1,000,000 gallons of fuel oil.

13. The frigate *La Jean Florin,* lost on July 2, 1751, ten to fifteen miles offshore. Any relic from her would be valuable.

14. The *Atlantic.*

15. The British armed sloop *Beaver,* was lost on Aug. 28, 1763. Any of the military stores aboard would be saleable to collectors.

Snags, mud flats, sandbars all are among the navigational hazards that have resulted in freshwater ship sinkings.

two hundred tons of the red metal comprises a fortune! There also are literally fortunes in antiques aboard some of these vessels. Any sunken wreck that has aboard the ship's chinaware that might be a century old automatically holds a fortune, if one considers today's antique prices.

When thinking of sunken treasure, even when there is known to be no fortune aboard, one must think also in terms of the salvage values. One treasure hunter points out that ordinary building bricks sell these days for upwards of thirty cents each. A shipload of such construction materials is worth investigating. A ship's anchor that might be used for the base for a coffee table or even a lawn decoration is worth hundreds of dollars.

Collectors are a prime market for such salvage and, should one find a vessel loaded with old hand tools, these would be much higher in price — assuming they are fairly well preserved — than new tools of the same type. The blocks, pulleys and other equipment used in the rigging of old sailing vessels automatically constitute value, for there are collectors who covet this type of artifact, especially if there is a story that goes with it as to how the vessel was sunk. Even the handmade nails used in some of these old ships will bring up to $1 each!

The amateur tends to think in terms of famous treasure ships, but most of these — if the location is known — have been worked over years ago. Old newspapers and periodicals, however, constitute a source that can mean paydirt. Most newspapers keep files going back as much as a hundred years; some even have clippings cataloged, making the chore of research simpler. The old newspapers, in recent years, have been microfilmed and the editors often are willing to allow you to search the films, using the equipment at the newspaper's offices. The U.S. Government Printing Office also sells a series of wreck charts that are fairly accurate.

But once a lead has been discovered, additional research is in order. The wreck chart usually will afford basic information such as the date of the wreck, the name of the ship, the value and type of cargo by standards of that day. Navigation charts also are available and should be checked before becoming involved in any full-scale and expensive hunt.

These charts give one an idea of where the dangerous areas are as well as those that mean clear sailing. If a wreck is reported in an area where sailing is approved, chances are either it didn't happen or a wrong location has been reported. These charts are available from the U.S. Corps of Engineers, 630 Federal Building, Detroit, Michigan 48226.

Before you get carried away with searching for Great Lakes' treasures, be certain of your target. All too often, the cargoes of such ships have been salvaged and an expensive search would be nothing more than that: an expensive search.

As an example of what is meant, take the case of the Westmoreland, a propeller steamer of steel-hulled construction, which went down near Sleeping Bear, Michigan, on December 7, 1854.

This particular vessel was alleged to carry a cargo of gold and whiskey that was valued at more than $100,000. Also, it has mistakenly been reported as having foundered off Green Bay, Wisconsin, and also in the Straits of Mackinac Islands. Truth is that the gold and whiskey both were recovered from the vessel as long ago as 1869. If located, there might be some artifacts that would prove of value to collectors, but little else.

One of the best-maintained legends involves a ship called

Following the Revolutionary War, the British were allowed to search the Hudson River for their sunken ship that allegedly carried a payroll in gold. Thus far, the treasure — if it exists — never has been recovered.

the Atlantic, an old sidewheeler that went down in Lake Erie near Erie, Pennsylvania, in August, 1852. The vessel is supposed to have carried some $338,000 in gold in her safe. However, four years later, the ship's strongbox was brought up and opened. At that time, some $36,000 in paper money, bonds and gold were recovered. As for the balance, there still are treasure charts that list this as a gold ship, but the truth is that the discovered $36,000 was the full extent of the recovered wealth. The balance never existed.

Still another favorite treasure tale of the Great Lakes involves the wooden-hulled steamer, Pewabic, which went down after colliding with the Meteor of Thunder Bay in Lake Huron. This happened, according to old records, on August 9, 1865.

Legend held that the ship carried some $40,000 in gold in her safe as well as three hundred tons of copper in the hold. The stories continued to build until May, 1917, when the safe finally was recovered. When opened, there was no gold at all. Instead, there was a mass of rotting paper money. Of this, exactly one — repeat, one — five-dollar bill was recovered.

Of the copper aboard, fifty tons were recovered but, after that, the salvage operation was abandoned as being too dangerous. There are dangerous currents that run through Thunder Bay the year around and the area is subject to instant storms at almost any time of the year.

So, the three hundred tons of copper — minus that taken more than half a century ago — still remains to be salvaged. There are countless fortunes in metals and goods waiting at the bottom of these lakes for the right salvage team that operates under the correct set of circumstances.

In November, 1770, a British gunship — Her Majesty's Ship Hussar — sank in New York's East River. According to

one of the seamen from the downed ship, there were fourteen cartloads of silver and gold coins hidden aboard the vessel at the time she went down. The treasure has been estimated at more than five million dollars.

Today, somewhere off the Port of New York, the world's busiest port, lies what is left of that old ship and the two hundred-year-old treasure.

As for the details, the twenty-eight-gun, 114-foot vessel was moving up the Hudson, when the captain heard that there was a riot going on in what was to become New York City. The captain immediately ordered the ship to reverse course but, at a point known as Pot Rock, the vessel ran onto a single underwater spire and began to take on water. As the tide changed, the floundering vessel was swept off the point of rock into deeper water.

In an effort to make a landing, the captain ordered the vessel into the mouth of a small stream emptying into the river, but the warship ploughed into another water ledge, which ruptured the bottom and she sank almost immediately. Before England could think in terms of salvage, the growing hostilities that led to the Revolutionary War began to blossom and it wasn't until the early 1800s that the British crown asked that they be allowed to salvage their warship.

The colonies agreed, although they couldn't understand why one would want to salvage a gunboat, considering the expense and risk of underwater operations of that time. Whatever the reason, the British salvage ship and her crew worked for several weeks in the area, finally giving up and returning to England.

American observers, however, had heard the tale of treasure and, by the 1840s, there had been four more major attempts to salvage the vessel, all of them falling short of

During the last century, sidewheelers, utilizing sail as well as steam power were popular in lake, river trade.

success. A number of items such as glassware, pewter plates and cups, and even a branding iron for marking African slaves had been recovered. But the treasure — allegedly hidden under a layer of white ballast stone taken from the white cliffs of Dover — had yet to be found.

Several more attempts were made and a number of precious coins were found amid the wreckage, but little more. In 1900, another diving crew went after the sunken ship, but all they found was the anchor. Rot and the tides had disintegrated the hull, spreading her up and down the East River, parts of the waterlogged hull probably being swept downstream to the Atlantic, more of it buried beneath the silt.

One Simon Lake — to become renowned for his contributions to submarine design — began collecting research material on the sunken Hussar in 1933, finally receiving a salvage permit from the U.S. Treasury Department.

Lake, using inventions of his own, spent three years searching, finally announcing that he had found the final resting place of HMS Hussar.

"She is in silt off 135th Street in seventy-two feet of water," he informed the Treasury Department. However, there was a complication. The silt was covered by a rock-hard substance resembling tar. This was a puzzle until it was determined that it was the by-product of a gas manufacturing plant that had been dumping its residue into the river. In spite of this, Lake and his crew began chipping at the hard covering shell, while his bank account dropped each day.

By 1937, Simon Lake was down to his final financial resources and all he had to show for it were several truckloads of the black, tar-like substance. However, he decided on one final attempt.

By this time, a gentleman named Henry Ploger had contacted Lake, telling him that he was searching the wrong site. For one million dollars, he offered to show Lake the actual location of the wreck. Lake explained that he could not come up with that kind of money at this late date; most of his resources had been expended, but he did agree to award Ploger five percent of any treasure found.

To the amazement of all, Ploger ordered Lake's work boat moved to a point off 149th Street. As it turned out, Ploger had been a commercial fisherman and had fished many times over an underwater wreck that other fishermen had always identified as that of the old Hussar!

Lake's crew put down a probing drill and brought up ancient waterlogged timbers. But the searchers' elation was short-lived. Other drillings revealed nothing but more mud and silt.

By this time, England was well into World War II and it was becoming obvious that the hostilities would affect America. Lake, flat broke, returned to inventing and became involved in the defense industries of the time, trying to recoup his lost fortune. But before the war ended, Simon Lake died, never having achieved his greatest goal of locating the Hussar treasure.

F.L. Coffman, a noted diver and treasure hunter who has

become wealthy through tracking down legends until he has the gold in hand, estimates there is $275 billion in sunken treasure waiting to be reclaimed. He points out that since "1500 A.D., one-eighth of all the gold and silver mined has been lost in marine disasters."

The Griffon, a French vessel of sixty tons, was sunk on September 18, 1679 near Green Bay, Wisconsin. The ship had been engaged in the fur trade at the time she went down with her captain and five-man crew. More important to treasure hunters, of course, is the fact that she was carrying some $12,000 in gold for the payroll of military garrisons in the Upper Great Lakes region.

Several years ago, parts of the Griffon's wooden hull were thought to have been raised by a salvage expedition near St. Ignace, Michigan. Research allowed that the timbers raised were of the same kind used in the sunken ship; also that a peculiar type of wooden dowling utilized in its construction was used almost exclusively at that time by the shipyard in LaSalle, New York, where the vessel was built.

In spite of periodic searches since, however, no sign of the rest of the wreck — or of the $12,000 payroll — has been discovered.

The Lexington, a trading vessel, was reported sunk off Point Moullie in Lake Erie in 1846 with 110 barrels of whiskey aboard. Were this to be raised, one could truly say that he had the oldest "aged in the wood" whiskey in the world for sale. Of course, on the other hand, while the barrels have rotted and the whiskey has gone to intoxicate the fishes of the Great Lakes, there still is $300,000 in gold aboard the lost vessel to make the search worthwhile even for one who doesn't drink!

Several ships are known to have gone down over the years with cargoes of coal worth millions. The James B. Colgate was sunk in January, 1916 off Long Point, Ontario, in Lake Erie with a cargo of coal valued at $200,000; the William B. Davock, which went down in 1940 with coal in the holds worth $425,000 is reportedly in Lake Michigan little more than a mile off the town of Pentwater; the Anna Minch, which went down the same day, November 11, when it collided with the Davock, was carrying coal valued at $375,000. There are dozens of similar wrecks throughout the lakes.

There are at least six vessels lying on the lake bottoms with fortunes in copper aboard, waiting only to be salvaged. The Regina, which went down in Lake Huron off Hammond Bay in 1913 had copper cargo valued at $235,000 aboard; the Dakatah, sunk near Long Point, Ontario, in Lake Erie had a copper cargo of $500,000 aboard, while the Charles S. Price went down at the mouth of the St. Clair River in November, 1913, carrying $360,000 in copper. The G.R. Griffin, not to be confused with the wooden ship that sank in 1679, is thought to be lying two miles off of Lorain, Ohio, in Lake Erie, with her $525 of cargo still intact. She sank in 1896.

For the diver who finds the R.G. Coburn and the City of Detroit, double fortunes await. The former was sunk in 1871 with $75,000 in copper and $105,000 in gold and is thought to lie off Harbor Beach in Lake Huron. The City of Detroit went down near Barcelona, New York, in Lake Erie in 1873, carrying copper valued at $100,000 and an equal amount in gold.

Is This The Hiding Place Of Ancient
Pirate Gold? Fortunes Are Being Spent
In Learning The Truth!

Chapter 5

THE OAK ISLAND MYSTERY

ONE OF THE perennial treasures that has been eluding man for decades is the alleged horde located on Oak Island, Nova Scotia. If nothing else, it probably has constituted the most expensive hunt in history, inasmuch as it has been going on for more than 180 years.

Oak Island is only one of some three hundred islands scattered about the Canadian province's Mahone Bay on the Atlantic Seaboard. The island, only a mile or so in length and half as wide, is some four miles from the mainland. Since 1795, it has been the scene of an almost continuing search for the legendary booty of the infamous Captain Kidd, while others feel that the treasure said to be buried there probably is that of the English pirate, Henry Morgan; the loot taken from Panama and Maracaibo in the 1670s. Still others contend the wealth — if there is such — is that of Edward Teach, better known in history and legend as Blackbeard the Pirate. As he was about to be beheaded in 1718, he declared, "I've buried my treasure where none but Satan and myself can find it."

Oak Island can hardly double for Hell, but it has proved to have some of the same qualities for those who have spent lives and fortunes in an attempt to recover the supposed booty. In the past five years alone, for example, a syndicate made up of Canadians and Americans has spent well over half a million dollars drilling holes and shafts all over the island. In the past, engineers, scientists and geologists have headed up numerous groups that have attempted to find the treasure. In fact, there are those who say they know the location, but that removal is the problem.

The small island contains an extensive maze of man-made tunnels and caverns that engineers estimate would take a full-scale task force at least two years to complete.

The late President Franklin Delano Roosevelt was a partner in one of the expeditions, circa 1910, to find the supposed buried treasure. However, according to current accounts, little evidence of the treasure really has been found. These include bits of a parchment map, a couple of ivory bos'n's whistles, as well as several links of heavy gold chain. Also found have been pieces of milled metal and timbers that obviously were hand-hewn. The most unusual find, perhaps, is several tons of matting woven from coconut fibers. The chief question here, of course, is what are mats of a tropical fiber doing this far North?

According to popular legend, the continuing hunt started in 1795, when a trio of teen-age boys noted a strange depression beneath one of the oak trees. Supposedly thinking it might be an Indian burial site, they began to dig. Oddly enough, nearly a decade later, these same three were part of a syndicate that dug the first of many holes on the island. It was called, aptly enough, the "money pit."

The original three investigators were Daniel McGinnis, Anthony Vaughn and Jack Smith. Vaughn later told of the find, explaining that the spot was in thick oak scrub and had the appearance of having been cleared many years before.

According to Vaughn's recollections, the large oak tree standing near the center of the clearing was carved with odd-looking marks and symbols. One of the lower branches had been sawed off, the stub projecting directly over the center of the deep depression, which was about thirteen feet in diameter.

The three teen-agers began to dig at the center of the depression, soon discovering that they were working a previously dug shaft which had hard, solid walls, the old pick marks even showing. Meanwhile, in the shaft itself, the dirt was so soft that it could be handled with shovels and no need of picks.

By the time they had reached a depth of thirty feet, however, they became discouraged and quit — until nine years later. Sometime in 1802, the three youths — now

This is the residue of one attempt to locate the so-called treasure of Oak Island. Hundreds of thousands of dollars have been spent in the futile efforts to solve mystery.

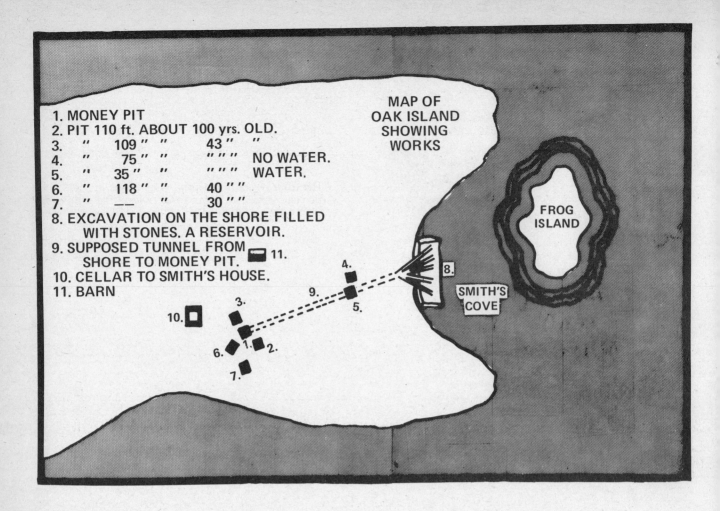

1. MONEY PIT
2. PIT 110 ft. ABOUT 100 yrs. OLD.
3.   "   109 "   "   43 " "
4.   "   75 "   "   " " " NO WATER.
5.   "   35 "   "   " " " WATER.
6.   "   118 "   "   40 " "
7.   "   —— "   "   30 " "
8. EXCAVATION ON THE SHORE FILLED
   WITH STONES. A RESERVOIR.
9. SUPPOSED TUNNEL FROM
   SHORE TO MONEY PIT.
10. CELLAR TO SMITH'S HOUSE.
11. BARN

MAP OF
OAK ISLAND
SHOWING
WORKS

FROG ISLAND

SMITH'S COVE

grown into men — told a Dr. Lynds of the shaft. He, in turn, organized the company of which the original three became members and the digging was renewed. With work renewed, the depth ultimately reached ninety-five feet, with marks every ten feet to indicate the level being found cut in the walls of the shaft.

According to Vaughn's report, at the ninety-foot mark, a flat stone measuring three feet long and sixteen inches in width was discovered. The stone allegedly was covered with marks or characters of a strange nature.

The stone, incidentally, was cemented into the fireplace in a house that Jack Smith was building at the time. It would appear that no one locally, at least, had any idea as to the meaning of the carved symbols in the stone's surface.

A number of years later, when the house was torn down, the stone was taken to Nova Scotia's capitol city of Halifax, where scholars attempted to decipher the markings.

As often happens with all treasure stories, legends and rumors were born aplenty. Whether the cuts in the stone ever were deciphered is not known, but there are differing stories to the effect that the inscription was translated to read: "Ten feet below are 2,000,000 pounds buried." Another version had it that the stone listed the depth at forty feet below where it was located.

As for the stone, itself, it long ago disappeared. The last indication was that it was being used by a bookbinder in his shop.

When the crew financed by Dr. Lynds' syndicate reached the ninety-five-foot level, they came to a wooden platform that extended over the entire surface of the shaft. As it was Saturday evening, they quit work for the rest of the weekend.

Returning on Monday, the workmen found the shaft filled with water to within twenty-five feet of the top, although there had been no previous indications of intrusion. Attempts over the next twenty-four hours to bail out the shaft met with total failure.

It was decided to sink a new shaft just to the east of the original hole, the idea being to go down 110 feet, then tunnel into the so-called money pit. This shaft was dug as planned and all seemed to be going well, until the workers started cutting into the area below the original shaft. The water burst through the partially completed tunnel's wall, nearly drowning the workers. Water soon filled this shaft as well and the syndicate abandoned the project.

A similar effort was made in 1849 and was abandoned when the pit, which had filled in the meantime, again was filled with water. Another attempt was made to bail out the hole, but this also was unsuccessful.

Finally, a crew was brought in that had a boring apparatus normally used in prospecting for coal deposits. A new platform was rigged in the pit some thirty feet below ground level and the boring began.

The wooden platform was struck by the drill at ninety-five feet. After boring through the five-inch-thick platform, the auger dropped a full dozen inches, then went through four inches of oak, identified by the shavings on the bit.

Finally, the bit went through twenty-two inches of

metal, bringing up on it three small gold links, which appeared to be from an ancient watch chain. Finally the bit went through another four inches of oak, then six inches of spruce, followed by seven feet of clay in which nothing was found.

In the next boring, the auger came in contact with what appeared to be a cask of some kind. When withdrawn, the bit held splinters of oak and what appeared to be coconut husks.

The crew's foreman, one James Pitblado, was seen to take something from the auger, wash it, examine it, then put it into his pocket, refusing to show whatever he had found.

Several days later, a friend of Pitblado's attempted to buy the whole area of the money pit, but sale was refused. It is assumed the foreman gave the would-be buyer some information, but Pitblado was killed accidentally and it never has become known what he had found on the auger.

A third shaft was sunk about ten feet from the original, this one on the west side, about 1850. The shaft was put down 110 feet then, as before, a horizontal shaft driven toward the supposed money pit. Again, water poured in, filling the shaft to a depth of forty-five feet in only twenty minutes or so.

Horse-operated equipment was used around the clock for several weeks in an attempt to lower the water level. Oddly enough, it wasn't until now that someone discovered the water was salty and they literally were trying to pump dry the Atlantic Ocean.

The truth began to creep into the minds of some of the participants and they began to investigate the shoreline of Smith's Cove, an inlet about 150 yards from the pit. It didn't take long to find a trench had been dug from the sea in the direction of the treasure pit. It had been filled with a tropical fiber, local eelgrass, then beach rocks deposited

This serial photo of Oak Island shows some of the heavy equipment that has been brought to the island in an attempt to discover the so-called money pit. Note that much of the island has been dug up, the foliage removed in the attempts.

Parts of Oak Island resemble a timber cut, all of the greenery have been removed in a less than subtle manner.

over the top to make passage of the high tide water through it plausible.

Actually, the system was shown to be something of a major engineering feat, for the water seemed to pass through a man-dug tunnel. The investigative work was destroyed by an extremely high tide and it was decided that it would be too expensive to start digging out the channel through the underground tunnel again. Instead, it was decided to sink a shaft in the path of the tunnel.

The first try missed the tunnel and the second attempt found the shaft filled with water, lending credence to the previous theories. Attempts were made to block off the tunnel with pilings, but this failed, too.

The Oak Island Treasure Company was formed in 1894 for another try. Some $60,000 was collected, half to be used for seeking the treasure, the rest for a three-year lease on that part of the island where the treasure was alleged to be buried.

The new engineers planned to cut off the water near the shoreline before attempting to empty the flooded pits. They exploded huge charges of dynamite near the tunnel, which created some interesting earthworks but didn't shut off the water.

Through an intricate series of experiments, they managed to pump red dye into the shaft, but it did not come out in Smith's Cove. Instead, it came out on the south side of the island, suggesting a second water-filled tunnel.

One of the staunchest believers in the Oak Island treasure was the late Frederick L. Blair, a native of Nova Scotia. He continued backing searches until his death in 1953. His contract with the Canadian government covered a fifty-year period, from 1894 until 1944. It was in 1909 that Franklin D. Roosevelt, than a young attorney, raised some $5000 to aid Blair to carry on his search.

One H.L. Bowdoin, a deep-sea diver of the era who also had developed a number of items of salvage equipment,

came up with the idea of sending divers down into the flooded pit, but the danger of cave-ins killed this thought. Meantime, far down, the drills had hit cement, and as boring continued, bits of the concrete — determined as being man-made — were all that were recovered.

According to Blair's records, he felt that he was onto the lost crown jewels of Louis XVI. According to legend, they had been carried away by one of Marie Antoinette's ladies-in-waiting before the king and his lady were captured and beheaded.

It may well have been sour grapes, but Bowdoin ended up by claiming there was no treasure, his theory being that no one would have buried a treasure so deeply. However, others contended the gold links could not be ignored.

Another who believed in the Oak Island treasure was one William Chappell, a Nova Scotia contractor, who was involved in three different attempts to find the treasure, the last in 1931, when he was 81 years old.

With a crew and a steam engine, a twelve-foot-square shaft was sunk to 160 feet near the original pit. They found no water entering the shaft, but they seemed to have missed the treasure by several yards. There were other attempts during the Thirties. Involved in one such effort was a copy of what was purported to be one of Captain Kidd's treasure maps. There can be little doubt that the shape of the island on the map and the shape of the actual island were similar, but the latitude and longitude on the map showed it to be somewhere in the South China Sea.

Ultimately, in the infant days of metal detectors, Colonel H.A. Gardner of Arlington, Virginia, came to the island with one of these devices; he found strong signs of metal in the vicinity of the so-called money pit. He was on the point of leasing the treasure rights when he died in 1949.

There have been many searchers since. In all, there are supposed to have been more than two hundred holes of one kind or another dug on the island. Robert Restall was working in one of the holes in August, 1965, with his son and two other men. They were overcome by carbon monoxide fumes and drowned.

One of the latest, working the island at this writing, is Dan Blankenship, who is partnered with several others. He says that he personally has invested more than $80,000 in the search. While he has yet to find riches, he has been encouraged by the fact that seventy-five feet down, he found a bit of wire, two inches of it. Tests show that it was made about the Seventeenth Century.

"We drilled a hole on the spot and, at a hundred feet down, we struck iron," Blankenship says. "We sat on it three days with the drill. We could not budge the drill to get a sample. Cast iron? Wrought iron? Whatever it is, it's hard as hell!"

A diamond drill was brought in and didn't help. Meantime, he and his partners were attempting to overcome the flooding problem — seemingly with no great success.

But Blankenship, unlike many others, doesn't necessarily buy the pirate theory.

"Spaniards were looting Indian treasures through the Sixteenth Century," he says. "It is known that the Incas at Tumbez, an ancient Peruvian city noted for its riches, outfoxed Francisco Pizarro in the 1520s.

"Inca history tells how the treasures were taken to the Atlantic Coast and loaded on ships that sailed North. Wouldn't it be something if we ran onto a treasure of that magnitude?"

There are almost as many theories about the Oak Island money pit as there are holes in the ground — but the secret still waits to be solved.

This drawing presumes to detail the manner in which the hidden loot has been buried and the reasons why it has been virtually impossible to this time to recover it. Actually, there is no real evidence that treasure does exist.

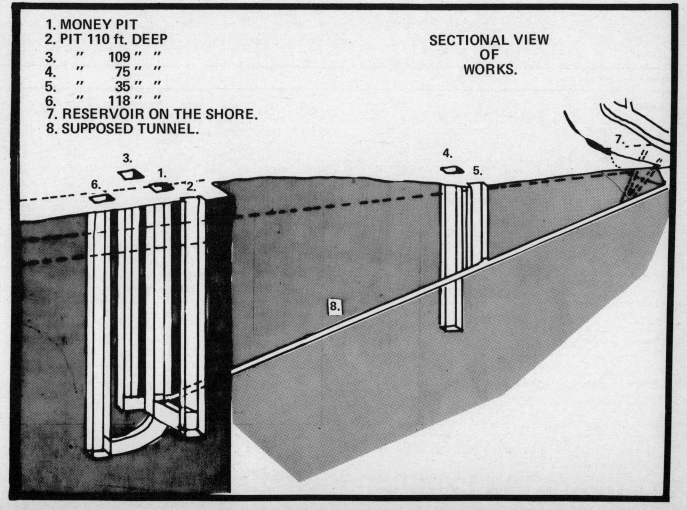

1. MONEY PIT
2. PIT 110 ft. DEEP
3.   "   109 " "
4.   "   75 " "
5.   "   35 " "
6.   "   118 " "
7. RESERVOIR ON THE SHORE.
8. SUPPOSED TUNNEL.

SECTIONAL VIEW
OF
WORKS.

THE LOST LOOT OF LIMA

There Is Every Reason To Believe That Cocos Island Still Holds A Fabulous Fortune; The Problem Is In Getting To It!

FOR MORE THAN twenty years, James A. Forbes, then of Arlington, California, carried on a campaign to find the fabulous, blood-spattered "Loot of Lima," which legend claims is buried on lonely Cocos Island.

In his continuing search, the mild-mannered but stubborn Californian launched half a dozen expeditions to the small, jungle-covered island located three hundred miles off the coast of Costa Rica, where the $60,000,000 treasure is supposed to be buried. All of his dreams and plans have been based upon a single piece of age-cracked yellow vellum parchment.

In spite of his lack of success in locating the fabulous treasure, Forbes feels certain he has been within a scant twenty feet of the multi-million dollar treasure that has taken thousands of persons to the island, daring illness, injury and even death to seek the hoard.

Until 1939, Forbes had never been to sea, although his family had been in California since the days of the caballero and the dons. He had been raised on tales of the Cocos Island treasure, listening to his father talk of the pirate hoard which lay buried there, but it was not until his father's death that he was left the vellum chart of the island which had been drawn by his great grandfather, James Alexander Forbes, a young British doctor.

The great-grandfather was aboard the ship, the Mary Dear, when it sailed from Callao in 1819, loaded to the gunnels with the treasures of the Cathedral of Lima.

Uprisings against Spain were spreading throughout Central America with Simon Bolivar riding at the head of the revolutionists.

The Spanish officials of the Peruvian city had started removal of the treasures to Panama and Spain, when the ship which Forbes was aboard was commissioned to carry the array of golden statues, gems and other valuables which had graced the cathedral.

Commanding the vessel was Captain Mary Thompson, who some forty-three years later declared on his deathbed: "We were tempted by the glittering millions and cut the anchor cable to put out to sea at night..." Once clear of the port, the crew seemed "puzzled about what to do with the treasure, so we buried it on Cocos Island," the captain's dying statement read. Thompson had sailed from Bristol, England, as mate aboard the Mary Dear which was bound for Valpariaso with a load of coal. According to his statement, he had assumed command when the ship's captain died on the voyage.

Although the California Forbes is pleasantly tight-lipped concerning parts of the information he dug up in more than a decade of intense research, he does admit that he is confident his great-grandfather sailed as mate of the Mary Dear when the crew set out to plant the treasure on Cocos. He had been on a world cruise when he joined Thompson's crew at Callao.

After the treasure was buried, Thompson and his crew were captured by a Panamanian man-of-war in the narrow strip of water between the island and the mainland and returned to Callao.

In his dying admission, Thompson said, "We were then tried for piracy and sentenced to be shot. The sentence was carried out on eight men, but myself and two companions were spared on the promise that we would reveal where we had hidden the treasure. We said the treasure was hidden on the Galapagos Islands. On the way out, we put into the Bay of Dulce, where nearly all the crew died, including one of my companions, of yellow fever."

Thompson and his remaining companion escaped from

The only evidence of the Cocos Island treasure found by Forbes and his crew was a bit of gold chain and petrified sail cloth.

the ship and made their way onto a New Bedford whaler which was also in the bay.

Some historians say that Thompson stayed aboard the whaler for several years. Others claim that he joined the Spanish cutthroat, Benito Benito. His companion, the young Dr. Forbes, made his way to the interior of Costa Rica and lived there for a time before moving northward.

According to experts on pirate treasure, the loot was made up of a life-sized gold Madonna, twelve life-sized statues of the Apostles, at least 100 statues of the lesser saints, 200 chests of jewels of all types, 350 jeweled swords, 150 jeweled chalices, 300 bars of gold and 600 bars of silver.

The present Forbes admits that these figures compare with his own knowledge gained through the charts and other ancestral papers left to him upon the death of his father.

"There is every bit of that in the treasure and possibly more," he avows.

The first known hunt for this fabulous array of wealth was in 1845, after Captain John Keating, a Newfoundland skipper, picked up a graying, middle-aged man on the Western coast of South America and carried him northward.

He told Keating he was Mary Thompson, skipper of the Mary Dear, also telling of the treasure. A voyage to Cocos Island was organized, but Thompson died before sail could be set for the island. It was during his last hours that his signed statement was made.

Keating, believing the old pirate, went ahead with the plan, arriving at Cocos with his crew and a mate named Benito Boig. Though history is somewhat fuzzy on this point, it is said that Keating and Boig attempted to escape from the island with a portion of the treasure in a small boat. Overloaded, the craft swamped in the surf and Boig was drowned.

Keating held on to the overturned boat for two days and eventually was picked up by a fishing boat which landed him at Callao. He made his way back to Newfoundland, and his crew, with the ship, also returned — but without the treasure. Keating was organizing another expedition in 1870 when he died.

Since the ill-fated Keating venture, there have been more than thirty known expeditions which have scoured Cocos Island for the Loot of Lima as well as other legendary hoards purportedly left by the whole piratical line, including Kidd, Swan, Davis and Captain Bartholemew Sharp.

Rumor says another four hundred expeditions have been made to the island but are unknown to the Costa Rican government which must pass on such searches and issues permits at a cost of $1000 per month.

The most laughable expedition was one led by a British sea dog named Captain Shrapnel in 1896. The naval officer sailed one of Queen Victoria's warships to Cocos, landed his three-hundred-man crew and "literally blew hell out of the island with dynamite." All the captain received for his effort was a stiff reprimand from the British Admiralty, which then issued an order that none of Her Majesty's vessels henceforth would be used for treasure hunting.

Forbes held little belief in existence of the treasure until he began to research records handed down by family ancestors.

COCOS ISLAND
(densely covered with trees and bushes)

NORTH PACIFIC OCEAN

COCOS ISLAND

East Point
Flathead Island
Tanner Point
Albatross Point
Dampier Head
Nautical Miles

The British lord, Fitzwilliams, who made an expedition
to the island early in the Twentieth Century, found an old
hermit named Gissler living there. He had been given
treasure rights by the Costa Rican government, but had
found only a single Spanish gold coin. He had, however,
uncovered an old encampment and rusty weapons.

Despite hearing of the treasure from the time he was a
child, James Forbes did not listen to the tales and vowed to
find the treasure when he grew up, as might be expected. It
was while casually talking over the maps and papers with a
neighbor after his father's death in 1939 that he decided,
"That treasure must be there!"

That was the beginning. The first trip to Cocos Island
was made in a small sailboat with a party of nine, only one
of them a seaman. Although the round trip took forty-six
days, they stayed on the island exactly nine days and didn't
even unpack their tools. The crew, made up of vacationing
businessmen, returned thoroughly discouraged. Forbes'
faith continued.

In the following four trips, Forbes located an area in
which he felt the treasure was buried. Misfortune, however,
traveled in his pocket.

In 1948, when a crew composed of nine men and one woman nearly perished in a storm on the return trip, it was nothing new. Blood has come to be synonymous with the treasure. On one occasion, rival treasure hunters engaged in a pitched battle over the undiscovered loot.

What made the chubasco, or Mexican hurricane, doubly effective was the fact that before the crew of the ship Malibu Inez had sailed for Cocos, another member had jumped ship, stealing a portion of the lead ballast at Newport Beach and selling it for junk. He had replaced the ballast with concrete blocks which did not properly balance the craft.

When this crew had landed on the island, the search had been under way in the vicinity of a creek mouth feeding into Chatham Bay.

Here was discovered a clue that left Forbes certain that the treasure was literally within their grasp. A length of tiny, exquisitely formed gold chain was found in the sand. The second clue was even more convincing.

In the papers handed down to Forbes from his piratical ancestor, it was written that they had covered the golden hoard with a spare sail. A piece of petrified sailcloth turned to limestone was found in the diggings.

The forces of nature defeated the hunters, however, for they were able to dig down only twelve feet. What had seemed a sandy creek bottom proved to be filled with boulders weighing several tons each. Unable to move the huge rocks and to cope with the tide from the sea, which backed up each day to fill the shaft with sand, gravel and water, they declared the trip a failure.

No actual records are available as to how many lives have been lost in the searches for the Loot of Lima. Legend is that an English expedition was completely lost when its sailing craft ran on a reef and sank. Histories of piracy show that strife among the early searchers was common. The affair of Keating and Boig is an example. There are those who claim that when Thompson, Forbes and the others buried the treasure on the island, the bodies of the Spanish officials who had been aboard the craft with the treasure were deposited at the same time for their spirits to guard the loot. Forbes feels he has been lucky in never losing a life although several men have been hurt.

In 1949, Forbes was back on the island with engineering equipment and talent including an engineer who had been instrumental in such projects as Chicago's immense Navy Pier. He was to clear the tons of rock at the bottom of the

The Malibu Inez is the vessel used by Forbes' group for its search of Cocos Island in search of fabulous Loot of Lima.

Forbes (upper right) was leader of the expedition to Cocos Island, appearing confident and happy as adventure begins.

creek and to sink the shaft to the treasure that they were certain was there.

The terrain is largely responsible for the treasure seekers' troubles. Sheer bluffs of 1900 feet rise from the creek to the highest point on the island. Although the jungle-cloaked isle is only nine miles long and four wide, some 3000 waterfalls return the torrents of the rainy season to the sea.

With some three hundred earthquakes during the past one hundred years, mountains of stone have tumbled down into the narrow creek bed.

The Californian's information follows closely Captain Thompson's deathbed statement in which he said:

"We anchored in the bay, landed on a sandy beach where a small stream runs out. Stretching back from the beach is a piece of level land about two acres in extent.

"We followed the stream and near its head, on a piece of level ground, we buried the treasure. There were ten boatloads of it."

Forbes is certain that the two-acre piece, due to topographical changes of the last century, is now under water.

It was the plan of the expedition engineers, reinforced by nearly sixty laborers from the Costa Rican mainland, to use a series of tubular cassions to sink the shaft down to the treasure. The searchers, though, were doomed to failure...failure they blamed on the lack of a telephone.

"The engineers we had were among the best in the world," Forbes relates, "but they were hundreds of miles from nowhere. Had they been in civilization and could have gotten equipment as needed, sinking the shaft would have been no problem. As it was, we didn't have enough."

The result was that the first cassions were sunk, but the rocks beneath kept the laborers from placing the smaller sections of the tube in position. At high tide, water poured in through the rocks, and seeped up from below. The pit dug to a depth of sixteen feet — four feet below the previous record depth — before defeat closed in.

According to Fortune Hunter Forbes, reason for calling off the search was the attitude of most of the men involved.

"Tempers had reached the explosive stages," he recalls. "It's hard to describe the thoughts of men when they may be a scant handful of sand away from a fortune.

"It doesn't take too many weeks of that sort of thing to turn anyone's mind into strange channels," Forbes continues. "An example of that was when the treasure turned Thompson, a supposedly honest merchant seaman, and my great-grandfather to piracy."

The trip was not without its rewards, however.

"We had locating equipment that would record the presence of metal to a depth of thirty-two feet," he explains. "We recorded the presence before we even started to dig. The shaft was only sunk to half that level, but I'm convinced we were within a few feet of the Loot of Lima!"

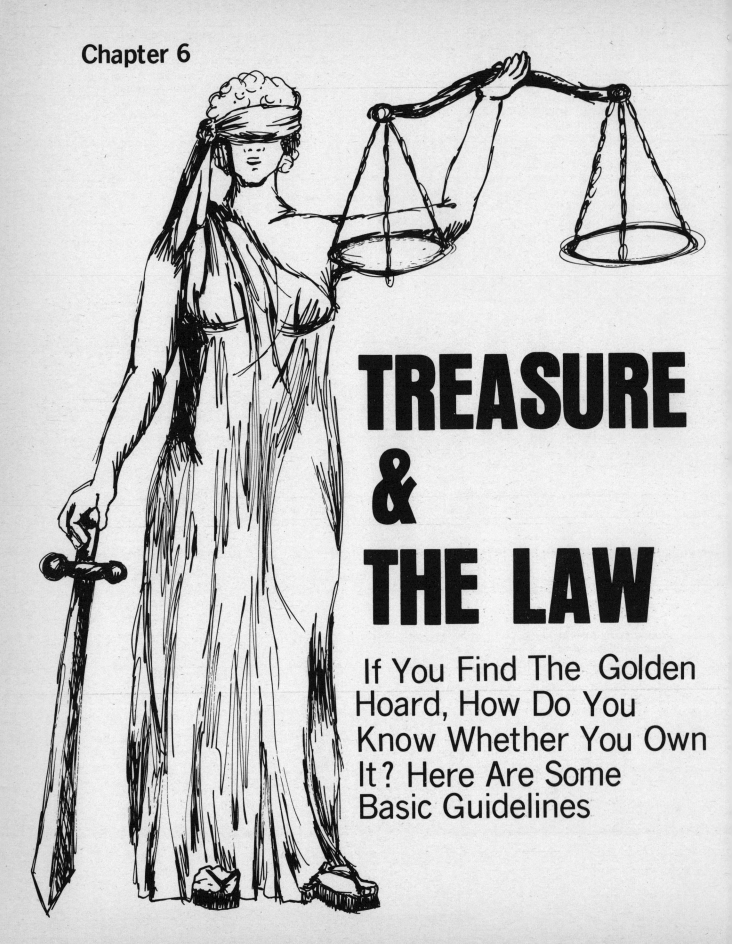

Chapter 6

TREASURE & THE LAW

If You Find The Golden Hoard, How Do You Know Whether You Own It? Here Are Some Basic Guidelines

LATE IN 1974, there was passed by Congress a bill introduced as Public Law 93-110, which repeals some sections of the Gold Reserve Act of 1934. Simply stated, that particular law made it illegal for the average citizen to own gold except in jewelry or collector coins.

The new law reads in part: "No provision of any law in effect on the date of enactment of the Act, and no rule, regulation or order under authority of any such law may be construed to prohibit any person from purchasing, holding, selling, or otherwise dealing with gold.

"The provisions of this section, pertaining to gold, shall take effect September 1, 1974." To offset the possibility of speculation, the United States auctioned two million ounces of gold to the general public in January, 1975.

Gold, with its rich, yellow texture and luster, is the king of metals. It's illustrious heritage chronicles wars in which men fought and died for its possession. Gold in large quantities is scarce. Although there are billions of ounces of gold dust suspended in sea water, no one has yet found an economical way to remove the gold from suspension.

In 1975, more treasure hunters have gone out to find it in its raw placer state. If economists are correct, the price of the king of metals will continue to steadily increase.

Americans had been restricted in ownership of gold, as indicated. Gold coins could be purchased or hunted as treasure, if they classified as "rare and unusual" under Treasury Department dictates. Any gold coins made after 1934 found buried in the ground or elsewhere were illegal to own unless exported, then re-imported with the proper customs declaration filed. Before the new law, the Treasury Department amended its gold regulations to allow gold coins minted before 1960 to be imported into this country. This ruling allowed for importation only and was not retroactive.

Gold award medals acquired through achievement, exploration or other means, could be kept only if more than one hundred years old.

Robert Marx is world famous as a treasure hunter and an underwater archeologist, but makes certain of ownership of the land he searches. He found these Spanish coins on a Texas beach with D-Tex detector.

Bullion was illegal to own except for that necessary for industrial manufacture and the arts. If the bullion was hidden, then discovered, one could keep it only if it was hallmarked before 1900. However, bullion is seldom found hallmarked.

F. Lee Bailey has been litigating for several clients seeking to explore the White Sands Missile Range in New Mexico for a purportedly hidden treasure of millions of dollars in gold bullion. Under the new law, they could keep it — after settling with IRS and the State of New Mexico.

Placer gold could be kept in any quantity — as long as it was not chemically acted upon or refined into a bullion substance.

Gold, for many generations, has been considered a storehouse of value. Gold often has defeated the attempts of world governments to inflate a currency of a nation, frustrated aims to direct the economy of a nation, given its owners a hedge against the erosion of the purchasing power of their currency.

A leading scholar wrote that it was for this reason that Americans lost their right to own gold in 1934, becoming "criminals" in the process if they retained any bullion. President Franklin Roosevelt and a compliant Congress agreed that only when civilian control of the economy was prevented completely (by ending gold ownership) could the Great Depression be successfully combatted.

To Americans, this decision bears importance. Many people rather than surrender their gold coins and bullion

Left: Bill Mahan has used one of the detectors of his manufacture with great success in searching old Civil War battlefields, but he gets proper clearances first.
Below: Mahan and Mel Fisher check an old Spanish map.

chose to bury their treasure. Burying one's valuables was a safety precaution against Indian bands, robbers and cowhands.

A hoard of gold was found buried on a Southern plantation site in Mississippi. The plantation house was burned and the owner killed as General U.S. Grant and his Union Army were advancing on Vicksburg during the Civil War in 1863. The plantation owner reportedly buried three caches, only one of which has been found. The unearthed hoard includes several $5 gold pieces, two eagles and one $20 coin. When the coins were buried, they had a face value of $70. Today, the gold content alone is worth several hundred dollars on the open market. The numismatic value of the coins is amazing. One coin, an 1844 $5 gold piece from the New Orleans, Louisiana mint, in uncirculated condition, has an estimated value of $400; an 1860 $5 from the Charlotte, North Carolina, mint has a value of $250; an uncirculated 1859 $20 gold piece from the New Orleans mint has a cool value of $2,000.

If you find American gold coins and need the quickest and most efficient way to determine the numismatic value, purchase a copy of R.S. Yeoman's "A Guide Book of United States Coins." The book costs $2.50 and lists the values of each U.S. coin ever struck in a variety of condi-tions. The book is an excellent investment, particularly if coins are your goal.

At current market prices, placer gold (which is more than ninety percent pure) can be sold at an outstanding profit. Gold coins have a more ready market. There are hundreds of coin dealers throughout the United States, and thousands of coin collectors.

American gold coins minted after 1837 are all .900 fine. Coins minted between 1834 and 1837 are .899 fine. Coins minted from the 1790s to the 1830s are .9166 fine.

Some gold coins are scarce from a collector's standpoint and some derive their value from their bullion content, with a small added premium for numismatic value. Generally, this bullion value situation exists with $20 gold pieces — double eagles — but it occurs in some cases with the $10 or eagles. The double eagle, the largest coin to be circulated in America, weighs more than an ounce and has a total fine gold content of .96752 fine troy ounces. This coin was minted from 1850 to 1933 and has dozens of dates and mint marks. Total production of the coin was more than $1.9 billion.

The $10 coin, weighing .48176 troy ounces, is another bullion piece. Most common of all gold coins are the $5 (or half eagle), the $1 gold piece and the $2.50 quarter eagle.

Old ruins such as this may seem excellent places in which to search for treasure, but many of them are privately owned and one should make an arrangement with owner on any find.

These coins were heavily circulated and were standard in an era that did not trust banknotes.

Treasure hunting is lucrative, exciting and entails many obligations — to the owners of lost items and property searched, to the government, to the general public and even to other treasure hunters. The novice treasure hunter may be overwhelmed quite understandably by the many and varied opinions given by self-professed experts.

The novice wants to know whether one owns the articles legally that he finds. If the item is found on private property, can the property owner claim your find? If the item is proved to have another owner other than the property owner, whose rights prevail? Can you hunt for treasure on government land? If the original owner is dead but does have heirs, what are their rights and yours?

In California, for example, there is no precedent or procedure for the disposition of treasure trove other than the statements contained in the Civil Code (Sections 1864 to 1872) relating to lost property.

Civil Code 1872 reads: *"This article is substituted for an act concerning watercraft found adrift, and lost money and property. (Sta. 1850 p 156) The material changes are:*

1. In establishing a uniform rule applicable alike to all kinds of lost property. 2. In vesting the title of the property in the finder instead of in the county on which it is found."

"It is certainly just that when property cannot be restored to the owner, the title ought to vest in the person whose care and expenditures has preserved it, and that no sufficient reason can be adduced for taking it from him and giving it to a county which has neither run risk nor incurred expense in relation to it."

When diligent research points to the existence of treasure on private property, what is the best way to proceed? Permission must be obtained before entering private property — usually an easy task if the request is made courteously and in a straightforward manner. Come right out with your purpose. If necessary, offer to share half the value of whatever items are found. An agreement in writing is a good bet, for often it will make believers out of uncooperative people and will protect you from the possibility of a lawsuit.

If the owner of found valuables is known, the treasure belongs to him regardless of who owns the land or who made the discovery. If the rightful owner is dead, then the treasure belongs to his heirs. If the owner is not known, the treasure belongs to the finder, regardless of where it is found.

Reference to this subject is made in Volume 34, American Jurisprudence, Pages 633-4 (Section 4). It states:

"The rule in this country, in the absence of legislation is that the title to treasure trove belongs to the finder against all the world except the true owner, and in this respect is analogous to lost property.

"The owner of the soil in which the treasure trove is found acquires no title thereto by virtue of his ownership of the land."

To avoid possible litigation, keep in mind that, unless an owner of lost money or merchandise publicly gives up his title to it, it remains the legal property of the owner at the time of the loss. The title to the trove is not relinquished when the official search for the missing property was abandoned.

In the case of sunken treasure, if the ownership of the ship and its contents is known, the property belongs to him. Section 2080 of the Civil Code provides a method

The laws of salvage may well apply should one run across a wrecked vessel such as this one on Padres Island, but it is wise to check the law before carting off any part of it.

whereby *"the owner of the vessel may recover the property upon paying the reasonable charges incurred by the finder."*

Kip Wagner, a construction worker of Sebastian, Florida, used the treasure he found from a sunken Spanish fleet to form the Real Eight Corporation. Over the years since this discovery on Jan. 8, 1961, his corporation has found five million dollars in treasure on the beaches and at offshore sites within a twenty-five-mile radius of his home. The State of Florida gets one quarter of all treasure found and a larger percentage for artifacts with historical value.

Wagner finds the "electric atmosphere" that surrounds the treasure hunter to be the greatest inspiration. "It is the exhilarating thrill of anticipation," he says, "that fires the incentive to keep searching when things look blackest."

Half the refined gold of the entire world lies scattered on sea, lake and river bottoms. Treasure exists on wrecked pirate ships, ships of state bearing payroll gold and modern wrecks with bullion aboard. All seas and rivers of the world. plus the Great Lakes, conceal valuable items of jettisoned cargo.

For the disposal of gold coins, the United States Gold Regulations state: "Gold coins of recognized special value to collectors of rare and unusual coins may be acquired, held and disposed of within the United States or any place subject to its jurisdiction without a license."

What is a rare or unusual coin? The regulations define this as being any gold coin which was made before April 5, 1933. Gold coins that were made after 1933 are presumed not to be rare. These coins cannot be held in the United States without a special determination that the particular coin has a special value to collectors.

If your treasure hunting takes you outside the country — into Canada or Mexico, for example — there may be special requirements, in some cases, for bringing gold back into the country. An April, 1969, amendment to the Gold Regulation allows the importation of any gold coins made before 1934, without license, provided the coins are genuine. For other coins, a special importation license may be required. Specific information on the regulations regarding gold coins can be obtained by making your inquiry to: The Department of the Treasury, Office of Domestic Gold and Silver Operations, Washington, D.C. 20220.

The disposal of gold in its natural state is another matter. In March, 1968, the U.S. Government stopped purchasing domestic gold. If you discover gold in a natural state, then, how do you dispose of it? The answer is quite simple.

Charles Garrett displays several items in his treasure museum in Garland, Texas. Bent rifle barrel is from Idaho battle site where Nez Perce Indians wiped out a cavalry regiment. Large melting pot came from an abandoned Spanish mine.

Take the gold to a private assayer. He will assay a mineral sample for a nominal fee, which usually depends on the process that is required to correctly evaluate the sample. If it is determined to be gold or some other form of precious metal, you may either hang on to it or sell it. The assay company may make you an offer for the metal. If it is gold, the price will be based on an average for the previous five days in the London gold market. The price will depend upon the state of the material. No matter where you live, there should be a private assayer somewhere in your area.

Part of the reason for the change in the gold situation today is the widespread use of gold and other precious metals in numerous applications. Gold and other precious metals are generally good electrical conductors, and are

therefore used extensively by the electronics industry. The various uses of gold and other precious metals doesn't stop here. In addition to the traditional uses, like dentistry and jewelry making, gold is presently being used in the manufacture of many everyday items such as small appliances and even childrens' toys.

As for the question of treasure hunting on government land, the California State Antiquities law states: "It is illegal to remove, injure, destroy, or deface anything of historic value on public lands." The decision of what is or is not of historic value is left open for discussion. However, the law further goes on to state that: "Upon finding that it will be for the best interest of the State Park System, the director may grant a permit to remove or disturb plants, animals,

Circle Rock at Dorrance, Kansas, was a favorite searching area at the turn of the century, although it was on privately owned ranch.

or historical or archeological materials." Any person who has been granted such a permit by the director of the park system — not just that particular park — shall not be liable for prosecution. Other states have similar laws. In the matter of treasure hunting on Federal lands, the National Parks Director may be reached by writing to the Department of the Interior, National Park Service, Washington, D.C. 20240.

The specific legal information you need can be obtained by writing to the Attorney General's office, in care of the capital of the state involved.

Treasure hunters who earn substantial sums from their hobby should seek the advice of a tax consultant. Though the Internal Revenue Service is not in business to tell citizens what they may or may not do to earn money, they do insist on the government's due for the money you earned — or dug up. Agents of the IRS will furnish information on reporting income from treasure-hunting activities. Every large city has the numbers of these revenue men listed in the phone book. Ordinarily, you will not be challenged if you report treasure trove on the tax form as miscellaneous income, but this classification does not provide any way to deduct expenses. The majority of treasure hunters treat money earned from their hobby as self-employment income and file schedule C with their returns.

A professional treasure hunter will be careful to avoid the stigma of vandalism by always cleaning up after himself. He will fill up holes in sod, replace tread boards from staircases, reinsert boards from door casings and paneling from walls. If you find yourself in a place that has not received this courteous attention, it usually is best to leave immediately. You could be blamed for the mess. It is a wise practice to leave a friendly tipoff in the form of tin cans or a few pieces of aluminum foil where you have searched. Though the next treasure hunter might be crushed that he didn't get there first, he will appreciate the many hours saved from fruitless searching.

The State of Florida feels that the sunken ships and their cargoes hold vastly greater wealth in knowledge than they do in monetary riches. Florida is proud of its historic heritage and is eager to share the "Florida story" with the nation's citizens. The state's heritage spans the turbulent years from the earliest explorations of the New World to the present. And the physical remains of that history that exist today are a resource, a resource that in most cases lacks development and interpretation. If Florida were to allow historical sites to be neglected or picked clean and sold to the highest bidder, then the state would lose a tangible and invaluable piece of its heritage.

Writer W. Havihurst wrote, "The past is not the property of historians; it is a public possession. It belongs to anyone who is aware of it, and it grows by being shared..." The State of Florida bases its stringent regulations on this philosophy.

"Field agents for the underwater archaeological research section of the Department of State's Bureau of Historic Sites and Properties are required to oversee all underwater excavations that are under state contract. Agents must be part scuba diver, historian, archaeologist, geologist, surveyor and photographer," according to Glen Couvillon of the Florida Development Commission.

All shipwreck material recovered under the contract salvage program, with the exception of obvious treasure trove, is sent to the Department of State's laboratory in Tallahassee, where it is cleaned, drawn, photographed, weighed, mapped, measured, recorded and then stored. All material recovered from state-owned bottomlands is the property of the State of Flordia.

However, provisions in the contract agreement allow for division of the recovered bounty between the state and the salvage contractor. Before dividing the artifacts, research and interpretation are conducted for each artifact and object recovered so that knowledge and information can be shared with scholars and researchers.

The treasure then is divided, with the State of Florida taking twenty-five percent of the findings. All artifacts, treasures and objects that the state receives will be housed in a museum to be completed in Tallahassee in 1975.

Salvaging companies, such as the Real Eight and Treasure Salvors, have been of immeasurable help to the nation and to Florida in tracing early history through findings of sunken relics. Because of the high caliber and unceasing cooperation of these companies, the state has been able to pass legislation that will leave this valuable legacy of history intact, rather than allowing it to be destroyed by greedy, profit-seeking and history-be-damned overnight treasure hunters.

Old houses such as this may well hold hidden fortunes, but if you are to avoid legal entanglements, be certain of current ownership.

Chapter 7

The Metal Detector & How It Works

FOR THOUSANDS OF years, people yearned for and sought reliable methods for pinpointing the location of buried or hidden valuables. Generally speaking, the results were disappointing until the invention of the vacuum tube paved the way for development of the science of electronics. Sometime around the 1920s, radio circuitry was invented and developed that proved capable of reacting to the presence of objects coming close to wire loops. This basic principle saw application for several uses such as burglar alarm circuits and systems to operate animated store window displays when a potential customer stood outside the glass.

The use of mines — concealed containers of explosive, hopefully to be set off by the unwary enemy — is well rooted in history and buried land mines saw extensive employment by most of the combatants in WWII. By that time, the state of the electronic arts had grown sufficiently sophisticated to produce mine detectors capable of locating such devices. As often proves true, the impetus of wartime emergency forced a rapid development of mine detector designs.

After the war ended, military mine detectors turned up on the surplus market and were purchased by hopeful souls who envisioned a profitable application for locating buried treasure caches through their use. Some success was achieved through the use of such devices, although they would seem quite crude and primitive in comparison to the equipment available today. Since the transistor did not commence to replace the vacuum radio tube until some few years after WWII, the surplus detectors incorporated several of the glass tubes and, as a direct result, required batteries that were heavy, bulky and expensive.

A few of those war surplus detectors still are in use, although the batteries have become difficult to obtain. Most of the military models have been modified to some extent to make them more efficient, convenient and inexpensive to operate. The cost of such conversion adds up to a figure that could purchase one of the modern, transistorized detectors and the latter tends to be markedly superior.

Modern metal detectors can be divided into various design categories, of which the induction balance (IB) circuit is by far the most popular, accounting for the major number of units sold and in use today. The induction balance detectors are a modification of the transmitter-receiver (TR) circuit and several of the induction balance instruments are referred to as TR designs in manufacturers' literature.

The true transmitter-receiver models are easy to identify, since they consist of two components, joined together by means of one or two horizontal bars at a distance of some four or five feet from each other. In use, the operator carries them along over the area being searched, using a handle or shoulder strap to keep them in position. The true TR instruments have little or no ability to locate small items, although they can pinpoint relatively large metallic objects at considerable depths; down to about twenty-two feet, depending upon the object and soil conditions. Most of their present use is by utility companies for tracing underground lines or similar purposes.

Another type of detector is the beat frequency oscillator (BFO). In usual physical appearance, it resembles the induction balance detectors, both having the disk-shaped coil at the lower end of a rod, connected by a wire to the box containing the power supply and operating circuitry. Typically, the box will have a handle for carrying and guiding the search coil at the lower end of the unit. In some designs, the circuit box is fastened to the operator's chest with straps, thus relieving the hand of weight and fatigue in extended operation or tricky footing.

Speaking in generalities, the induction balance detectors offer the attractive dual advantages of better sensitivity combined with simpler operation, as compared to the beat frequency oscillator designs. The latter offers preferable performance capability in certain underwater applications or when working in such places as a mine shaft, where the surrounding concentration of minerals would make the induction balance devices all but useless for locating small items.

As a rule, the BFO units are a poor choice if the operator suffers from any degree of hearing handicap, since effective operation depends to some extent upon judging the pitch and tonality of the audible signal. The IB units emit a beep in the proximity of the search-subject to their coil and, while this may vary to a greater or lesser extent, depending upon the given model, it is by no means so critical to be able to read the tone when using IB detectors.

Most units, be they BFO or IB types, incorporate a small speaker in the circuit box to emit an audible signal when the search-subject has been detected. Some models have a jack into which you can plug a pair of headphones. This offers a useful advantage when using the instrument in areas where there is a lot of background noise and it improves the ability to detect faint signals, although at a cost of cutting off the ability to hear other sounds from the world at large. For example, if you're prowling through rough country with your ears muffled by headphones, you won't be able to hear the warning whir of a rattlesnake.

Many detectors have a meter on top of the circuit box. In some cases, this provides a visual indication of the signal and its relative strength and it may be possible to turn off the speaker, relying upon the meter to indicate presence of search-subjects. This can be advantageous in certain situations, although, in others, it may be preferable to keep your eyes available to watch your footing, relying upon the audible signal instead. It should be noted that, in some detectors, the meter serves solely for testing the batteries and has no connection to the detection signal circuit.

Both the BFO and IB detectors must be tuned by adjusting the current flow through the circuit. This is done by turning tuning knobs or, in the case of some models, by depressing a button. If seriously out of tune, the detector may not be able to signal the presence of fairly large objects that come within a short distance from the search coil. Delicate tuning is the secret of optimum sensitivity and efficiency of operation. The BFO models tend to drift out of tune a bit more readily than the IB type and both are somewhat susceptible to loss of tune through temperature change. This can pose some amount of problems when operating a detector over sizzling desert terrain in midsummer, for example.

Metal detectors are, as the name implies, only capable of sensing the location of objects having some amount of

This Invention Has Revolutionized Treasure Hunting In Recent Decades!

By far the best approach in selecting the metal detector best suited for your individual needs is to shop in a specialty store carrying several different makes and models. Its personnel will be happy to counsel you as to the best size of search coil and similar important considerations.

metal in their makeup. The screening arches through which boarding passengers must pass at airport security checkpoints are a specialized form of metal detectors operating on essentially the same principles as the treasure hunter's faithful friend and companion.

Despite their limitation to detecting metals and metallic compounds such as oxides, metal detectors can lead the searcher to any number of valuable items that contain no metal, examples including old, collector-item bottles and jars. The reason for this is that such glassware — yesterday's trash and today's treasure — often was discarded in a small area, together with tin cans and similar metallic debris. While a rusted tin can may not arouse much enthusiasm, if its presence leads you to a nearby bottle worth several dollars, it will have served its purpose well.

The more efficient detectors will pinpoint the location of metal objects through layers of covering mediums including common dirt, fresh or decaying wood, leaves, grass, ice, snow, mud, water, concrete, asphalt, gravel, glass, plaster, brick, adobe and quartz. There are certain rocks that are more or less opaque to detector frequencies by reason of their content of metal or metallic compounds.

Several of the more sophisticated detectors embody a selector switch offering discrimination between metals and magnetic targets. At the metal-setting, a reaction will be obtained primarily for nonferrous metals, that is, those containing no appreciable quantity of iron.

The beginning operator soon discovers that all that beeps is not treasure. The aluminum pull-tabs from beverage cans, for but one example, are a bane to the treasure hunter's existence. Bottle caps and the aluminum foil from cigarette packages or candy wrappers likewise can waste a lot of time and effort, with a dampening effect upon your enthusiastic dreams of easy wealth.

While some manufacturers' advertisements make attractive claims for their detectors' abilities to discriminate between treasure and trash, a modest amount of reflection will suggest that this is not too probable. Detection depends to some extent upon the comparative conductivity of the given metal. Gold and silver are excellent electrical conductors, as are copper and aluminum to a lesser degree, iron offering somewhat more resistance to current flow. As noted, you can program some detectors to keep from getting overly excited over magnetic objects, including steel bottle caps, but aluminum is a nonferrous metal and an excellent conductor of electricity.

Although one of the most plentiful of all metals in the earth's crust, aluminum is not easy to extract from its parent ores and, for some years after its discovery, extraction was so difficult in terms of the techniques available at that time as to make it, if not a precious metal, at least a scarce and expensive one. Hence, it was used for making up a host of small objects definitely worth uncovering for the sake of their rarity, if not for their intrinsic value. It doesn't take much cogitation to conclude that, if a detector rejects pull-tabs, it would likewise ignore aluminum streetcar tokens from the turn of the century, for which some collector would be happy to pay a substantial price.

As anyone can testify who has unwarily touched a farmer's electric fence in the early, dew-sparkling morning, wet grass is a pretty effective conductor of electricity in its own right. Needless to say, this is a handicapping effect, so far as the depth sensitivity of a metal detector is concerned when operating over wet grass and several of the more elaborate detectors offer provisions that can compensate to some extent for unusually high-conductive cover, such as wet grass or partially mineralized soils.

Apart from probing for potentially worthwhile iron

Control box of this Rainbow Mach II detector carries a meter for visual signal, a small speaker for sound, as well as a jack for headphones, together with battery-check and other controls. Instruction book supplied with instrument gives details on operating procedures, which are not as hard as you'd think.

objects — buried guns are highly prized, for example — the magnetic setting can aid in locating pockets of black sand that often accompany gold in fine particles. Many of the older guns, by the way, used brass for some of their component parts, so that there is a chance of picking one up, even when the detector is operated in the nonferrous mode. In point of fact, most detectors will react to fairly large iron objects, even when turned to the metal setting, rather than the magnetic.

Performance and sensitivity of the detector is governed to a considerable extent by the size and composition of the target object. If you are looking for tiny gold nuggets, about the size of a BB shot — roughly .175-inch diameter — within two or three inches from the ground surface, best results will be obtained by using a search coil that is quite small in diameter; three inches or smaller. Such small coils will not perform well on larger objects, buried more deeply. If you're after comparatively large items, at a considerable depth, you'll need a search coil that is larger in diameter, twelve inches being about the largest size in common use,

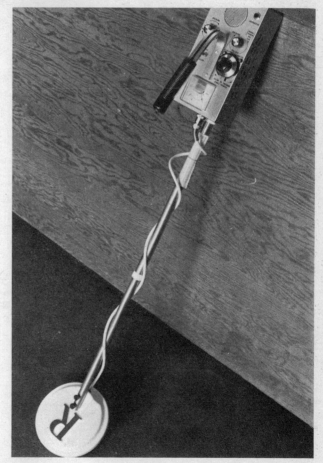

Overall view of Rainbow Mach II, above, shows telescoping rod. Search coil, left, is interchangeable for others of different size, so as to handle targets of varying size; most are waterproof.

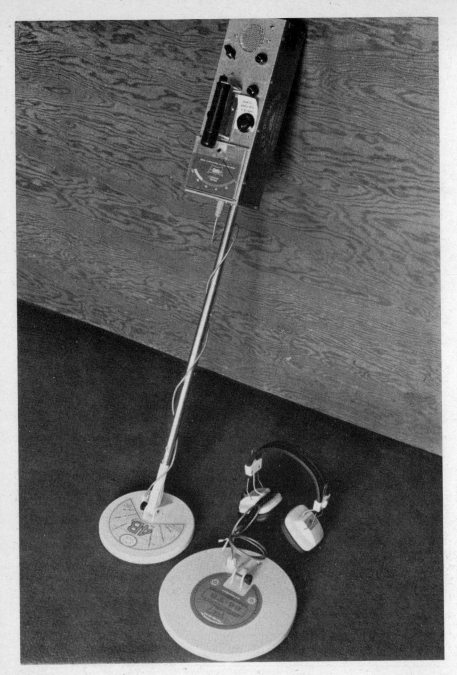

The Gold Master detector, made by White's Electronics, shown with two of several sizes of waterproof search coils for use on targets of different size or depth, with optional headphones, pros and cons of headphone use are discussed in the text.

although coils as large as twenty-four inches are available for some detectors.

Coils of about eight inches diameter probably are the most popular with typical detector operators, offering a good compromise between depth and sensitivity for small objects. Regardless of the size of coil and make or model of detector, it is well to establish the effective radius or width at which it can be relied upon to detect objects of typical size. This may be a swath represented by almost the full width of the coil, or it can be as narrow as about one-third of the coil diameter. Obviously, the wider search pattern will enable you to cover ground at a more rapid rate, but the important consideration is to program your sweeps so as not to leave occasional strips unscanned.

Gold, platinum and certain other elements in the platinum family are termed noble metals, meaning that they form compounds little if at all with other elements. Silver, copper, brass, nickel and most other metals oxidize more or less slowly when buried and the oxides spread

outward through the surrounding soil. In effect, this serves to increase the size of the target for the detector.

Were you to bury a brand-new dime in dirt as a practice object for detection, you'd stand a good chance of losing the dime, unless it lay close to the surface. If that happens, you may be able to mark the spot and locate it a year or so later, after the traces of oxidized silver have had a chance to spread through the dirt to offer a larger target.

Some detectors are capable of pointing to the location of voids in the earth underfoot, as well as metallic objects and they may react to covered potholes, old wells, channels cut by underground water flow and the like. This can be a useful ability when you're prospecting in gold country, since such undercuts can carry good traces of placer.

Most of the modern detectors operate on penlight cells, transistor batteries or similar power sources and the life expectancy of a set of batteries will vary with the make, model and design of the unit. Typically, they will operate for one hundred hours or more on a fresh set of batteries, affording ample service life for any ordinary requirement. If you are planning an extensive search operation in remote and inaccessible areas, it is a good idea to take along a fresh set or two of batteries as a backup. Few if any detectors are designed for operation with rechargeable batteries of the nickel-cadmium type. The modest cost and lengthy service life of the expendable batteries simply do not warrant the greater cost and inconvenience of using the rechargeable type.

A casual riffle through the pages of the magazines on treasure hunting will show that a large number of manufacturers are offering a considerable number of metal detectors and selection of the one make and model best suited for your personal needs can be rather bewildering. One fact soon becomes apparent: Few manufacturers are intensely critical of their own products — a general observation, by no means restricted to makers of metal detectors! — and it becomes even more difficult to select a detector objectively, based solely upon its maker's advertising claims.

One of the better approaches is to visit a dealer who sells metal detectors, if such merchants are listed in the classified section of your phone book. Generally, such stores are located in the larger cities, although you may find some detectors displayed in small-town stores in those regions where the hunting is apt to be a little more encouraging.

If a dealer who stocks one or more makes and models of detectors is accessible to the place of your residence, it is an excellent approach to visit the shop so as to see and discuss the comparative merits of the different choices. If the dealer is knowledgeable and obliging — and most of them are — he can answer your questions, give you the benefit of his own personal experience and perhaps even let you try out a sample or two.

Some dealers have detectors that are available for rental, possibly with the option of applying the rental cost against the purchase price. Others avoid involvement with renting, though most dealers will take a used detector in trade against some other model and, as a result, may have used detectors in stock at a substantial saving over the cost of the same unit, brand new.

Another approach is to build your own detector from a kit. These are offered by several manufacturers and distributors of electronic equipment. Here, your choice should be governed by a realistic appraisal of your expertise and familiarity with electronics and allied subjects. After completion of the project, it would be an excellent idea to compare its performance against that of a typical ready-made detector to see how much — if any — sensitivity you have sacrificed in going the do-it-yourself route. As with any detector, if you're going to be missing good finds at the limits of detection, you'll want to know you're doing so.

As with most other categories of merchandise, in detectors you tend to get what you pay for to some greater or

Here's a closer look at the signal intensity meter of the White's Gold Master detector shown on the facing page. It offers an accurate reading on signal strength, which the experienced operator can use in judging value of hidden target, combined with the ability to verify that batteries are adequately fresh.

Compass Electronics, of Forest Grove, Oregon, offers both induction balance and beat frequency oscillator units, in a variety of designs and degrees of sophistication. The detector shown here is their Model 77B.

lesser extent. True, the highest price does not always go with the best machine and some excellent units are priced well below the average. Some of the cheapest kits and units — particularly those based around the beat frequency oscillator design — are hardly better than no detector at all in terms of comparison with the more expensive but correspondingly more sensitive and capable instruments.

The sensible approach is to look for the detector that will satisfy your personal needs in terms of the use you plan to make of it. Having found your ideal machine, you can inquire as to its cost and make peace with your budget as best you can. Try not to let yourself be talked into a detector that falls somewhat short of your personal specifications, merely because it happens to cost ten or forty dollars less. Even if it means going home to drop quarters into the sugar bowl for another month or three, it's better in the long run to hold out for the machine of your first choice.

Remind yourself that, by missing but a single find, the lower-priced detector could wipe out its entire saving in cost over the model you picked as your favorite. If you remain discontented with a cheaper second choice, you're apt to end up trading it in on the one you wanted in the first place and the total outlay will cost you considerably more in the long run, to say nothing of the rankling thought of the goodies your bargain may have been unable to pick out for you.

Once having come into possession with a metal detector

fairly well fitted to your personal requirements, it comes time to consider the places and ways in which you can put it to work to the best advantage. While you may have had romantic visions of sniffing through ghost towns of the Old West, there may be some rewarding sites for prospecting that are closer and much more accessible throughout the year, rather than during the fleeting weeks of a vacation holiday.

Parks, playgrounds and schoolyards are fertile hunting areas for metal detectors. Small children, in their tireless tumbling and cavorting, lose quantities of coins, rings, jackknives, jewelry, house keys and kindred items, as any parent can confirm. If the object is not sighted soon after its loss, it tends to get buried to shallow depths, making a generous sprinkling of small, metallic items beneath such locations.

A few words of cautious council are in order, however. If you are seen prowling about community property, burdened down with an assortment of picks and shovels, in addition to a metal detector, the local police are likely to engage you in detailed discussion of your activities and intentions. If you leave your hunting grounds looking as if it had been assaulted by a roving band of giant moles, it tends to throw you into disrepute and, what is even worse, tarnishes the good name of other treasure hunters.

Most of the modest treasures buried in parks or schoolyards can be turned up by using a discreet screwdriver or similar tool, with a minimum of disturbance to the terrain. It is more efficient in terms of time and effort and it is much less apt to run you afoul of duly constituted authority.

Before you commence exploring beneath the surface on private property, it is a good practice to obtain permission from the owner. In some cases, this can lead to disagreement as to the ownership of any noteworthy valuables found in such places, but failure to obtain permission can get you embroiled in a charge of malicious trespassing or similar legal inconvenience.

On most public beaches, there is little or no objection to the use of metal detectors and the moist sand makes for easy excavation. However, it never hurts to inquire from a custodian or lifeguard as to the attitude on such activities.

In addition to your detector and digging equipment, you will want to have some type of rucksack or container in which to deposit your accumulation of found items. You will find it handy to provide a few compartments for the sake of being able to segregate coins or other valuables from items of lesser worth. Quite probably, you will consider it worth the modest effort to pick up even the junk and debris that you find, discarding it in a refuse container where it should have landed in the first place. Not only are things such as rusty fishhooks hazardous to the unwary bare foot but, if you plan on prospecting the same area again, each piece of recovered trash is another false lead that won't waste your time and effort next time. Thus, it serves your enlightened self-interest and, if it comes to a discussion with hostile custodians of the area, you can show them that you are improving the environment by policing up dangerous hardware.

As with so many other pleasant hobbies, thoughtless and inconsiderate behavior of a few people can make life unpleasant for the majority whose conduct is beyond reproach. This is as true in the case of treasure hunters as with, for example, hunters or motorcyclists. If you encounter unwarranted hostility over your possession of a metal detector, it may be that it's because of the depredations committed by some member of the boorish minority.

Look at the situation from the viewpoint of the property owner: What would your own reaction be if you looked out the window and saw someone going over your back yard with a mysterious-looking gadget whose purpose you didn't recognize?

In the more extreme instances, there have been reports of treasure hunters being fined, with confiscation of the items they'd found and their detectors and equipment being confiscated, as well. That sounds pretty rough, and it is, but it points up the wisdom of making sure there will be no objection to your activities before you commence them.

After all, when you've gone to all the trouble and expense of selecting your detector and paying for it, you'd like to look forward to many years of enjoyment in using it.

Items appearing here are but a small portion of the Compass collection of articles found with the Model 77B, opposite page, and similar models.

Chapter 8

THE WHY, HOW & WHERE OF COIN SHOOTING

Here Is A Way To Riches That Dates Back To Biblical Times, Taking Minimum Equipment But A Degree Of Patience!

Probing an old streambed in a public park can be fruitful inasmuch as coins and valuables dropped there when it held water often can be located with a metal detector.

ALTHOUGH THERE ARE beachcombers who have managed to exist for years on the proceeds and coin shooting — as it is called — is an activity that goes back to Biblical eras, the hobby or business of hunting for lost coins has gained popularity only since the advent of the metal detector less than half a century ago. And it has reached today's level of interest only in the last half decade.

The current high level of interest has resulted primarily from the interest created by clubs across the country; in recent years, all sorts of publications and advertisements have done everything short of guaranteeing instant wealth for those who take up the hobby. Most of these advertisements, of course, are puffs for specific metal detectors and neglect to state that it's not all that simple.

Nonetheless, there are those who have literally turned

Once the metal detector has indicated signs of metal, if in a public area, one can use a screwdriver or similar instrument to probe grass or dirt for coins or valuables. Be certain to replace the sod, when search is completed.

coin shooting into professions. For example, one Eric Perrin, a Minnesota resident, worked for only three years in his home state and the adjoining state of Wisconsin, concentrating largely upon lake front beach areas. In that time, he managed to fill a fifty-gallon whiskey barrel with coins and various types of jewelry. A California searcher, Darrell Reid, has collected more than a hundred diamonds. These he found while searching Los Angeles beaches and public parks, using nothing more than a metal detector, which he had built himself in his spare time.

A Florida coin hunter, Steve Browning, is said to have found more than 5000 old Spanish coins along his state's beaches, as well as nearly that many more Cuban and American coins in city parks and playgrounds.

In the old Colorado ghost town of Primero, a Minnesotan, Walter MacLaren, found a five-cent piece that was worth $40 to a collector, as well as a dime valued at $9, all within a few weeks. But several weeks later, another search-er found three $5 gold pieces lying on top of a dirt-covered building foundation in the same town.

For literally decades, some Southern California teenagers have made their spending money by hitting the beaches on summer Mondays, after the weekend throngs had departed. They would take sections that had been heavily populated by sun worshippers, then would mark it off with six-foot squares in the sand. They then would begin to sift the sand for a depth of an inch or so through a wire mesh, collecting the coins, jewelry, watches and cigarette lighters that did not pass through. In later years, they abandoned this tedious method for the efficiency of the metal detector, which allowed them to cover considerably more ground — including the time spent in discarding bottle caps!

There are literally thousands of similar stories of success in coin shooting, but there still are many beaches, playgrounds and areas across the nation that never really have

This mixture of coins was found on a Southern California beach in only a few minutes, using a metal detector. Several were buried in the old jar.

been scanned by today's electronic metal detecting devices. Even more important is the fact that, as long as people continue to use these areas, the supply of available valuables is continually being replenished.

There are coin shooters who equip themselves with more gear than a platoon of Army engineers out to clear a mine field, but this really isn't necessary. For efficient work, about all one really needs is a metal detector and a screwdriver or perhaps an ice pick.

As mentioned elsewhere in this book, digging up public property and leaving unsightly holes is frowned upon and can find one in court. Therefore, keep in mind that most of the coins you are likely to find are no more than two inches beneath the surface. Once located with your metal detector, it is a simple matter to probe for them with your screwdriver or ice pick, until you make contact, then use the instrument to help lift them out of the ground by angling it under the coin's edge.

It doesn't take a great deal of experience in handling the metal detector to determine precisely where a coin is located, as one passes the coil back and forth across an area, where he is getting a reading.

As with beaches that are searched before a tide covers the sand, most other recreation areas that have loose soil, such as fairgrounds, rodeo grounds, race tracks and carnival grounds, invariably have lost coins that are barely covered with loose soil. Once located with the metal detector, one usually can uncover the find with his toe or, at least, by sifting the sand or loose dirt with his fingers, if he doesn't have a mesh screen at hand.

For more specific ideas on where to look, the profession-

Above: Pro uses detector on a public beach at Vancouver, B.C. (Below) The scene of a massacre, Apache Peak in New Mexico is type of location where odd items often may be turned up.

als favor looking under picnic tables and park benches and, when searching playgrounds, check the worn and grass-free spots under swings, teeterboards and other recreational equipment.

At fairgrounds, carnivals, rodeo grounds, et al., run your metal detector over the areas around the ticket booths as well as under the bleachers or other seating areas. Also, unpaved parking lots usually yield a variety of coins and small jewelry. Church yards, ranging from the front door to the street, also can provide good pickings.

There are few country schools still in existence, but the grounds still are there. Checking out these areas can prove profitable, since numerous generations of children tended to lose their lunch money there. Amusement parks also are becoming a thing of the past, but some of these make lucrative search areas even though they may have been closed for years.

On a more modern note, the rest areas constructed along most of today's interstate highways also make good search-ing, as do the less formal picnic areas found along lesser highways. Lovers' lanes — and every community has at least one — have been found to be profitable searching areas. One Iowa college student helps pay his tuition by treasure hunting. He found more than $100 in coins, plus some valuable jewelry, along one such deserted lane near Des Moines, Iowa.

In the past, many rural areas held community picnics, harvest festivals and similar celebrations. An example of how lucrative searching these areas can prove is indicated in the experience of two gents, John Gilson and Frank Slater. They went into an area known as Woodlawn, some four miles from Miden, Nebraska. This actually was a grove of trees in which the annual Fourth of July celebrations and festivals had been held for decades. However, there had not been such an event in more than a quarter of a century and the area had reverted pretty much to the wild state.

Nonetheless, in a single day of searching, they found more than $500, including enough valuable Indian head

Old wash basin and drinking cup were turned up at the site of an old Girl Scout camp in Southern California that had been abandoned in the 1920s.

Coin shooting is a type of recreation that requires little in the way of investment, yet can be enjoyed by the entire family and one doesn't have to venture far from city.

pennies to fill a quart jar! Needless to say, this no longer is a prime area. Since their find, it has been gone over repeatedly by other hunters.

Historical monuments and the areas around which local legends have been generated usually can provide good hunting. For example, at the site of old Camp Floyd, near Provo, Utah, searchers found approximately four dozen gold coins. These were especially valuable, since they were of Mormon origin, having been formed in the days when firms and groups were allowed to mint their own money. This particular site, however, no longer is open to treasure hunters. Some who didn't know when they had a good thing, dug holes all over the historical site, not bothering to fill them up.

At Fort Kearny, Nebraska, there was an area across the road that apparently was a wagon camp in the pioneer era. Since then, it has been used for camping by tourists. This has shown itself to be a lucrative area, with old coins and artifacts being uncovered along with the small change and jewelry dropped by more recent visitors.

There are any number of other areas that are excellent for searching. Trailer parks, for example, have provided ample returns for a little time invested. Check the car parking areas, as well as along the concrete ramps for each trailer space. The lawns, swimming pool areas and parking lots of motels also are good. We know of one treasure hunter who invariably is able to pay a night's motel bill simply with the money he locates on the premises.

The manager of a drive-in theatre in south Georgia became interested in treasure hunting and bought a metal detector. He paid for the device in only a few days, check-

Wagon Mound in New Mexico was the site of the last camp before reaching destination on the old Santa Fe Trail. Historical areas make excellent areas for coin shooters.

Charles Garrett family and Hardrock Hendricks explore an old bottle dump near a Colorado ghost town. The search produced trade tokens and several valuable old bottles.

ing the gravel-covered parking area. In Venice, California, one teen-ager concentrates almost entirely in searching the areas in front of beach-front hamburger stands.

A Colorado treasure hunter found more than $500 simply by running his metal detector over the parking lot and lanes at the tourist viewpoint above Wolf Creek Pass. Among the items he found was a three-cent piece — valued by coin collectors — more than fifty pieces of jewelry, a Spanish piece-of-eight, a Mexican peso and a money clip with $75 in it!

On a more parochial note, Clarence Hill simply walked around his block the first day he had his metal detector, searching the grassy areas on both sides of the sidewalks. In that single trip, he paid for the metal detector, as he found several wristwatches, an antique lodge emblem watch fob and an emerald ring that had been lost several years before. The owner of the ring paid a $50 reward for the return of the ring, but the resultant publicity was of even more help,

since Hill has been called upon since to help find numerous lost items of value and has been suitably rewarded when successful.

The experienced treasure hunter has found that he recovers more copper pennies than perhaps all other types of coins combined, but there are several reasons for this. First, more pennies are lost than other types of coins. Following this theory, more silver coins are lost than gold.

But much of the ratio of discovery has to do with the chemical stability of the various types of metals contained in the coins. For example, copper begins to literally dissolve as soon as it is covered by dirt. After a few months, a minute part of the copper has leached out into the soil surrounding the coin. Thus, when the metal detector passes over a coin, it reacts not only to the coin but to the area of the soil that has been contaminated by the leaching. A penny that has been buried for several months will cause the detector to react as though a coin the size of a silver dollar was buried.

Deluxe model All-Pro digger can be an excellent aid in finding coins. It is marketed by Indian Territories Supply Company located in Tulsa, Oklahoma.

Right: Bill Vesters and Ed Moody of White Electronics display some 200 coins found in St. Lewis park on one Sunday afternoon. (Below) Picnic areas, where company celebrations were held also make excellent spots in which to seek long-lost valuables.

THE DENVER · DRY GOODS · CO.
ANNUAL PICNIC · TOLLAND · D & S L RR · JULY 17 1915
PHOTO BY WISWALL

Silver leaches much more slowly and gold, being affected by few chemicals in the soil, does not offer so large a clue. As an example of what can happen, more gold jewelry is found than actual coins, although it stands to reason that many gold coins have been lost over the centuries. However, gold jewelry contains more alloys that react to chemical action of the soil and weather, thus making a larger target for the metal detector to hit, so to speak, when the other alloys leach into the soil.

The examples furnished here as to likely places to search for coins constitute only a small number. The field is as broad as the imagination of the coin shooter, for there appears to be lost money almost everywhere.

In loose sand such as on a beach, it is possible to find coins with hands, after initial location has been made with the use of a metal detector.

One can get an excellent suntan at the same time he or she is paying expense of an extended visit to exotic beach.

Making Treasure Hunting Pay Off

Chapter 9

Treasure hunting can be an excellent hobby for women as well as men. It has Lucile Bowen of Spokane, Wash., who won the women's treasure hunt during a convention of the Prospectors Club of Southern California.

There Is More To It Than Simple Discovery; Here's What To Do About It!

Housing projects and expansion of civilization are covering much of this nation's good treasure hunting areas, but there still are countless sites available, where the serious treasure buff can make his finds.

WHEREVER PEOPLE HAVE gathered to play and work there are valuable things hidden or lost close by. These treasures can vary in size from a cluster of coins found around the first base bag on a sandlot ball diamond to a two-karat diamond engagement ring lost at a local swimming beach. Jewelry, tools, antique auto parts, knives, historic firearms, cannon shot, spent lead, steel bullets and coins are but a few of the exciting finds waiting to be unearthed. A meteorite can bring in as much as five dollars a pound or even more.

Successful treasure hunting, like all skills, requires a considerable amount of practice and knowledge and the importance of careful research cannot be over-emphasized. Get into the habit of haunting your local libraries, newspaper offices and the records found in your courthouse.

Kip Wagner found 4,000 Spanish pieces-of-eight at the site of a sunken Spanish fleet, thanks to the information he found in "Concise Natural History of East and West Florida." This book was published in 1775, just sixty years after a hurricane had sunk the Plate Fleet. The book not only provided generous information on the fleet but included an accurate map to the site.

Next to research, the metal detector is the treasure hunter's best friend. Get to know your metal detector backwards and forwards. There are dozens of metal detectors on the market made by as many different manufacturers. A good way to learn about them is by sending for literature on every unit available. Study this information carefully and pick a unit in a price range you can afford that will do the type of work you have in mind. Pay special attention to claims made about detection range. Some manufacturers may mislead you into thinking that because a detector has a loud signal tone, it is the sign of a powerful unit. This is not necessarily true.

This loud signal — if you're using a BFO unit and have the volume turned too high — could prevent you from hearing the minute change in tone that can mean contact with buried metal. Most treasure hunters prefer a detector with

This hoard of coins and jewelry was discovered by members of treasuring hunting club, who specialized in searching shallows at public beach.

One should be especially careful of the con man who has a treasure map for sale. The game is almost as old as treasure hunting and depends on human greed.

A.B.FROST. 1887

volume that can be turned down for secretive detecting, if necessary, without affecting the sensitivity of the unit.

A good detector will have interchangeable search coils that can be switched easily when the user encounters different conditions. A search coil with a large diameter is used for locating large objects buried deep in the ground, while a small coil will detect smaller objects located close to the surface. It is wise to have both a large and a small coil, as this will prepare you for anything for which you might possibly want to search.

Once you have a detector, you will be ready to plunge into treasure hunting. Where do you start? Believe it or not, the best place is right in your own back yard. What you find may surprise you. After going over your yard, start checking out the lawns up and down your block next to the driveways and sidewalks. In the Summer, children with coin-in-hand stand in these places waiting for the ice-cream man; a great deal of coins never make it to the ice-cream truck! Another good spot is around parking meters if they're located in a grassy area.

One of the best spots is your community park. Be sure you use only a hunting knife to dig and always replace the turf exactly as you found it. Use an icepick or a screwdriver with a rounded head and probe until you touch the object, then slide the blade of your knife down alongside your find and remove it with the least amount of digging possible. The best areas to search in parks are around the bases of the baseball diamond, the foot of the slide, under the monkey bars and around the swings. In addition to the many coins to be found in parks, you may also acquire a nice collection of jewelry. However, check local laws covering such searches before you get carried away.

As you gain experience, you will want to start going after the big treasures that are out there waiting for the right person to come along.

Professional treasure hunting is just like any other business. It can't succeed unless it is properly financed. Is it possible for the average man, with a wife and children, to become a professional treasure hunter? Yes, if you go about it in the right way, allowing the little finds to finance the big ones.

There are many facets to treasure hunting and any one of them can pay off if you set up a program and follow through with it. One must decide what type of treasure hunting he likes and pursue that activity at every opportunity. Before you know it, those various little finds will accumulate until you have quite a store of valuable items which can be sold to finance larger, more expensive expeditions.

Many hunters prefer seeking out important relics rather than the various forms of precious metal. A well-preserved frontier pistol or a Civil War rifle often bring in a higher price than a like amount of silver. There is hardly a corner of the North American continent that — at one time or another — has not seen troops on the march or armies in battle. Old forts and military bases often are rich hunting grounds. Though some of these historic sites are national parks with no hunting or digging allowed, often the real goodies are found outside the park areas where the oldtimers used to dump their trash. Perhaps you've heard the saying among treasure hunters that "yesterday's trash is today's treasure." It's true! Many early military artifacts bring fantastic prices. Buttons from period uniforms, for example, may bring anywhere from $1 to $35. There is also money in old emblems, guns, swords, spurs, canteens and many assorted pieces of military hardware. Among the battlefield artifacts bringing good prices are old cannon balls, bullets, shrapnel pieces and you name it.

Another favorite in treasure hunting is any old, abandoned house or building site. One beginning hunter, Charles Coker of Hugo, Oklahoma, recovered an estimated $30,000 in gold and silver coins while searching an old house site!

In searching any of the thousands of old houses around the country, a system should be followed to help insure complete coverage of the area. Start by searching the outside of the house, especially around the fireplace and under what might have been the bedroom windows. If there is a storm cellar, check it thoroughly, as this is always a likely spot. Investigate the walls and floor of the cellar, especially in the corners. If there was a chicken house near the dwelling, check it out, too. Money hidden always was well protected; if the chickens were disturbed, either night or day, they would create such a commotion that they would alert anyone in the house. That might well have been the original alarm system!

Another area to check around older houses is the top of

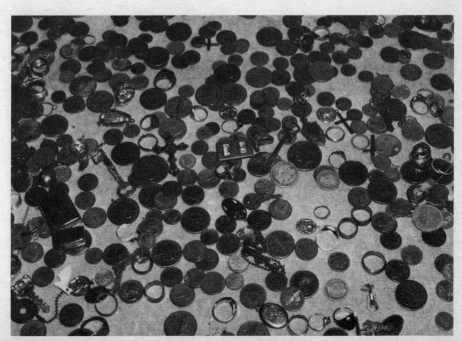

The hands tend to shrink in water. This results in a great deal of valuable jewelry being lost, but it can be recovered with the types of metal detectors used underwater.

A variety of old spoons were found in the remains of a long-forgotten house fire. One on the left was polished by an unknowing finder and its value was lowered, as proof marks showed it to be one of the original Hallmark silver design. Polishing removed the silver plate, leaving only the brass underneath.

the foundation. Most old houses were built up on either wooden posts or pilings of stone cemented in place. These were usually twelve to eighteen inches high. On these were placed stringers that made a natural shelf all around the house. Many items have been concealed — and forgotten — on such shelves.

Inside the house, pay special attention to the stairs if the structure is a two-story building. Any one of the pegs could be a secret hiding place that still holds the valuables of the occupant who could have died without disclosing the location to his family. Also, check the baseboards that run all around every room. The short ones near the corners are the most likely places. Be sure to investigate all windows and doors. The facings were easy to remove and made ideal hiding places. The old houses had metal weights on ropes attached to the windows to assist in opening them. These

weights were hung inside the window frame so don't be surprised if you get a reading at this point. In one case, a window weight had a real treasure wrapped around it — $500 in old large bills! No doubt about it, there are good finds to be made in old houses and you will seldom have to travel far to find one.

If you are the hearty outdoors type, don't overlook the possibilities in gold prospecting. This activity is for individuals who can afford to invest in a moderate amount of specialized equipment. Contrary to general opinion, you do not have to go to the Far Western states. Gold is found in varying amounts in many of our Eastern states and was discovered first in Georgia. With a good metal detector, dredge, sluice box and gold pan, it is possible to find profitable amounts in many areas. If your state carries on any type of mining activities, you can get books and maps from

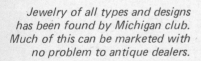

Jewelry of all types and designs has been found by Michigan club. Much of this can be marketed with no problem to antique dealers.

your state's bureau of mines and geology that show where to look for placer as well as vein gold. The Bureau of Mines in Washington, D.C., also carries a wealth of readily available information.

It is quite possible to make several hundred dollars a month finding lost diamond rings. You can send your business card to all the insurance companies in your area or run a small ad in the classifieds of your local newspaper. You can draw up a simple contract with a no-charge clause if you cannot locate the object and a ten percent of the insured value if you do.

The day may come when you run across a well-documented treasure lead that will really excite you. Going after treasure sometimes may involve detailed searching, especially if the area is several acres in size.

Assume that you've heard a treasure story or found a lead in an old newspaper about a miser who was wealthy but never was known to have kept any of his money in banks. Suppose he lived on a farm or ranch and had a vegetable garden that was his pride and joy. He worked in it daily and had a secure fence around it. He never allowed anyone else to work the garden or pick his vegetables. Upon

Author surveys the overgrown ruts that mark the path of the original Santa Fe Trail through New Mexico. With the thousands of wagons that passed this way, it should prove an excellent area for relic hunters.

his death, none of his reputed wealth was found. His relatives all assumed that he had buried it and the logical spot was in his garden. With random digging, they had found nothing and finally gave up the search.

Now you've heard the story and are eager to search for it yourself. Grabbing your metal detector, you go out to the site to have a look in hopes of digging up your first large treasure. You arrive at the site and find that the garden area consists of one or two acres of land where you could wander around all day and not find a thing!

In checking out several acres, it is possible to miss as much as twenty-five percent of the given area even though you feel you've covered it completely. The so-called "grid method" guarantees complete coverage in any given area. This method takes only a small amount of inexpensive equipment and may mean the difference between success and failure.

Before going out into the field, make up a bunch of eight or ten-inch stakes one-inch thick and buy a dozen rolls of cheap kite string. These materials are used for making up the grid.

Next make up about a dozen markers which can be of 3/8-inch dowel rod available at any lumber yard and most hardware stores. Cut these dowels into six-inch lengths. Drill a small hole in one end of each, then fill it in with wood glue and drive in a small nail to fit tightly. When the glue dries, grind the head off the nail and make a slight point extending out about one inch. It's best to paint these stakes a bright color so that you can see them in the field.

In the supposed miser's garden, start out on one side of

Bottles, jars and bits of crockery that once were quite common, today are sought by collectors and bring respectable prices.

Mike Grumka of Michigan Prospector's Club probes bottom of stream for an indication of lost valuables.

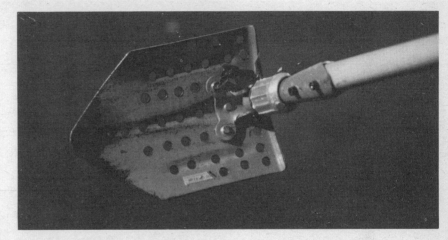

An old military entrenching tool, with holes drilled through it to allow water to escape, is great for digging in water-covered area.

Michigan Prospectors Club members plan how they will sweep a public beach. Each does specific chore.

Club members look over a find made during a Sunday outing at Pontiac Lake, a nearby recreational resort.

the plot, driving the grid stakes into the ground at five-foot intervals along the edge of the area. Go to the opposite side of the garden and drive in more stakes at intervals in line with those on the other side. Now take your kite string and tie it onto one of the corner stakes. Cross the garden and wrap the string around its matching stake on the opposite side. Move on to the next stake and wrap the string around it, again to the next matching stake. When you finish staking the area in this manner, you will have a series of marked rows five feet wide that reach across the entire garden.

Start with your metal detector on one corner, swinging the search coil all the way across the five-foot-wide row. Swing and take a step, again and again. Work back and forth across the area between the strings just as though mowing your lawn. Searching this way, one isn't likely to miss anything in the area.

Every time you get a reading with the detector, stick one of the marker stakes into the ground on the spot. After you have covered the entire area, you then can go back over it and dig up the objects that gave you readings. If you have a partner, you can work twice as fast; one man can locate and the other can do the digging. The grid method of searching

is great for covering a large area completely in a short time and should assure success if the treasure is there.

There are thousands of treasures in this country, large and small, waiting to be found by some lucky treasure hunter.

Two members of the Michigan Prospector's Club, Mike Grumka and Ray Sadowski, have found success in an unusual way of locating treasures both large and small. Where? In the most obvious place...their local state parks and private beach areas right out in the water, going as deep as they can walk out into the water without becoming buoyant.

Both believe more treasures are recovered in the water than on the beaches. More items are lost in the water due to the shrinking effect water has on your hands, while swimmers are frolicking, throwing frisbees or balls, or just plain fooling around. Once Mother Nature claims her treasure in the water, it is usually lost to the owner and left for recovery by the water treasure hunter with the proper equipment and technique.

By proper equipment they mean waders, wet suits or bathing suits — depending upon the weather — a long-

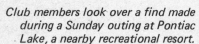

handled GI shovel drilled with holes to allow sand to sift through, earphones and most important a good metal detector. Both Compass and White's have available body mount-style detectors that are suited to this type of treasure hunting. The unit or transmitter box can be strapped either around the chest or floated in a device such as an inner tube adapted with a plastic pan in which to carry the unit. The loop and wand are separate from the transmitter box and are attached only by the cable which for these purposes should be six to ten feet in length. Add large scoop with a long handle and you have treasure, although a little work is also required.

Working in the water requires a basic grid pattern in covering an area just as working on land. The slower the pattern is worked, the greater the degree of success for the treasure hunter. Listening for the slight tone variation which indicates a deeper target will aid the treasure hunter in his recovery efforts. Experience will teach any individual how to scoop at each indication — which will include bathing cap snaps, bobby pins, belt buckles, any metals lost by those who have used the swimming area over the years — but, along with the trash, treasure is to be found such as gold rings, coins, watches, medallions, bracelets and miscellaneous valuables. As in any type of metal detecting, the more experienced one becomes with the use of his unit, the more success he will enjoy. The bulk of the items found in the water are approximately two to six inches deep.

Mike Grumka, the Michigan Prospector's Club president, and Ray Sadowski, owner of the Old Prospector's Shack in Union Lake, Michigan, have enticed the other members of the club to get out in the water and they have enjoyed numerous outings past summers to several Michigan lakes.

One story concerns a ring found by Grumka and presently being worn by his pretty wife, Sue, in a lake not too far from his home. This ring contains eleven diamonds with the center stone being a carat and one half. It is valued at approximately $2500. Two charter club members — both women working together with their scuba gear recovered a gold ring with one small diamond on one of these Sunday outings.

In inclement weather, the club also works old farmhouses and school grounds and various other locations decided upon by club members. While working a school ground on an outing, one club member, who holds the club record for the most coins and goodies recovered on each outing, came up with a Bulova watch that was about three inches down and was still in running condition. He also beat everybody out on the final outing for this year, a charter boat cruise to Sugar Island, with a super find of an 1834 half dime.

Anyone interested in working the water or in any of the club activities contact The Old Prospector's Shack, 5077 Elkin Road, Union Lake, Michigan 48085.

Completely discouraged from her lack of finds at a local club treasure hunt the day before, Cookie Bevins, wife of

Equipment for searching shallow water for lost items of value is simple, inexpensive except for detector.

This array of coins and jewelry was recovered by members of the Michigan Prospectors Club during their series of weekend outings.

Cookie Bevins discovered this hoard of old coins, while checking out a new metal detector in public park, within walking distance of home.

Leon Bevins, vice-president of Indian Territory Supply Company in Tulsa, Oklahoma, was determined to get to know her new detector better. The purchase of a different detector only days before the hunt had convinced her that a lack of use of the new unit was her problem. Up at 6:30 and out at 7:30 Sunday morning in an old Tulsa park where she and her husband had previously found several coins, tokens, and jewelry, she was eager and determined.

Although going his separate way, Bevins kept an eye out for her during their hunt through the large park. Several times Cookie would ask for assistance in tuning her new detector and each time the cry for help was heard, her husband would respond with less and less enthusiasm. He had been picking up a few older coins and needed no interruptions.

After several hours of searching, they were about fifty yards apart with a large evergreen tree between them. For the "umpteenth" time the familiar, "Leon, come here," was heard. Reluctantly, her husband walked around the evergreen to find her on her knees in the middle of a well-worn path digging in the sandy soil. A hole about eight inches across and some ten inches deep was apparent. At least three coins had been found and Cookie was excitely running her metal detector over the hole, saying, "More! More!"

Bevins laid his detector down and started digging in the hole. After digging up coin after coin, the total coins taken from the one hole were: 1823 dime; 1874 three-cent piece; 1862 half dime; 1853 dime; 1889 dime; 1867 five-cent piece; 1897 five-cent piece; 1907 five-cent piece; 1890, 1897, 1904 and 1906 Indian head pennies. Cookie's take from this one hole in this park was fourteen coins, ranging in dates from 1823 to 1907. How these coins came to be in this one spot in this park is still a mystery.

All the coins, other than those of silver, were corroded beyond recognition and it was only after quite a lot of cleaning that they were identified. Were they part of the fill that this park has had over the years or were they buried by gypsies who camped in this area? Maybe they were buried by some youngster or possibly they are part of a larger cache still in the area.

The local treasure club awarded Cookie Bevins first prize in the Find Of The Month contest and awarded her a 1921-S silver dollar.

In the same park several weeks later, her husband found a 1917-D and a 1904 half dollar, both together, about six inches deep.

Unless you have located the Mother Lode, there are three general markets for your so-called treasure finds. These are collectors, dealers and the public at large. And let

There are countless publications available to serve as a guide in determining value of old relics.

it be pointed out here that there isn't much value to any find unless you have a market for it.

As might be suspected, selling to a dealer usually is the fastest way, but he is going to pay you only half or so of what your finds may be worth. One treasure buff, Fred Hollister, tells of finding some four dozen old whiskey bottles buried in the foundation area of an old, burned-out frontier saloon. These bottles all were the same and, at that time, were cataloged in collector journals as being worth $6 each. However, he found that an antique dealer was willing to pay him only $2 each for them. The fact that he had a large number of identical bottles also tended to drive the price down.

Selling to collectors takes time, but the margin of profit does increase — depending upon how one goes about it. Also, the average collector is not interested in four dozen identical anythings; he is interested in only one or two such items to help fill out his collection.

By checking specific collector publications, one often can make contact with individuals seeking specific items. Or one can place small advertisements in such journals, telling what he has to offer and inviting inquiries from collectors.

Selling to the public is the most difficult method of the three in realizing a profit. For success in such efforts as this, it helps if one has a gimmick. Take the whiskey bottles, for example. One could sell them as old bottles to a dealer or even a collector, but if he could come up with an authentic story of romance, describing the historical significance of the discovery site — suggesting that Billy the Kid may have drunk from the bottles, since he actually did hang out in the saloon — the bottle then gains stature in the eyes of the public as an interesting relic.

The aforementioned Fred Hollister somehow obtained a number of bricks that had been recovered from a shipwreck in Lake Michigan. He sold these for as much as $1 each to those interested in specific history of the area. He feels that to a collector or dealer, they would simply have been bricks.

One of the basic rules mentioned several times in this tome is never to change the condition of what you find. If you find a rusty, old gun, for example, for the amateur to attempt to clean it up can mean that the value is destroyed. There are specialists who do this kind of work, but you would do better simply to sell the item to a gun collector and let him instruct the specialist as to how far he wants

Ray Sadowski uses army entrenching shovel attached to long pole to bring debris — and valuables — off the bottom of a local pond. The electronic unit is carried on an inner tube with wooden platform.

the work carried out. With coins, never attempt to clean them; don't soak old stamps off envelopes, as the postmark and the envelope are parts of the overall value.

There is a market for almost anything that might be considered junk by the uninitiated. In your own attic, you may find milk glass, old cast-iron piggy banks, shaving mugs, straight razors, ad infinitum. And each of these has a definite market, if you know where to locate it. In the case

Sadowski's effort proves successful, for he holds an ancient Liberty head quarter in excellent shape.

of gems, have a jeweler appraise your find, but don't tell him it's for sale.

Below is an alphabetical listing of some sources of information that may be of help:

Autographs:
Walter R. Benjamin Autographs, 790 Madison Avenue, New York, New York.
Charles T. Hamilton Galleries, 25 East 53rd St., New York, New York.

Barbed wire:
Barb Wire Times, P.O. Box 442, McAlester, Oklahoma 74501. (This source can give you the names of numerous dealers in such wire.)

Books:
The Booklover's Answer, Box 157, Webster, New York 14580.
Carnegie Book Shop, Incorporated, 140 E. 59th Street, New York, New York 10022.
Phillip Duschnes, 699 Madison Avenue at 62nd Street, New York, New York.

Bottles:
American Bottle Collecting Association, P.O. Box 467, Sacramento, California 95820.
Old Time Bottle Publishing Company, 611 Lancaster Drive, N.E., Salem, Oregon 97301.

Buttons:
National Button Bulletin, Hightown, New Jersey 08529.
Just Buttons, 500 N. Main Street, Southington, Connecticut 06489.

Coins:
Guide Book of United States Coins, Whitman Publishing Company, Racine, Wisconsin.
Coin World, 110 Court Street, Sidney, Ohio.
Numistmatic Scrapbook Magazine, 7320 N. Milwaukee Avenue, Chicago, Illinois 60648.

Currency:
Stack's, 123 W. 57th Street, New York, New York.

Gems:
Gems & Minerals, P.O. Box 687, Mentone, California 92359.

Guns:
National Rifle Association, 1600 Rhode Island Avenue, N.W., Washington, D.C.
Shotgun News, Columbus, Nebraska.

Newspapers:
Newspaper Collector's Gazette, 53-F Curie Road, Cornwall-on-Hudson, New York 12520.

Stamps:
Linn's Weekly Stamp News, P.O. Box 29, Sidney, Ohio.
Scott Publications, 461 Eighth Avenue, New York, New York.

While not aimed at specific subjects other than simply collecting, there are other publications that can be of interest to the treasure hunter as they usually include potential markets among their advertisers.

Antique Trader, P.O. Box 327, Kewanee, Illinois 61443.
Collector's World, P.O. Box 654, Conroe, Texas 77301.
Collector's News, 606 Eighth Street, Grundy Center, Iowa.
Hobbies, The Magazine for Collectors, 1006 S. Michigan Avenue, Chicago, Illinois 60605.
Treasure, 7950 Deering Avenue, Canoga Park, California 91304.
Western Treasures, 6660 Reseda Boulevard, Reseda, California 91335.
Yankee Magazine, Dublin, New Hampshire 03444.

And there is the obvious source: your local library, which should be able to help you in determining authenticity of any item you find, as well as help generally in establishing its worth.

Accept that fact that you cannot help but find a lot of jewelry that is junk, but there is that occasional find of great value!

Knowing Topography Of The Area You Intend To Search For Hidden Wealth Can Save Time And Trouble!

IN TREASURE HUNTING, most of us tend to think in terms of ancient parchment-drawn maps showing where the Loot of Lima is hidden or the Lost Dutchman Mine secreted away among the Superstition Mountains.

However, the maps that will lead one to treasure are much more easily come by. These are the simple topographical maps published by the U.S. Geological Survey, which is under the Department of Interior. Also important are the serial maps used in aircraft navigation, since searching for likely treasure areas by airplane can save one countless days of traveling and often disappointing results,

when he ends up a blind canyon to find that there is nothing there but a wall of rock.

How can these topographical maps be of help to a serious treasure hunter? Chances are, if he is serious and has been hunting treasure for a time, he already knows the answers. However, these maps show all sorts of natural formations, including rivers, streams, mountains, lakes, as well as indicating steep slopes, valleys and canyons. But more important, they show the location of almost every large construction that is man-made, unless the structure is so recent that it has not been incorporated.

To obtain an accurate reading with a lensatic compass care should be taken to hold the compass steady. Above is the most acceptable hold position.

Map Your Success

Chapter 10

The close contour lines of the topo on the left indicates an extremely rough and high area. This is an area that should be avoided by most hikers.

A Silva Ranger model is excellent for map work. It has a declination setting that can be locked in for an area with a screwdriver. This compass usually is used by the more serious-minded off-trail hikers.

Included on these maps are trails, roads, railroads, bridges, dams, towers and, in some cases, even fences. More important, included are schools, churches, barns and even homes, not to mention mine shafts, wells, parks, mine dumps, old cisterns and just about anything else created by mankind. The man-made objects always are shown on the Geological Survey maps in black, which makes them easy to pick out and identify.

Most individuals with a military background should have no problem with reading these maps, since they are, for the most part, the same type used by ground forces in small unit operations. However, to the uninitiated, a topographical map may present a puzzle until he has looked it over and come to read the legend explaining how to read it. The wavy lines, for example, usually marked with numbers, indicate elevations, the distance between the lines indicating a difference of one hundred feet.

Unless one is looking for mineral wealth in its natural state, those man-made signs will mean more to him than anything else on the map. But perhaps more important may be the signs that are not there. For example, in the past thirty years, the United States has ceased to be rural-oriented. Literally millions of people have deserted the land, moving to the cities. As a result, the back reaches of this country are dotted with old, deserted, tumble-down houses. The old, fallen house, where there may be little to tell it ever existed except for an old stone or brick chimney, usually is

*By using your compass and the magnetic declination angle
on the standard map (to left of the compass in the
photograph) you can adjust your compass reading to find
your true direction. All topos will have this diagram.*

not shown on the newer topographical maps. For this reason, it often is better to obtain older editions, if possible. If you can get old and new of the same area for the sake of comparison, so much the better.

Checking a map certainly is not going to take the place of visual reconnaissance of the area you want to search, but it can give you an excellent idea of places that would be a waste of time. If you are unfamiliar with such maps, the best idea would be to obtain a topographical map of the area right around your home. If one lives in a city, he could order a map covering an adjacent rural area, of course. But by working with a map that covers an area with which one already is familiar, it gives him an opportunity to become acquainted with the relationship between what you see on the paper and the actual ground involved.

Before one can order topographical maps, he has to know what it is he wants; the confines of the actual area involved. Thus, one should order what is termed an "index map," which is available without charge to cover any state.

For those east of the Mississippi River, the index map is available from the Distribution Section, U.S. Geological Survey, 1200 S. Eads Street, Arlington, Virginia 22202.

For those west of the Mississippi River, the index map can be obtained from the Distribution Section, U.S. Geological Survey, Federal Center, Building 41, Denver, Colorado 80225. For those covering Alaska, write to Distribution Section, U.S. Geological Survey, 310 First Avenue, Fairbanks, Alaska.

The so-called index map covers the entire state, with smaller maps superimposed, each given the name of a physical feature or perhaps a town or city, which is on the specific map covering the area. These maps, in turn, should be ordered from the same facility from which the index map was ordered. Order blanks come with the index map and it can take from two weeks to a month or so for the specific topographical map ordered to arrive. Inasmuch as the printing on the index map is exceedingly small, one should use a magnifying glass in looking over the area in which he is interested before ordering the larger scale maps.

The best topographical map for treasure hunting purposes is perhaps the seven and one-half minute series, which has a scale of one to 24,000. This means that one inch on the map is the equivalent of 24,000 inches on the actual terrain. The maps printed on this scale, incidentally, cover an area of approximately sixty-three square miles.

The maps arrive in tubes, tightly rolled. When removed from the tube, they are difficult to handle, since the rolls tend to snap back into place. The easiest way, experience shows, is to flatten them out, then fold them into a convenient size that can be carried in a pack, the hip pocket or filed. The serious treasure hunter may have a number of these maps and sooner or later devises a filing system so that he can locate specific maps when he wants them.

Those who use these maps a great deal usually end up with a device called a map measurer. This is a device with a small wheel that can be run along whatever route one intends to follow, or it can be used to measure distances along riverbeds or other relatively flat surfaces. When the measurement has been made, the device tells the exact distance — on a flat plane, at least — from one point to another. It does not, however, take into consideration such things as contour lines, which would indicate one is walking a long way upward or downward in order to move a few feet forward. These devices are available for a few dollars in most stores or shops that specialize in camping gear.

For the serious treasure hunter, who intends to take to

An inexpensive compass is normally all you need. This one would not be good for map work, since scale is in five-degree increments. It will get one from point A to B, however.

Higher priced compasses will have added features and will normally have a cover to protect the rose. A cover is not absolutely necessary, however.

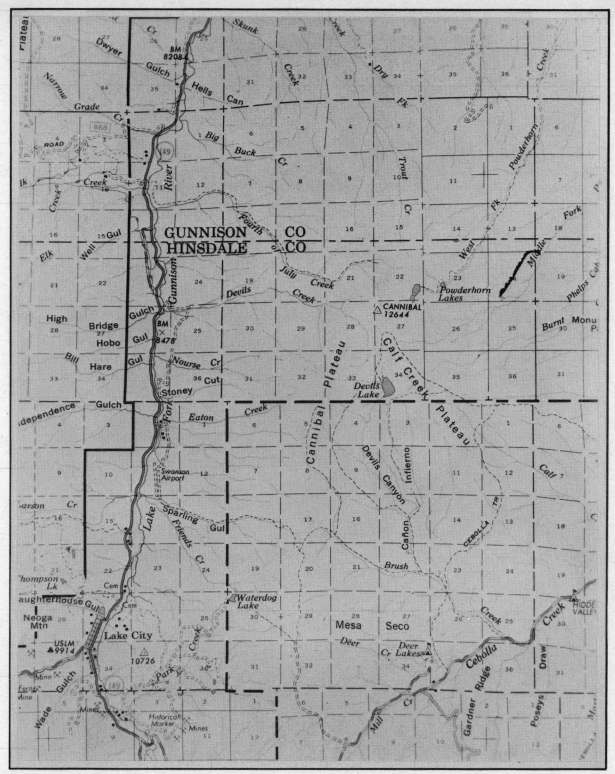

Maps published by the U. S. Forest Service are handy, but they do not have the contour lines that are contained on the topographical maps. They can be used, but to get a true picture of the terrain, a topo is much better.

the wilds with his map, a compass is almost a necessity. If you are going to be searching in familiar terrain, the compass becomes less important. Incidentally, familiar terrain with well-recognized landmarks is where one should go to learn to use a compass, if he isn't familiar with the techniques.

As mentioned earlier, for the individual interested in known treasure grounds, there are plenty of maps available. In fact, there are several companies that specialize in this type of material. One of the leaders is Varna Enterprises, P.O. Box 2216, Van Nuys, California 91404, which publishes a number of such collections.

There is little doubt, for instance, that California has more lost mines and treasures than any other state. Based

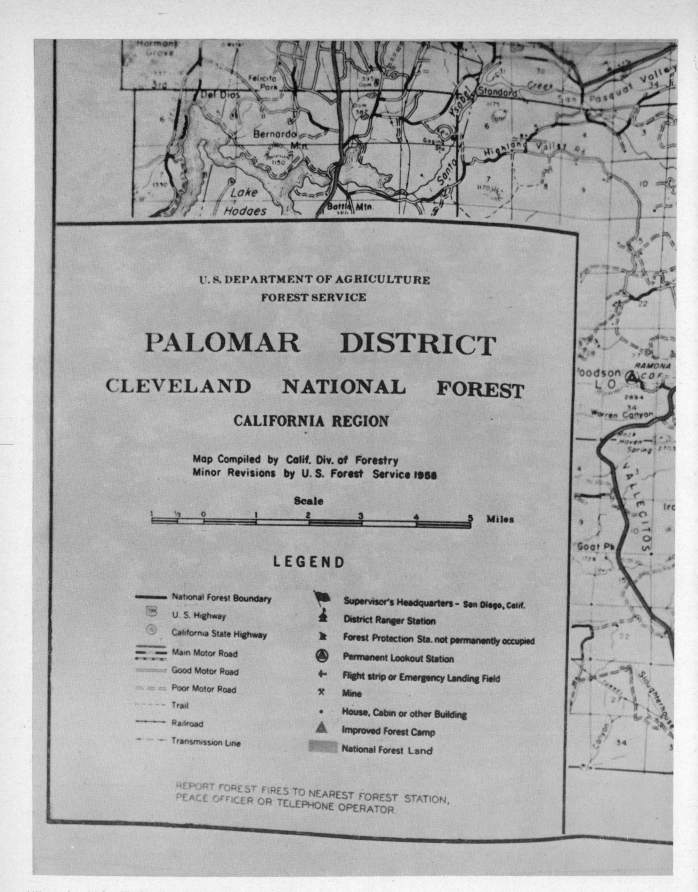

U.S. DEPARTMENT OF AGRICULTURE
FOREST SERVICE

PALOMAR DISTRICT

CLEVELAND NATIONAL FOREST

CALIFORNIA REGION

Map Compiled by Calif. Div. of Forestry
Minor Revisions by U.S. Forest Service 1958

Scale

1 ½ 0 1 2 3 4 5 Miles

LEGEND

National Forest Boundary
U. S. Highway
California State Highway
Main Motor Road
Good Motor Road
Poor Motor Road
Trail
Railroad
Transmission Line

Supervisor's Headquarters – San Diego, Calif.
District Ranger Station
Forest Protection Sta. not permanently occupied
Permanent Lookout Station
Flight strip or Emergency Landing Field
Mine
House, Cabin or other Building
Improved Forest Camp
National Forest Land

REPORT FOREST FIRES TO NEAREST FOREST STATION,
PEACE OFFICER OR TELEPHONE OPERATOR.

*Hikers should familiarize themselves with the symbols
used on the particular map that they are using. All
maps will have a legend in the lower margin. To save
time on the trail, you should study them before starting.*

124

A simple direction compass with a folding cover is the type used by most backpackers. The cover protects the sensitive insides from dust and dampness.

upon this premise, the firm has published "Roadmap To Lost Mines and Buried Treasures of California." The map lists 127 lost mines and treasures, covering both Northern and Southern California, but to the would-be prospector, the areas marked in pink probably are more important. These areas indicate the known gold regions, many of which have not been overrun with prospectors as yet.

A companion map published by the same firm is "Roadmap To California's Pioneer Towns, Ghost Towns, Mining Camps." It does fill a need in offering a detailed guide to the hundreds of defunct mining camps and ghost towns that dot the California landscape. There are more than four hundred listed in alphabetical order, listing current population — if any. Included on the map are such long forgotten communities as Grub Gulch, Lousy-Level and Celestial Valley.

The same publisher also has a map covering the Oregon Trail, showing all the landmarks and campsites along the trail that ran from Kansas City to the Oregon Territory. Listed are the various forts along the route that even in recent years have been the sites of some historic finds by treasure hunters scouring the old ruins.

Varna Enterprises also has published a map covering virtually all of the pioneer trails that existed across the western United States and northern Mexico between 1541 and 1867. The actual routes probably vary considerably from what the map has to offer, although it is obvious that considerable research has gone into this effort. However, if you are thinking in terms of treasure, this map and the one on the Oregon Trail probably will make better den decorations than practical guides to fortune!

Numerous electronic firms, makers of metal detectors, offer similar maps and booklets as a part of their public relations effort. For example, Thrifty Electronics, Incorporated of 5760 E. 26th Place, Tulsa, Oklahoma 74102, publishes "Treasure Hunters Map of Oklahoma Ghost Towns." It lists more than 650 such abandoned communities, showing their locations.

It is common sense that whenever such a booklet as this makes an appearance, if the towns haven't been picked over long ago, it attracts attention to them and the rush begins. However, when you have 650 towns to choose from, there has to be something worth finding in some of them!

The Fireball Electronic Metal Detector Company of 3528 Fairlane, Odessa, Texas 79760, is another firm that has come up with an interesting map called the "Texas Prospectors And Historians Map." It covers the old forts, the pioneer trails and some of the lost treasures. It also tells you which of these are on private property and whom to contact, if you want to make a search of the area.

Often you will hear oldtimers say that they would never use a compass; that their compass is built into their heads. If this is the truth, they are fortunate. Most of us, although we may never become lost, find that there are times when we become turned around and lose our sense of direction.

With a compass, a topographic map and a bit of innate instinct, this situation can be rectified quickly. Only the very young or very foolish wander off into an unknown area without means of finding their direction should they inadvertently become "turned around."

Compasses basically fall into three classes...all of which will do the job, but some of which are a little more sophisticated.

The first type would be a simple needle with a compass rose under it in a carrying case. The case may be brass or the ever increasingly popular, plastic case; with this case

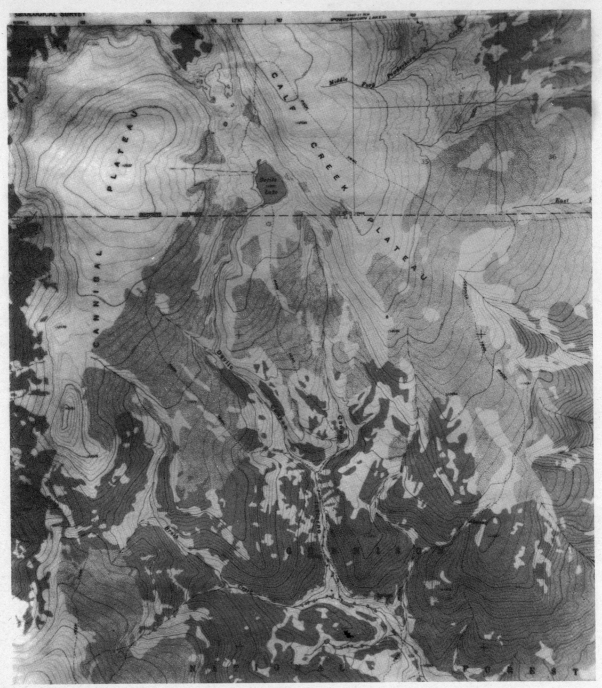

A larger scale map gives the hiker much more detail and a better idea of the terrain. The map above is a large scale, which shows the contour lines very clearly.

housing the needle and compass rose. The metal units have a lever to dampen the swing of the needle when the hood of the case is closed. The hood is used primarily to protect the glass over the needle and at the same time keep the unit clean.

The plastic models normally will be filled with a liquid such as alcohol or glycerine, which will not freeze in extremely cold temperatures. Purpose of this liquid is to help slow the swing of the needle while taking a bearing. This is a handy time saver, but is not necessary and is not always found in your cheaper models. The price of these simpler models will run from approximately one dollar to

five dollars, depending on its construction. The scale of degrees on this compass will read clockwise from zero moving around the dial to 360 degrees. This type of compass will be more than adequate if your budget is a bit tight.

Another type of compass is the military or lensatic compass. This has the same clockwise degree scale, but has the added feature of a sighting system for taking a bearing on an object at a distance. Another feature allows you to look at the scale at the base of the finder and read the bearing with the aid of a small lens in the viewfinder. This is extremely handy and this model as a rule is a better compass. It does cost a few additional dollars, but some find that it is much easier to use. Others will find that the extra gadgetry only confuses them and is more of a hinderance than an aid.

The third version of the pocket compass is used by the forestry service, surveyors and other professionals. This compass has the degrees going counterclockwise on the dial and is used in a different manner than the other two types mentioned.

If you plan to do serious work in the field, or want to lay out lines or other map and compass problems, this compass should be your choice. This model is often called a cruiser compass. However, if you are a beginner, you are better off staying with one of the first two types described. The cruiser is mentioned only so that you can distinguish the difference should you desire to purchase a new compass and are not familiar with this style.

Many beginners will purchase an excellent compass, then allow it to rest at the bottom of the pack, never used. Not only can a compass be a necessity sometimes in an unknown area, but practicing with it in a known area can become a great sport. By doing this, you become thoroughly familiar with how it works and when the day comes when you really do need it, you will have no problems.

Before getting into how to use both a compass and a map, let's first discuss the simple use of a compass. This is where you want to simply get from Point A to Point B, then return to Point A. This is a relatively simple process.

Before leaving your car or base camp, remove the compass from your pocket and, holding it steady, take a reading. If you have the model with the swinging or rotating marker such as the lensatic model, you can set it to point in the direction of camp on the reciprocal heading. This means that when you leave camp, for example, you may be going north and to return to the camp, all you need to do is go south.

This sounds simple. However, once you leave the road or camp, you may not be able to travel in a straight line due to impassable creeks, downed timber or other types of obstacles. To reach your destination, you may have to go around them, in a direction that is entirely different from that which you originally intended.

With a good compass and topo map, the treasure hunter should be able to find his way regardless of what type of terrain he may encounter.

If this happens you need not worry about true north or other situations you will encounter in map reading. All you need to do is follow the arrow as you lay it out. To do this, when you meet an obstacle and must go around it, take a reading on the compass; move approximately one hundred steps or whatever it takes to get around the obstacle; clear the obstacle and use the reciprocal heading to return the one hundred steps or more to the original line of direction.

You may not have to count your steps if you have a good landmark to use for direction; however, if you don't, you may forget to use the compass and you may find yourself in deep trouble. The landmark may become obscured by fog, a hill, a line of trees or almost anything that can block your view.

If you do not know how far you have gone off course, it is difficult to get back to the original line of direction, especially if the landmark you have chosen is no longer visible by the time you are able to to get around the obstacle. It is always best to use your compass and if, when you get around the obstacle, you still can see your landmark, well and good: You will have a double check. Once back on the original line of direction you can continue on your way.

There are no set rules for the use of compasses, but the one discussed is the easiest and the best for just getting from one point to another without using a topographic map. The use of a compass in conjunction with a map will be discussed later in this section.

Many treasure hunters fear becoming lost in mountainous areas, because they are so vast and are rarely traveled. Here you can spend the entire outing without ever seeing another person. So mountainous areas should not be avoided strictly because of a fear of becoming lost. This is why you have a compass and if it is used properly, you should have no difficulty finding your way no matter what the terrain.

Other hikers prefer the mountainous areas, because should they be in a forest area for awhile, when they come out into a clearing they can use the mountains as a landmark. When they went into the forest the peak was on the left for example, and upon emerging into a clearing it is now in front or to the right of them. By zeroing in on the mountain and hiking in that direction, they can find their way back to their original line of direction.

These people also should use their compasses, because if you do much backpacking at all, there is going to come a time when there is nothing in the terrain that can be used as a landmark. In this situation, the only thing that is going to get you heading back in the right direction is a compass.

A phenomenon which often occurs and can give the treasure buff trouble, is that anything that is iron or steel in your pack can have an effect on the needle in your compass. If you carry an ax or anything with a large mass of iron close to the front of your pack where it is near your compass, it can throw your compass reading off. Most pack frames are made of aluminum and will not affect the

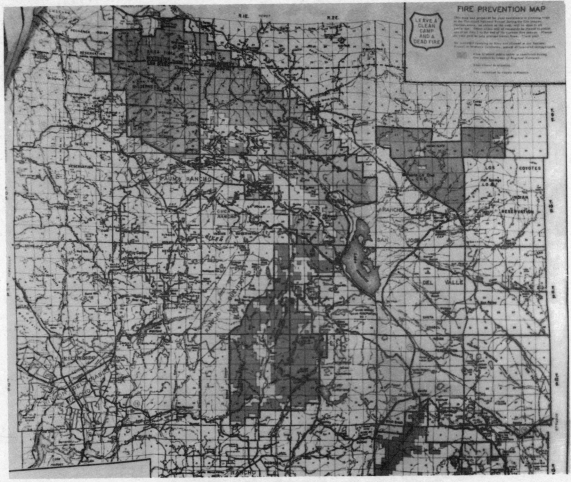

The Forestry Service map above shows the drainage system of the area, but without the contour lines of a topo, it gives too little information on terrain.

Compasses come in all sizes, price ranges. The style you select should depend upon need and your budget.

needle, but anything that is of iron or steel in the pack definitely will, if too close to the compass.

Should you find yourself continuously ending up to the right of your objective, you should check whether you have something metallic on the right side of your pack. If so, it should be moved to the pack center where it will not affect the needle. This metal mass deviation should not be confused with compass declination, which will be covered later. The deviation is an error in your compass reading caused by an abundance of natural ore in the area, or as mentioned, a metallic mass in your pack.

This deviation of the needle works by the inverse square law theory. This means that, if the metal object is one foot from the compass, it will deviate quite a bit and be obvious to the user. However, if the metal object is two feet away, it will exert four times less attraction on the needle and the needle will not swing in its direction quite as noticeably.

If you move the object three feet behind you, it would then have nine times less attraction, so it would be barely or not at all noticeable.

If your compass continues to behave erratically, check for metal in your pack and, if there is none, then you can assume that the needle is being affected by a natural ore deposit in the area.

Stars are another means to determine your direction and they can be helpful in checking the accuracy of your compass. If you are out after dark on a clear night, you can check the compass deviation by finding the North Star and sighting the compass on an object or imaginary object at the base of the star. If the needle is not pointing north on the dial, however many degrees you are off is your compass deviation and you can adjust your direction accordingly.

Some compasses have luminous dials for night use, but, if yours does not, you shouldn't worry. Luminous dials are fine for military night maneuvers, but for the average person lost at night, the last thing he should do is to move. It is best to make yourself as comfortable as possible and wait for morning, unless, of course, an emergency necessitates your trying to find help.

A compass that is going to be of any use should have a graduation of degrees not less than units of two. A graduation of one degree is difficult to read and one that is five degrees will not be accurate enough, but will have a variation that will throw you off your target point.

The most common style of compass used by backpackers is the pocket compass, but there also is a wrist compass available. A disadvantage of this style that you might want to consider is that it becomes covered by your jacket and is difficult to read. There is also the possibility that it might be caught on a limb and be pulled off without your knowing it. In fact, it might not be a bad idea to carry two compasses in case one might get lost.

Some compasses have grid scales that can be placed on a map for reference. These are helpful, but for the compass to have them it must be bigger and the larger size is sometimes more of a hinderance than what the grid lines are worth.

A word of caution concerning your maps: Often these topographic maps are ten years or older and do not show current roads or other man-made structures. Should you be hiking and run into a road that is not on your map, don't be concerned; chances are the road was built after the map was published.

Naturally, it is a help if they do contain the roads, and many maps will; however, the primary purpose of a topographic map is to show the contours of the terrain. They are made from aerial photographs of the area and by using stereoscopic viewing methods and special machines, map makers are able to project the actual contour lines on the map.

When looking at a topographical map, in the lower left-hand corner you will find the date that the aerial photograph was taken. You will find that many are made in the mid-Fifties and early Sixties and one should keep this in mind when moving over unknown terrain. The rivers, streams, hills, valleys and mountains will be shown, but more than likely many of the present roads and other man-made structures will not appear. Use the map for determining the terrain, and shift with the roads and other structures as you come upon them. One time through the area and you will be familiar with these also.

The U.S. Forest Service and the Bureau of Land Management (BLM), also publish maps, but many times these will not have the contour lines. They will have streams and drainage systems, but not the contour lines of the terrain. These should be used only when the other type of maps with contour lines are not available.

An inexperienced map reader may be overwhelmed when he first looks at a topographic map. To him the map looks like a bunch of mysterious squiggly brown and green lines drawn in no apparent pattern. However, with a little knowledge these soon begin to take on some meaning.

The first thing you should check is that you have a map of the right area, which is written in the lower right-hand corner of the map. Maps are normally named by landmarks or particular areas: for example, Cannibal Plateau, Colorado quadrant. Just left of the quadrant name is a map of the state in which the section map appears and a dot that

A lightweight roll of sponge-like plastic can make a bed softer in the wilds, but will pack easily.

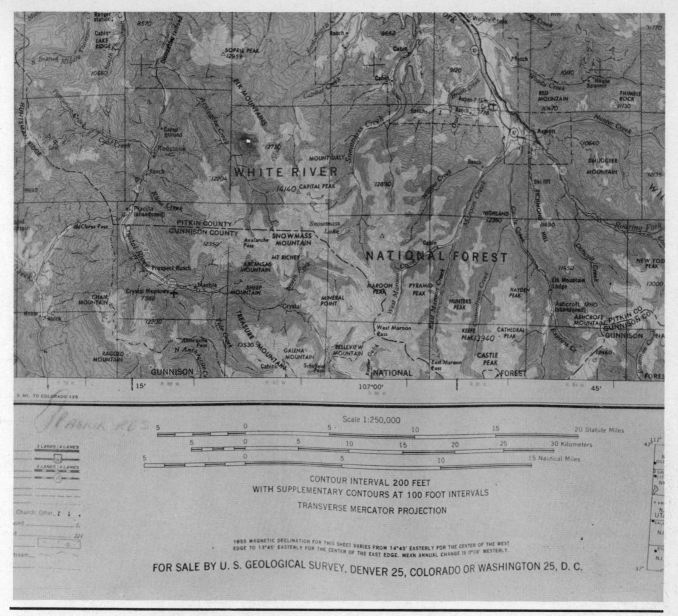

Scale 1:250,000

CONTOUR INTERVAL 200 FEET
WITH SUPPLEMENTARY CONTOURS AT 100 FOOT INTERVALS

TRANSVERSE MERCATOR PROJECTION

1955 MAGNETIC DECLINATION FOR THIS SHEET VARIES FROM 14°45' EASTERLY FOR THE CENTER OF THE WEST
EDGE TO 13°45' EASTERLY FOR THE CENTER OF THE EAST EDGE. MEAN ANNUAL CHANGE IS 0°03' WESTERLY.

FOR SALE BY U. S. GEOLOGICAL SURVEY, DENVER 25, COLORADO OR WASHINGTON 25, D. C.

*All topos will have a distance scale in the lower margin.
These normally are in either feet or miles; however,
some maps will have both measurements for more convenience.*

represents where the section is located within the state map.

Moving to the left of this, there is the scale for that particular map. These scales run from 1:1,000,000, a small scale map, to one of 1:20,000, a very large scale map. There will be a distance line marked off in scale for miles or feet and in some cases both. This is an aid in plotting map distances before starting out. For example, prior to leaving, you can determine your night's campsite by using the maps to plot the distance and your average miles covered per day.

An important item on the map is the magnetic declination diagram normally shown in the margin towards left of the map. This will have a star with a straight line representing the North Star and a line to the right of it or left of it, depending on the area, to denote the magnetic declination you must apply to correct your compass in order to use the map for true headings. Another line with a GN will also appear, which represents the Geographic North. The North Star is actually one degree to the east.

The diagram is used to compute your true direction by compass on that particular map. There are a few basic rules to follow in order to do this.

To change magnetic to true heading you will add east declination and subtract west declination. If you want to convert from true to magnetic, you will subtract east and add west. This appears confusing, so let's use a map of a western state as an example. The topographic map has a declination angle at the bottom of the page, which shows true north by using a star and a straight line, as mentioned above. The declination for this particular area for example, shows a fourteen-degree east declination from true north. A reading with the compass will give a magnetic north and, if this is followed, you would end up fourteen degrees too far east. To convert magnetic north on the compass to coincide with true north on the map, add fourteen degrees to whatever reading is obtained on the compass and you will be back on course.

Along the edges of the map will be latitude and longitude markings, but the hiker will have little need for these markings.

In the middle section along the edge will be the name of the next quadrant that matches your map. If you plan a long hike or one that may take you into the adjacent quadrant you should have both quadrant sections with you. These can be cut and taped together to make one large map or they can be used individually.

On the face of the map, one will find the actual terrain markings. These will show you the features of the terrain such as streams, peaks, rivers and forests. In addition, once you have learned how to read the contour lines, you will be able to predetermine the slope of the terrain, which is the beauty of a topographic map. It saves one from hiking many miles only to find that you have run into an impassable peak or cliff. By using the contour lines, one can plot his course to go around these obstacles prior to setting out and this can save many miles of backtracking.

In looking at a topographic map, you will notice that areas are shaded in various colors. These colors play an important function in map reading. Black stands for man-made objects, such as roads, towns and buildings. Blue represents rivers, creeks, lakes and other bodies of water, as well as permanent snow and ice. The color, brown, is used for all contour lines, except those in an area of permanent snow and ice. A darker brown line is used for altitude checks and will have the altitude written in small print alongside the line. An area shaded in green represents a forest area, with lighter shades of green used for a sage or lighter foliage area. A tufted green area indicates marshes or a swamp area. Red is used for subdivision boundaries and more important roads.

A quick look at a topographic map will tell you where the timber is; where the water and roads are; and with a careful study of the contour lines, you can determine the steep areas that should be avoided.

When the brown contour lines are close together and it's difficult to tell them apart, it means that you are looking at a virtual cliff face. Unless you are a rock climber, this would be an area to avoid.

Where the contour lines are farther apart, it means the slope is more gradual and the walking should be easy.

By using these contour lines and taking compass bearings before setting off on your jaunt, you can preplan your entire trip.

Should you get turned around, a good way to find your location is to check the contour high points on your map (peaks), then look around you for these peaks. By using them as a reference, you can determine where you are in relation to your map. You should use two or more check points, since this will enable you to better pinpoint your actual location.

Topographic maps also show jeep roads, pack trails and some even include hiking trails. There will be times when you find a trail that is not shown on the map. The reason for this is that often where there is too much traffic on a particular trail, these trails will be left off the map in order to help lighten the traffic in the interest of ecology.

By preplanning with a topographic map, you can mark each day's move before you leave. However, if you plan to camp at a stream shown on your map, take along a canteen and keep it filled anyway. These streams can be dry during certain times of the year or it may have dried up completely since the map was made. You should never rely completely upon your map without obtaining current information from other sources. A good source would be a local game warden or forestry service office in the area where you plan to hike. It is also a good idea to check in with

them and let them know who you are, where you plan to go; how long you plan to be there. If something should happen and you are late in returning, there will be someone in the immediate area who might become alarmed and come looking for you. With this in mind, be sure to advise them when you are leaving their area.

Much of the back country is laced with trails. These often are marked on your map, but there are times when they are not, for various reasons. Ranchers will use trails to move their livestock and these normally are not marked on the map, but often are confused as hiking trails. If you are somewhat familiar with the area they are no problem. If not, be careful not to take one, thinking it's the hiking trail on your map and wander way off course.

As stated earlier, topographic maps are made from aerial photographs of an area. If you have the interest and the time, you can purchase such aerial photographs before your trip. These usually will be about nine inches square and will be sent to you as a contact print. There is a data section at the bottom of the photograph, but that is all the reference material there is.

You can take two of these vertical prints and by using a stereoscopic viewer you can see the full area in a three-dimensional view. This can be helpful if you know how to read aerial photographs, but for the average hiker they are difficult without some training. However, the aerial view affords an idea of what goes into making a topographic map. It takes hundreds of photographs to make one topographic map, so it could turn into a costly project if you attempt to get all the photographs for a large area.

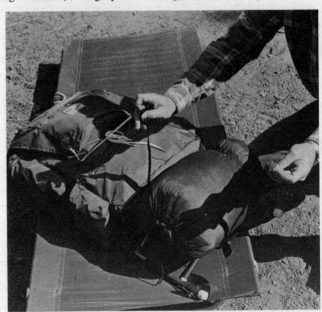

With the exception of the detector unit, all a treasure hunter needs to investigate even the wildest country can be carried in a pack.

Another source of maps, although they are not topographic maps, is the Department of Agriculture. These are used by the Forest Service, which is more interested in land management than in terrain features, so they do not have the contour lines. They do show access roads and all man-made structures, however.

These maps are free of charge from specific national forests, wilderness areas and range districts. To obtain the maps you should ask for brochure No. FS-13, "Field

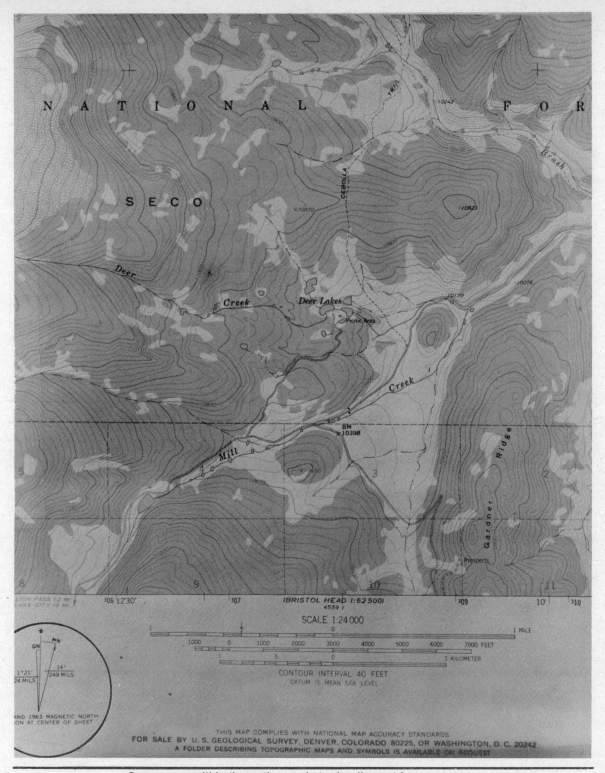

Some topos will indicate distance in both miles and feet,
as well as contour intervals. The magnetic declination
diagram is also shown very clearly in the map above.

Offices of the Forest Service." This brochure contains the ten regional offices from which maps may be obtained. These are usually in short supply, so be reasonable in your request. The address is: *U.S. Dept. of Agriculture, Forest Service, Washington, D.C. 20250.*

If the use of aerial photographs sounds interesting to you, they may be obtained from the Map Information

Office, U.S. Geological Survey, Washington, D.C. 20242. You should ask for the free publication, "Status of Aerial Photography." This booklet will tell you where to obtain the photographs. They are often in the hands of the company who contracted for the aerial photographic work and the prints must be made on order, so you should allow plenty of time for them to arrive.

To many of us, methods of dowsing for treasure — or the use of radiesthesia, speaking scientifically — seem as far removed from reality as reading the future in a crystal ball, but the technique appears to have foundation.

Chapter 11

There Seems To Be Definite Basis In Fact For This Little Understood Means Of Treasure Finding!

DOWSING: TALENT OR WITCHCRAFT?

Map dowsing is a technique used by some treasure buffs, who say they can segregate likely looking areas without ever being close to them.

THE MYSTICAL ART of dowsing has been around for an estimated 8000 years, since a drawing of a dowser doing his thing was discovered on the wall of an African cave with other pictures of life of that period.

The Sixteenth Century brought dowsing into active use in several European countries — including Italy, Germany and England — as a means of discovering deposits of ore. In the Midwest, variations of the art still are used to find water at shallow levels, thus selecting sites for drilling wells. But the art goes a great deal beyond that.

"It has been found that the younger you start dowsing, the greater your chance of getting the dowsing reaction and the easier it will be to become an expert," according to Gordon MacLean, Sr., a chemical engineer who has made a life-long study of the techniques.

According to MacLean, children of about 5 years of age are almost a hundred percent sensitive to the reaction and are extremely easy to train.

"The day may come," the engineer adds, "when physicians and the American Medical Association will recognize the value of dowsing for diseases, thus allowing us to catch up with England and the Continent in this respect."

According to L.H. O'Loughlin, president of the Southern California chapter of the American Society of Dowsers, "We try to take all the mysticism out of dowsing. We teach the basic techniques and work with a student as long as he wishes, but once he begins to get the hang of it, we let him develop his own techniques. Some people can dowse without using any equipment at all. They can do it bare-handed."

The last is in reply to the suggestion that there may be those who are attempting to capitalize on dowsing by selling special pendulums and rods that are individually tailored to a person's "vibrations."

There are several devices that can be used in dowsing — or radiesthesia, if you want for a more affluent term — to

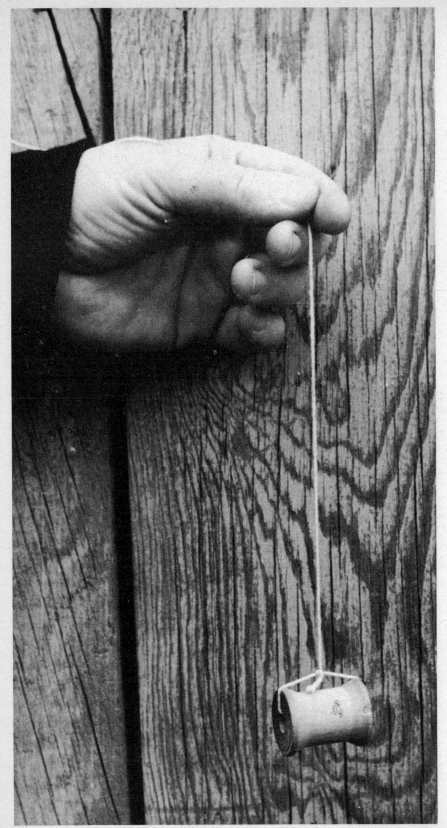

For the serious dowser, the type of materials used for the pendulum is not important, although faith is a necessity if one is to be successful

help in locating items. Some individuals prefer what they call an "L" rod, others use a simple pendulum, while still others favor a quartz crystal in what is termed a "ray gun."

One of the most amazing examples of radiesthesia is credited to a Swiss abbot, Father Alexis Mermet of Saint-Prex. A group of monks in a remote monastery of Colombia, South America, wrote Father Mermet for assistance. The monks lived in an area where it was impossible to obtain water, their spring was almost dry and the day was drawing nearer when their school would be forced to close down.

Father Mermet wrote it would be impossible for him to

While the so-called divining rod is best known for locating water for wells in the Midwest and South, it also is utilized for finding gold and other types of man-made treasure.

make such a long trip but perhaps he still could help them if they mailed him a map of the monastery grounds and surrounding lands. A map of the cloister was prepared and sent off to Switzerland.

Using a pendulum over the map, Father Mermet carefully dowsed for water. He placed an X on the map and wrote the monks that water would be found at eighty feet, nine inches. The water would be good and produce at the rate of five hundred litres a minute. The monks had nothing to lose by following Father Mermet's strange instructions. As Mermet predicted, at almost the exact depth, a strong flow of good water boiled out of the earth at five hundred litres a minute.

Mermet had sensed the presence of metal just outside the area covered by the map. A larger map was sent to him and he pinpointed a wild, rarely visited spot on a mountain. It was here that the monks found the remains of ten priests buried in tin coffins.

This incredible incident was carefully documented by the late Robert Ripley in his syndicated column, "Ripley's Believe It Or Not." Though Mermet's case is an extreme example of radiesthesia, it does lend proof that seemingly miraculous finds can be made by a talented dowser.

Mermet compiled his studies of dowsing in a book, "Principles and Practice of Radiesthesia." The book has known more popularity in Europe than in America and can be found in foreign book stores and libraries.

Mermet developed the hollow ebonite pendulum. A sample of what was being sought, water, gold, lead, etc., was placed inside the pendulum. In his later years, when unable to travel far, Father Mermet perfected the art of map dowsing. He also utilized pictures and photographs to locate lost persons, and animals and objects.

The secret of map dowsing did not die with Mermet; it is still in use today. Science has not come up with an accepted theory for the success of dowsing. Experienced dowsers have successfully located water and other objects from a map or representation of the earth's real surface.

It has been estimated that two people in ten have an innate ability for radiesthesia. Some experts believe that most people can dowse if they develop the ability. To test your ability, try this old folk game of dowsing for sex. Tie a fairly lightweight object, like a bead, stone or plumb bob, on the end of a string. This experiment works best in a group. Hold the pendulum with the weight over the hand of the person, being careful not to move the string. If one is a good dowser, the pendulum will inscribe a clockwise circle over the hand of a man. It will revolve in the opposite direction over the hand of a woman. This test provides a high degree of accuracy, except for a few rare people. For

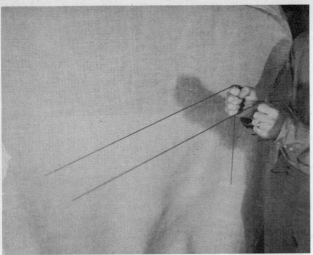

Ordinary welding rods or other lengths of metal can be used in dowsing. They are bent at right angles, then are held parallel to each other as walk-down is made.

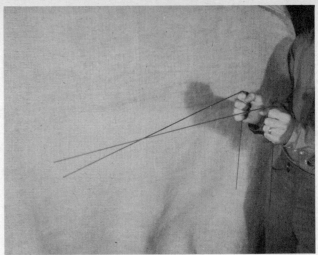

When the material being sought is directly below, the matched pieces of rod will swing in the grip to cross, if one can believe the enthusiasts who advocate the use.

example, it is possible to get a misreading if the person has Rh negative blood.

To predict the sex of an unborn child, use a large sewing needle, doubling the thread in the eye, making it about ten inches long. Knot the thread, then grasp it between the thumb and forefinger, letting the needle hang free. Holding the needle thus, place it over the mother's abdomen. The pendulum should give a "yes" reading on the sex of the mother. Attempt this test first to insure reliability. With the mother's pattern established, hold the pendulum over different areas of the abdomen. Because of individual variation in the art, you may have to check for a specific gender, say, female. If the pendulum doesn't react, the child is probably not a girl. Ask the pendulum if the child is a boy by stopping any motion. The pendulum should then give a male reading by turning in a counter-clockwise direction. Be careful not to start the pendulum yourself. If you do, the usual result is a gradual slowing down of the instrument until it stops. Conversely, when started in the test pattern that is correct, it will keep moving of its own accord.

Some dowsers claim the pendulum can be used to count the number and sex of children a mother has had, as well as the number and sex of children the mother will have in the future. To do this, continue to hold the pendulum as you did previously, then, after a short time, the sex of the mother's last child should be detected. After a short period the pendulum will stop. If there is still an older child, it will start up again and so on until all of the mother's children have been accounted for. Now, the pendulum should start once more, giving the number and the gender of the mother's future offspring.

The pendulum has proved most successful in finding water, water pipes and oil. It seems to work less well in locating gold and other metal objects.

One of the oldest known instruments made for dowsing has been the simple forked stick, which is cut from a tree or bush. There has been great discussion over the years as to the best kind of wood for this use, but the experts say there is little difference. Many dowsers in the past have favored willow forks, but this seemingly was because willow was readily available. Actually, any wood that has enough spring in it to bend without breaking will work adequately.

In fact, in recent years, even fiberglass and nylon have been found to work well in the hands of some believers.

According to the experts, the fork usually is cut so that the legs are about two feet in length, with the butt, where the branches are joined, thick enough to take the violent twist that usually results.

One grasps the two branch ends as he would a steering wheel. Thus, the forepart of the arms are straight out, horizontal with the ground, the elbows touching the sides of the body. The hands then are moved upward so the butt end is swung forward slightly, at the same time turning the wrists upwards. This tends to increase the twist to the branches.

As the butt end of the fork rises, a bit of nervous tension will be felt in the arms. The more you raise the butt, the more tension. When the butt end is sticking straight out, you are ready to start searching or "walking down," as dowsers put it.

If the would-be dowser is to make the trick function at all, he needs a bit of unconscious relaxation as he searches. This will cause the butt of the rod to dip when it reaches the goal. According to observers, there have even been cases of the force of the dip tearing the skin on the dowser's hands.

One theory advanced by dowsers is that "the central nervous system really controls the muscles and, when you give control over to your pineal gland, it takes on the chore despite what your conscious mind might desire of it. Break the hold and you break the tie."

But how do you know that the fork is reacting upon the specific material you seek? Could it be pointing downward to water rather than gold?

According to those who are experienced and swear it works for them, this is where the subconscious mind comes in. You must concentrate upon the material you seek. With the proper degree of faith, they insist it will work.

Those who are devotees of the art are quick to point out that no particular dowsing instrument will work for everybody. In fact, there are many persons who simply are not adapted to the art. If one doesn't have the talent, the experts say, no matter how expensive the rod or instrument he buys, there will be no results.

A gentleman named Dan C. George in Pierce City,

Missouri, is considered one of the finer practitioners of the art these days and he started as a non-believer.

His talent came to light in 1962, when a local Indian was using dowsing methods to attempt to locate water on George's property. Once the Indian had marked the site, George picked up the forked stick. To his surprise, the instrument literally twisted out of his hands. Since then, he has made a continuing study of the art and has been successful in locating water, natural gas, oil, precious stones and even lost mines.

George feels that the art depends upon the health of the pituitary or pineal gland. According to medical sources, if these glands are not healthy, their state cannot be improved; therefore the person is not going to be successful at dowsing.

According to George, "This gland's duty, in the dowsing function, is to initiate signals to the nervous system, to eventually cause the muscles to react ever-so-slightly. The dowsing rod or device merely is the instrument that amplifies this minute activity into a visible display."

As an experiment to determine his adaptability, one can tie a string of about fifteen inches in length to an ordinary bolt. This is your pendulum.

Then, using the hand with which you normally write, hold the end of the string between the thumb and forefinger. Hold it over the palm of your other hand several inches. Close your eyes for concentration if you have to at first, but imagine the pendulum moving in a circular fashion. Raise and lower it over the hand, watching to determine at what range it makes the broadest circle.

With practice and by concentrating, a dowser supposedly can cause the pendulum to halt and reverse the direction of its circle.

According to Dan George, such exercises help to awaken the pineal gland, transmitting information to the subconscious mind.

For some, this may never work, but don't give up immediately. There are slow starters and it may take several sessions before you begin to see results — if you have the talent at all.

Another simple instrument involves two identical rods of about sixteen inches in length. They may be as small as one-eighth inch in diameter. Making a bend four inches from the end of each, hold the short ends of the rods — one in each hand — so that the long ends are extending in front of you, horizontal with the ground.

In walking slowly over the ground, if you are qualified as a dowser and have a specific target in mind, the rods will act in an unusual fashion, according to those who have had experience with them. When you encounter your target, the two rods will tend to point toward each other or even cross. However, they usually will react differently with the individual.

There are some problems with the rods, however. In a stiff wind, they may be influenced by the swaying of your body as you walk, bracing against the breeze. However, they are easy to make and you can carry them around in your hip pocket, if you are looking for convenience.

To learn whether this divining rod — as it sometimes is called — is your bag, you might lay out several newspapers on the ground, having someone put a coin or several other items of value beneath just one of the papers.

Then, holding the rods in the prescribed manner, walk down the papers until you feel the tug, concentrating on your goal at the same time. With a little practice — and again, if you have the talent — you should be able to strike it rich!

When looking for treasure, it helps if you know what you are after, according to the experts. Just going out with a dowsing device in hopes of finding something is a waste of time. As it is explained, if you don't know what it is you seek, your subconscious isn't likely to know either.

With this in mind, many treasure dowsers use old treasure legends and maps of the area to help them with their homework before they ever venture afield. If a treasure of some sort is supposed to be in a specific vicinity, they find a map of the area then dowse over it. This is said to give them an idea of whether the treasure really is there. If there is no reaction from the dowsing rod or pendulum, they either write it off as a tale of total fiction or go to maps of the surrounding area, inasmuch as directions often are muddled, especially if the treasure was hidden in haste or under stress.

This may only confuse the beginner, but there probably are as many methods of dowsing as there are dowsers. For example, some insist that they are dealing with magnetic fields or fields of radiation. Yet, the map dowser is proving something that is in direct contrast, showing that it is more of a psychic situation.

Some dowsers carry what they call a "witness." This is material similar in nature to what they are seeking. For example, if one is searching for gold nuggets, he should carry a gold nugget in his left hand. If looking for fine gold, a small pouch of it held in the hand is supposed to be of help.

Others say this may help, but simply forming a strong mental picture of what you are after does as well; others suggest you draw a picture of the treasure and concentrate upon it before you start looking.

One also will learn in time how deep into the ground or into water his dowsing instrument will operate, although this again would appear to be in opposition to the map-dowsing theories.

All of this, of course, is intriguing, although there are hordes of treasure hunters who swear by the methods employed. At the same time, there is one expert who states that, while dowsing certainly can lead one to treasure, that doesn't mean you should retire or sell your metal detector. The latter instrument can be used to pinpoint the actual treasure location!

A forked willow branch is considered standard for the dowser who uses this particular technique, but several other types of wood seem to work equally well for the true believer in this technique of treasure hunting.

THE GOLD DIVERS

Chapter 12

With Today's Underwater Equipment,
Anyone Can Dive For Sunken Treasure
But Technique Helps!

THE SEA HAS been described as the treasure chest of the world. This is based upon the fact that, for nearly three hundred years, there were continual voyages from the New World to the Old as the treasures — gold, silver and jewels — were looted from the Indians and taken to the coffers of the European nations of the time: England, France, Holland, Portugal and particularly Spain.

As an example of the wealth, Spain alone is alleged to have shipped an average of some seventeen million — that's 17,000,000 — pesos per year over a period of three centuries. Records show that more than ten percent of this wealth ended up at the bottom of the sea. Only a small percentage of that wealth has ever been recovered.

In more recent years, hundreds of vessels — ranging from pleasure boats to men-of-war — have been sunk through bad weather, wars, structural or mechanical failure and even human error. Most of these ships carried valuables of one type or another.

These treasures — many of them of archeological as well as monetary value — have been protected through the ages by the simple fact that man had been unable to breathe beneath the water and even the early efforts to invent underwater breathing devices presented problems because of the bends, euphoria and other dangers.

Treasure diving became reasonably practical about the time that the diving suit and hard helmet were invented and perfected.

This consisted of a watertight suit, a weighted belt and lead-soled shoes, as well as the round helmet with a window through which the diver was able to survey his surroundings, although vision was restricted. Air was fed into the helmet by means of a hose from a compressor unit on the surface.

More within the reach of the average diver and treasure buff has been "scuba" gear, the letters standing for "self-contained underwater breathing apparatus." In the beginning, as divers entered the sport, they began to discover treasures on the floor of the sea, ranging from barnacle-encrusted anchors to Spanish treasure chests. In more re-

cent years, divers have formed teams not only to find treasure but to work with outstanding educational organizations such as the Smithsonian Institute in recovering items of archeological interest.

Most treasure has been discovered accidentally by sport divers, most of them working in teams, as diving alone is considered a hazard not to be undertaken. Also, as outlined elsewhere in this book, one doesn't have to stick to the depths of the ocean floor. There is plenty of treasure to be found in lakes and rivers of this country and, if collecting artifacts, these usually are better preserved than when exposed to saltwater.

The most popular type of underwater treasure site — and perhaps the most difficult to locate — is the sunken ship. While shipwrecks are found in great numbers along some hazardous sections of coastline and along the recognized shipping lanes, there often are so many of them that choosing a specific target is difficult.

While shipwrecks can be located in any sea of the world, the largest concentration of treasure ships undoubtedly is located in the Caribbean, where the Spanish treasure ships worked their way from one island to another. Bermuda is especially rich in sunken treasure ships, as evidenced by the number that have been found there. The area surrounding the Florida Keys also is well populated with old Spanish hulks or the piles of ballast stone that mark their passing. The entire area, of course, is loaded with coral reefs that make navigation a hazardous business, even in this modern day.

As mentioned, freshwater areas also can offer prime treasure hunting sites. In each case — whether fresh or saltwater — one is wise to conduct his searches in the area of the reefs, snags, sandbars and similar navigation hazards. It was such problems as these that usually caused the ships to sink.

Searching at random, of course, can consume a lot of time — and let you see a lot of water. A better method involves research, which can be extensive, too, if you are looking for the old Spanish galleons. The records concerning lost Spanish ships are found only in the Archives of the

According to historical records, ten percent of Spanish treasure fleet was sunk with the wealth aboard.

Diver uses an underwater camera to record the location of a wreck. This can be invaluable information for planning recovery operations. Note the old anchor.

Indies, located in Seville. The background on English wrecks is in the Public Records office in London. For that era, Lloyds of London the international insurer, also maintained records, but these also are located in their London headquarters.

In the matter of wrecked ships off the United States' coasts, there are charts available from the Director, U.S. Coast and Geodetic Survey, Department of Commerce, Washington, D.C.

But before one gets all carried away with buying a wet suit, a scuba outfit and rushing off to plunge into the depths, perhaps he should consider the wisdom imparted by Glen Couvillon of the Florida Development Commission. He is something of an expert in these matters, insofar as the Florida treasure grounds are concerned.

"Recent publications touting discoveries of Spanish treasure beneath the Atlantic Ocean off Florida's shores have brought about a new outbreak of treasure fever, tempting man's usually rational mind," says Couvillon, who has watched treasure hunters come and go.

"Visions abound of beaches paved with gold doubloons, waters laced with silver bars and treasure, treasure, everywhere, just waiting to be scooped up, sparkle in the dreamer's eye. After all, could there possibly be an easier way to get rich, quick?"

The simple answer to that question is an emphatic yes! You may realize quicker profits if you start a paper route, pump gas or sell matches on a street corner in the bitter cold of more northern climes.

As in most cases, mixing a little fact with a lot of fiction makes a more sensational story than what is actual fact. According to stories that have circulated in the Florida

Wet suits have become standard for the serious diver, as they protect against cold at the deeper levels.

Detector units have become common in spotting the locations of loot that has been long lost beneath sea.

Keys alone, the Spaniards lost more treasure galleons than they had in their entire navy.

For each diver who has found enough treasure to pay even his operating costs — and this excludes any profit — there have been dozens of hopeful, would-be millionaires who have lost their shirts and their dreams for no more than a couple of silver coins and cannons, which flake into rust in their backyards.

When a ship wrecked, it usually went aground on a reef or shoal in water less than thirty feet deep. When the Spaniards came to salvage the wreckage, they brought Indian divers who could dive to depths of one hundred feet for three minutes or more.

"Treasure hunters today hope to find skeletons of ships that the Spanish and Indian salvors missed. But it takes a trained eye just to recognize a wreckage site. All exposed wood has been eaten away by teredo worms, and sand and coral covered everything else within a matter of a few

Most of the treasure ships went down in rather shallow water, since they hit reefs or snags. Light rubber boats such as the one shown can be used to advantage.

years," Couvillon contends. "Novice treasure hunters have actually sat on a cannon without realizing it wasn't part of a natural reef."

Probably the most dramatic treasure strike in recent years was that made by the late Kip Wagner and the Real Eight Company in 1963, fourteen years after Wagner made his first attempt to locate a wreck site.

The most commonly held theory about the Real Eight discovery is that it was part of a fleet of Spanish ships that sank off Sebastian Inlet, along Florida's mid-East Coast, during a hurricane in 1715.

Historians explain that many treasure-laden fleets would sail from Cuba, catch the Bahama channel to the Florida Straits and then head up the Florida coast to Cape Canaveral for fresh water and supplies. They would then continue up to the Carolinas, where the prevailing trade winds helped propel them across the Atlantic Ocean to Spain.

Captain-General Don Juan Esteban de Ubilla, commander of the ten-ship New Spain Armada, followed this route along Florida's coastline, near the site of what has come to be called the Kennedy Space Center complex. His cargo of gold, silver, precious jewelry and rare Chinese porcelain was valued at some $14 million. Some sources estimate that an incalculable amount of booty not listed on the manifest — an often-used ploy to avoid paying a twenty percent tax to

Diver uses an underwater flashlight to inspect ancient fossils located in depths of Wakula Springs in Florida. Such finds often are of importance in scientific study.

These silver dollars were found with aid of BF-8 Goldmaster Amphibian, one of numerous underwater detectors.

the king — would up the total cargo's worth to approximately $60 million.

For two years, Ubilla had been delayed in Vera Cruz by supposedly laggardly slaves whose slowness in minting the gold and silver was surpassed only by their reluctance to load it. Further delays in Havana, where the commander joined the second half of his New World silver fleet, meant crossing the Florida Straits during the peak of the hurricane season.

In addition to the existing weather hazards, Ubilla was obliged to allow the French ship, El Grifon, to accompany his ill-fated flotilla as a protection vessel — a sure sign to cutthroat privateers that the fleet carried highly valued cargo.

Ubilla's desire for a speedy journey was not unfounded. On the evening of Tuesday, July 30, 1715, just south of the present site of Kennedy Space Center, ten of the vessels were smashed against the jagged reefs by hurricane force winds, scattering the $14-million fortune along the coral-studded Florida coast. El Grifon was the only ship that escaped the shoal.

The treasure sank to the bottom as the ships were battered farther inshore, their precious cargo draining out slowly through gaping holes made by the combined forces of nature. Some treasure plummetted to the ocean's floor, locked deep in ship hulls, and some cascaded like a glittering waterfall over the ever-shifting shoreline sands.

A thousand men went to the bottom along with the treasure and a thousand more crawled to the beaches to await relief that finally came when the salvage fleet arrived from Havana.

"The Havana treasury eventually recovered approximate-

The late Mel Fisher, probably best recognized underwater man in history, shows gold coins he found with D-Tex detector.

ly $6 million from the wrecks. This, however, was certainly less than the amount of recovered treasure. Undoubtedly a large portion of the recovered treasure stuck to the fingers of Spanish officials," Couvillon opines.

"But even greedier fingers soon arrived on the salvage scene! During the salvage operation, a temporary blockhouse was constructed on Cape Canaveral, where recovered bullion was stored under military guard while awaiting shipment to Havana. News of the salvaging operation soon reached the ears of the unscrupulous buccaneer, Captain Henry Jennings."

Jennings, along with several hundred of his kindred spirits and a salvaging flotilla of their own, sailed to Cape Canaveral where they murdered the guards, broke into the blockhouse and made off with nearly half a million pieces-of-eight.

For nearly 250 years following Jennings' heist, the doomed silver fleet was left to rot away in ghost-like quiet on the ocean floor.

The first serious effort to regain yet unsalvaged riches from the 1715 fleet began when Kip Wagner found his first coins on a deserted Sebastian beach in 1959. After much research, he deduced that he had found the site of the 1715 disaster.

Real Eight has come a long way since that day on the beach in 1959. The following year, the group discovered but a few dozen silver wedges, which didn't begin to pay for the thousands of dollars invested for equipment, not to mention the time involved.

In 1961, divers found 4000 silver coins in one day; and in 1964, nearly 2000 gold doubloons were found in two days. (Before anyone starts doing mental arithmetic on how many coins could be found in 365 days, it should be noted that there were only five good diving days in that year.)

The following year, the group found more gold coins, eight-escudo pieces and a valuable four-escudo Imperial. In October, 1964, Real Eight auctioned some of its coins, realizing $29,000 from the first sale. But the annual salvage operation costs had far exceeded the auction take.

Since the formation of the company, Real Eight has recovered approximately $8 million in treasure and artifacts. And the company, in return, has spent a small fortune in salvaging expenses as well as dedicated years of work.

The Real Eight Company built the Museum of Sunken Treasure in Cape Canaveral, which features a sight-and-sound program depicting the loss and recovery of the doomed 1715 silver fleet's treasure.

The museum also houses an impressive million-dollar collection of gold, silver, jewelry and priceless porcelain pieces

Robert Marx (left), one of the nation's outstanding treasure divers, discusses operation of a detector built especially for him with Bill Mahan, Jr. It will operate at depths of a hundred feet down from a boat.

that date back to the Kang H'si Dynasty of 1662. Highlight of the museum is a large treasure chest that contains the greatest single find in Real Eight history: 1133 gold coins, five hundred silver coins and other artifacts.

Treasure finds have set a number of precedents, created new state laws and challenged old ones, brought salvaging companies into court as defendants in some suits and as the plaintiffs in countersuits. For those who plan on running out to buy scuba gear and a treasure map to join in the hunt, unauthorized recovery of sunken treasure and artifacts will get you a term behind bars of iron, not gold.

Persons or firms attempting salvage operations on a wreck in Florida's waters must be under contract with the Department of State. Anyone failing to comply with this law faces a stiff fine and/or a jail sentence.

In most cases, shipwrecks occur in shallow water, thus the easiest method of searching is visual, as one often can see down two hundred feet or so, when the water is clear and the sun is in the right position for maximum light penetration. If one sees some kind of square angle, this usually is a dead giveaway, as natural underwater formations rarely take on such form. Or one may see some of the ballast stones from what once was a ship.

When a ship sinks, it invariably is buried partially in the sand. In fact, the sand often covers it in a short time. The wood of the old ships was attacked almost immediately by teredo worms, which ate it into nonexistence. In time, tides and weather will sweep away other parts of the ship and perhaps its cargo. Rarely, however, do the ballast stones move much. If they do not remain covered by sands being moved by tides and currents, they often are visible in a pile on the bottom.

A glass-bottom boat would be ideal for surveying the bottom, but most of the amateur divers and treasure hunters simply settle for a water-tight box with a glass bottom. This is held over the side of the boat, partially submerged, as the diver watches for telltale signs.

In recent years, more modern equipment has been used. For example, Teddy Tucker, one of the best known professionals, has used a balloon in Bermuda waters, communicating with a boat below him via radio. Numerous light aircraft now are being used, as are pontoon-equipped helicopters. Most of these, of course, are out of the reach of the sport diver, who becomes interested in hunting for treasure while below.

In more murky waters, such as those along the northern Atlantic seaboard and in many lakes and streams, grappling hooks are favored. A course is laid out so that the boat can cover an entire area, not repeating itself, then the hooks are used to drag the bottom as the boat moves slowly over the course. Only when there is evidence that something has been caught on one of the hooks is a diver sent below.

The biggest problem is that this system is less than efficient. One is dragging a narrow channel to start with, which means there is plenty of room for missing. Also, it is good only on smooth bottoms. If there is a great deal of kelp, seaweed or a rocky bottom, one would spend more time disentangling the grappling hook than searching.

If something is discovered, a buoy usually is attached to

An airlift is being utilized to remove sand from area that is suspected of holding treasure.

mark the spot and the boat is anchored at the site or nearby, depending upon conditions, so that the find — whatever it is — can be inspected more closely.

There are numerous methods of covering the bottom of the sea or a lake in a pattern that guarantees coverage, but most of these are being replaced by sophisticated equipment that can range in price from a few hundred dollars to many thousands.

The recording depth finder, which marks the pattern of the bottom's surface on scaled paper as the boat moves over an area, is perhaps the best bet. Whenever a large obstruction that obviously is not a normal part of the watery bottom appears on the scale, divers are sent below to investigate. This method is much faster and allows one to cover much more area in the course of a day.

Should one be searching an area for a wreck that might be covered with silt or sand, a magnetometer or metal detector would be the answer, since the depth recorder would not register. There are any number of underwater models with detection units that can be towed from a boat. Some of them will indicate metal as much as fifty feet away. Smaller models can be carried below by the divers themselves.

If a wreck is discovered that is partially or totally covered with sand or silt, it may seem beyond the capabilities of the weekend diver to investigate it. However, all one really needs is an airlift. This is nothing more than a long open tube into which one pumps compressed air. The air enters the tube near the bottom and is blown back toward the surface. This, in turn, creates a vacuum, which lifts the sand and silt. Small units can be used to move the sand, while one watches for small items that are uncovered.

The propeller of the boat also can be used to remove sand, using a device known as a prop-wash. This unit is simple to make and is nothing more than a metal tube — elbow-shaped with the two sections at right angles. Usually of aluminum to make it easier to handle, it is fitted over the boat's propeller and attached to the transom for stability.

The boat is moored with four anchors, two at the bow and two at the stern. When the engine is running, the sediment below is removed to drift away on the tides. Speed of the engine can be regulated for the best efficiency. The deeper the water, the wider the diameter of the excavating action. A word of caution, though: If not controlled properly, the prop-wash unit can break up rotted wood and perhaps will wash away artifacts of value.

With the development of modern self-contained underwater breathing apparatus, the hardhat divers of old are considered to be archaic. However, rig still is used for deep dives in many parts of world.

Diver pauses to inspect a coral-encrusted find in Caribbean. This is resting place of much of the Spanish treasure fleet of old.

Once most of the sand has been removed, the light sand left can be removed simply by fanning the sand with the closed hand or a flat object like a wooden shingle.

In some areas, of course, coral will have covered much of the wreck, calling for additional measures. There are some experts who choose to set charges and blast away this tough covering, but this can be dangerous and destructive, as well. Underwater explosives are not for the amateur. Also, the blast often tends to destroy valuable artifacts if it is an old wreck.

While it is slower and tougher going, hammers and chisels can be used to remove the coral. There also are power-operated chisels that can be used, as can high pressure water jets, if the search operation is big enough and well enough financed to afford such exotic equipment.

One of the greatest problems in recovering artifacts from the sea — or even from freshwater — is preservation. Gold suffers little from submersion or even being buried. Gem stones, porcelain and glass rarely are damaged, although they may become coated with coral. This can be removed with a ten percent solution of nitric acid.

Silver, at the other extreme, is converted into silver sulfide by the electrolysis of saltwater on the metal. Often it can be preserved, if a collector item, only if encased in plastic. At the other extreme, if the silver has been in contact with another metal on which the electrostatic action works more quickly, it may be preserved completely. In such a state of preservation, silver can be cleaned in a bath of fifteen percent ammonium hydroxide, followed by rubbing it with a combination of water and ordinary baking soda.

Iron and steel, however, suffer the most damage from sea water. If one is collecting artifacts from ancient vessels, he should remember that the moment iron or steel items are exposed to the air, the action begins to convert the metal to iron oxide, which is rust, anyway you want to spell it.

The result is that, unless these artifacts are treated properly — and rapidly — they can be reduced to a pile of red-colored powder.

The best way of treating against this rust is to place the artifact in a solution of ten percent sodium hydroxide, leaving it there for as long as six weeks. The solution then is renewed, with mossy zinc metal being added. After an hour or two, you probably will see a bubbling effect in the solution, but that does not mean your metal is being dissolved. Instead, after about three weeks in this solution, the item will have a coating of zinc, white in color. This can be cleaned off with a solution of five percent sulfuric acid, then the object is soaked in freshwater for several weeks, the water being changed as it becomes cloudy. When the water no longer clouds, the artifact can be removed, but it should be coated with clear lacquer or a spray plastic as added protection.

Scuba diver inspects the remains of a wrecked ship off the Florida Keys, where most Spanish treasure is found.

Mrs. Mary Brooks, director of the U.S. Mint, displays the stacks of gold in the Federal Depository at Fort Knox, Kentucky, during an inspection tour by Congressmen. Prospectors accounted for much of the bullion located here.

How To Pan For Gold

Chapter 13

Although almost any type of pan can be used for panning for gold, one of plastic with a series of riffles in it makes separating sand and gravel from gold easier.

THERE IS AN old saying that everyone has heard, 'Gold is where you find it.' This statement is absolutely true and it is possible to find gold in more than ninety percent of the earth's surfaces! True, it may not be in paying quantity but, nonetheless, it still is there. You can take an earth sample from about any place you please, even from your own backyard and, with either the X-ray defraction process or by spectrographic analysis, gold will show up as a trace element.

"Hardly anything to get excited about, because it would take thousands of tons of this soil to produce one ounce of gold."

Those are the thoughts of Bill Mahan, one of the pioneers in electronic treasure hunting, who has made a fortune from the lost and hidden wealth he has discovered over the years as well as making his mark in the metal detector field with his D-Tex instruments.

His are the words of an acknowledged expert in virtually all phases of treasure hunting, be it finding lost treasure or seeking the Mother Lode!

In the early days, as the pioneers spread and covered the North American continent, they were ever on the alert for the necessary signs that would indicate mineral deposits.

Thousands of valuable gold and silver mines were discovered and the many ghost towns of the West still stand as mute evidence of the wealth that was dug from our Western mountains. Today, it still is possible to find these veins and fissures of gold but, even if you do, the finding is not even a beginning. Before you could get started it would be necessary to spend thousands of dollars in equipment: air compressors, jack hammers, drill steel, ore cars, rails and many, many other expensive pieces of equipment. Also, in all probability your find would be miles from any road and to get the equipment to the location it would be necessary to get bulldozers to cut roads to the site. Also, if you were many miles from a mill or smelter, you would have to consider hauling the ore to some railroad for shipping. At today's prices, the hauling and shipping eat heavily into the price received for the ore. So, you have another consideration: install a small mill or concentration plant at the site; again, thousands of dollars in equipment and in buildings for installation.

With the discouraging facts understood, one may wonder how anyone ever did find gold. It was done by "placer mining."

Over the millions of years since our own Earth was

Considering The Current Price Of Gold, What Once Was Considered Too Poor An Area For Consideration Now Is Prime Panning Country!

Bill Mahan's wife uses a metal detector to determine the location of mineral deposits worth further investigation.

formed, the forces of nature, using water, have been crushing rock, grinding it fine and concentrating it.

We have the constant erosion of the surfaces by rains. In the winters, water soaks and seeps into rocks and crevices and, in freezing, the water expands, further pushing the rocks apart, thus allowing more water to get in the cracks and crevices. With constant freezing and expanding of the

water, the action on the surface rocks is exactly the same as a small explosion in slow motion.

As this breaking away and erosion continues, the melting of the snow and the rains all tend to carry the broken and eroded materials down the hills and mountains into the rivers and streams. Everyone has read the accounts of the discovery of gold in the mill race at Sutter's Mill that set off the Gold Rush of California. Millions of dollars were taken from the streams as a result and this was the beginning of the extensive placer operations of California.

Placer mining is the most practical way for the individual today to do a little mining and recover some gold himself for fun or for profit. It is possible to purchase all sorts of lightweight, efficient equipment for starting your own dredging activities. But, here again, money. To get completely equipped with a small dredge, all miscellaneous and sundry equipment as well as the scuba diving equipment used by our modern-day prospectors, you again have spent several hundred dollars even for limited equipment. At this point, if you are wanting to go gold prospecting for a vacation and possibly spend only one or two weeks, it would be foolish to purchase all the equipment. In all probability, you are ready to give up in disgust.

But there is still another method to use which is both inexpensive and quite interesting and it is almost a certainty that you will wind up with anywhere from a few grains to several ounces of gold dust and nuggets. As to the equipment necessary for your prospecting venture, we will assume that you are familiar with the necessary items for just average camping and will list only the items used in prospecting and placer mining.

The modern metal detector is the most important piece of equipment you can take along, as it can help you locate deposits of metals as a start.

Other items include a round-point shovel and a small pick. Both of these usually can be purchased from war surplus outlets. They fold up and take little room for storage or in carrying into the area.

Mahan suggests one take at least two gold pans — one of ten-inch diameter, the other eighteen inches — a small magnet, long tweezers with flat points, several plastic bags, an ordinary ear syringe that can be purchased at any drugstore, a one-gallon plastic bucket, plus several small plastic pill bottles for holding and storing the gold you find. Other necessities for serious gold panning include a magnifying glass, two or three ounces of mercury — see Chapter 18 — and a small plastic funnel.

After filling pan within an inch of top with sand, knead it as with bread dough, allowing gold to gravatate to bottom.

After kneading, the pan is hit sharply on its side with an open hand to aid in moving the heavy metals to the bottom.

"This list of equipment is sufficient for a successful small placer operation. For a larger operation, a Georgia cradle could be added at small expense," Mahan contends.

To decide just where to go, write to the Department of Mines in one or several of the Western states known to have placer gold. Request all pamphlets, handbooks and maps available on placer gold location as well as the law pertaining to it. Select an area where there still is open government land (does not have mining claims) and there is still plenty of it.

When you arrive in the area, find a spot readily accessible to the road and to the stream or river and put up camp as conveniently located to both places as possible.

The success or failure of the whole venture is completely dependent on the prospector and his metal detector. Most detector manufacturers state that their units will detect gold nuggets the size of a pea. It is highly improbable that you will find any that size. Usually you can classify the average finds as match-head size, pinhead size and dust.

The first thing you must learn and remember: gold being the heaviest of materials you will find in the streams, it will always be in the bottom of pockets or fissures. Another "heavy" you will encounter is "magnetite," commonly called "black sand."

Magnetite is a sulfide iron material, is magnetic and most always is in small particles like sand. We now know the two "heavies" and one thing of most importance is to remember: Placer gold is always found in and associated with magnetite.

Don't let this confuse you: the presence of magnetite does not always denote the presence of placer gold.

Mahan's method is to tune his D-Tex detector for the mineral setting, then set out to locate the beds, pockets and fissures that contain ore or magnetite. He then sample pans the magnetite to determine whether it contains gold. He digs to the bottom of the magnetite, taking a small sample, panning it down.

"If gold is present, I work out the entire mass. If not, I don't waste time. I move on to a new location."

In this type of prospecting, start your search along the edge of the stream around the base of boulders or rocks, check all crevices or faults that cross the stream. Check the inside of the bend where the stream turns and all the logical spots for heavy material to accumulate. As you find the pockets or crevices of magnetite, your detector should indicate it. Then carefully dig out the magnetite all the way to the bed rock. Place this in the large gold pan and, placing it

Mahan pauses to inspect an ore sample in a gold mine that he discovered, worked for a number of his younger years.

under water, work it quickly and vigorously for a few minutes. This will cause all the heavies to go to the bottom of the pan.

After washing vigorously, you can start sluffing off all the larger pieces of rock. As soon as it is worked down enough, pour all the contents into the smaller pan. With the rocks and sand in the pan, you should shake it from side to side and, at the same time, cause a rotary movement with one hand.

Begin actual panning in calm water, moving the pan in side-to-side motion, allowing sand to be flushed over edges.

As dirt is washed out of the pan, bottom becomes visible, slow the action so as to be certain gold isn't washed away.

Young Bill Mahan, Jr., points to gold-bearing ore found in the mine, which his father discovered, then worked.

start washing to the low side of the pan. Suddenly you see that it is leaving a shiny tail on the high side of the pan. If so, you have found your first gold!

If it is large enough, you now take your tweezers and carefully pick up the largest nuggets. Have one of your plastic pill bottles full of water, place the lip of the tweezers in the water and drop in the nugget. As you have worked down the pan, you notice some of the gold still stays in the magnetite so now we take our ear syringe and, with the pan tilted, we gently use the syringe to wash the black sand away from the gold. You finally dispose of most of it but some still remains behind, intermixed with the gold. Now to completely clean it, we again fill the pan with water. Take the magnet and place it in one of the plastic bags, or just wrap it with plastic. Slowly and gently pass the magnet around in the pan and you will see that it is picking up the remaining magnetite. As the magnet gets loaded with the black sand, hold it to one side and away from the pan, and remove the plastic. The magnetite falls away and you are ready to repeat the performance until your gold is completely clean.

Now take your small plastic funnel and, placing the end of it inside the pill bottle of water, hold the pan tilted over the funnel to pour the gold into the bottle. If the gold won't pour, use the syringe again, gently washing the gold out of the pan and into your bottle.

As a beginner, it is easy to work several pans of high grade gold and not see or save a single grain. In other words, to be successful in gold panning, you need some good practice.

Mahan practices gold paning without actually having any gold. To do this, get yourself a small wash tub or large dish pan. Find some construction site where they are pouring concrete. Borrow about one-half gallon of the gravel they use and about one gallon of the sand. Pour this into the tub or dish pan and cover it with several inches of water. You now have a nice placer gravel bed much as you would find in a stream. Fill the small pan with the sand and gravel — for gold, borrow a few BB shot from a shotgun shell. The object is to pan back into the tub all the sand and gravel and none of the shot.

For large amounts of amalgam or black sand concentrates containing gold, you can employ the services of a mill. A mill will have equipment such as an automatic gold panner, an ainley bowl, counter-stroke sluice, a water wheel or clean-up wheel and a Stephans concentrator. Check in the yellow pages under mining and milling, with a mining supply house or a gold diver's equipment firm.

As you sluff off the top layer of rocks and sand, you should hold the pan under water; or at least its front edge. Then, while working the pan, let the material slowly pour out. When you finally get it worked down you will find that it appears that nothing has remained in the pan but the black sand. With water in the pan, gently shake it and lean the pan slightly to one side. This causes the black sand to

As gold is separated, allow only a little water in one end of the pan, trapping gold in the ridge at bottom.

At this stage, the pan again is rapped sharply with the side of the hand, helping to separate sand from gold.

Roy Lagel of Lewiston, Idaho, uses a Garret metal detector to aid in searching for gold in the Salmon River. Much time can be saved in panning, if one knows that the gold is there; a far cry from the techniques of Forty-niners.

You may sell your gold to a dental lab or to a licensed gold buyer. Some jewelers purchase gold. Knott's Berry Farm in Buena Park, California, buys placer gold for their gold panning attractions. Large nuggets can be sold to a collector for a better than normal price. Electronic firms manufacturing Space-Age equipment and private industries use large amounts of gold.

When finished and as much sand removed as possible, the gold is trapped in the groove in the bottom of the pan.

With the exception of the dredge and wet gear, all of the equipment used in wet placer prospecting and recovery will apply to dry placer prospecting. A good way to prospect for dry placer is with a dry washer or concentrator. The type that knocks down for backpacking allows you to do your testing right on the spot. A dry washer consists of a hopper to shovel the gravel into. The gravel is metered out to a shaking screen where the coarser tailings fall off. The fine material goes through a chute to a lower shaking screen that does not allow air to blow through, but holds the fine material. Mining journals and prospecting magazines cover the many different types of machinery used for mining dry placers.

Prospect in mineralized land that is open for prospecting and have the proper equipment. Do your research first and study your maps. When taking samples for testing, number your samples and mark them on a map. It is a good idea to put a marker close to the place where the sample was taken. If you cannot qualify a sample, bag it for future testing. Disregard well-meant advice, unless you are sure of the advisor's reputation. Do not litter, but burn leftover food and trash and bury the containers. Obey all state and Federal laws regarding prospecting and placering. Travel in pairs, if possible, and take along plenty of water, spare automotive parts, first aid kit, survival kit, maps, compass, signalling mirror, a snake bite kit, a plastic water still and emergency rations such as beef jerky.

Gold, silver, platinum and mercury are virtually the only elements that occur in the metallic state in nature. That is

Steve Samson perhaps pans more gold than anyone in the nation today. He is official gold panner at Knott's Berry Farm, a Southern California amusement center, where 1500 people may try their luck with real gold dust on a busy day. He helped with photos to show panning techniques.

why you cannot analyze a sample simply with a pocket magnifier and decide it is no good. The sample must be analyzed chemically or by a lab qualified on assaying. Sometimes valuable elements look like pyrites and the rare elements may look like the common varieties of iron.

A study of geology and mineralogy is invaluable when wildcatting in an area that has had no previous discoveries. To be worthwhile, your area should have black sands or galena. When you prospect a dry wash, take samples at various spots across the wash and on each bank. Dig several feet or more at each location. A metal detector will pick out black sand deposits below the surface. A good place to check with your detector is along the canyon wall at the point where the rainy season water level meets the bedrock area at each bank. Take samples from the small tributaries and side drawers. If you have a companion, you can carry a portable dry washer and concentrate the samples on the spot.

Back at camp, classify the concentrates by screening through several, different sized mesh screens, window screening or nylon hose stretched over an embroidery hoop. Use a mineral light to check for fluorescent minerals.

Items to check for:

Zirconium — bright orange under the short wave.

Rare earths — peculiar shade of grass green — use the short wave with the filter removed.

Uranium salts and minerals — lemon yellow, light green.

Scheelite (tungsten ore) — bright blue, white or golden color — use the short wave.

You can operate a 110-volt mineral light with a convertor by plugging it into the cigarette lighter of your car or have a small 12-volt battery to run the convertor.

A wet placer, where gold is found, becomes a dry placer due to erosion of lode veins, upthrusts, faulting and the disappearance of water. Dry placers are found on basins, hilltops or on auriferous riverbeds raised to a higher level due to lava flow and upheaval of earth.

Some placers that received a hundred feet or more of overburden through faulting and erosion have been cut through by a canyon — pushing the original gravel bed high on the canyon walls.

For those not familiar with the term, placer, it perhaps is described best as a glacial deposit containing particles of gold, in this case, or other valuable minerals.

Sometimes the exact opposite occurs. Red Rock Canyon, in California, had a rich placer of gold on bedrock, sixty feet below the surface of the present-day stream bed. Some dry placers are replenished annually from small, sparsely disseminated veins or stringers in the mountains and hills by the yearly rainfall and natural erosion. These placers usually are small in size and require some experience to find. In tracing a dry riverbed, watch for placers where

This chest-carry instrument is ideal for operation in rugged terrain, as it is easily portable and works on land as well as in the water. Such an aid in detecting deposits of metal can save time and effort in the search for raw gold dust and ore.

Youthful weekend prospector Tom Forrest sinks his gold pan in Southern California stream to settle the sand.

the ancient water made an eddy or took a sudden drop over a fault or perhaps formed a pothole below a waterfall.

Placer deposits result from decomposition and the wearing away of mineral or metal-bearing rocks, being carried by water and glaciers from the higher terrain down into catch basins, faults, creeks, rivers or beaches. In cold climates, water soaks into the ground and cracks of the rocks. When this water freezes, it expands, causing the rocks to break

off; the scales and dust are transported down the streams and rivulets. The action of this kinetic water separates the mineral portion from the lighter constituents and the mineral's greater specific gravity causes it to sink to the bottom much sooner than the dirt and dust, which is carried farther downstream. The larger pieces of mineral sink first, along with portions of the gravel. This is the reason why coarse gold and mineral deposits are never at a

Second, faster panning method begins same way, kneading sand so that the heavier metal moves to the bottom.

Holding pan in one hand, swirling motion allows water to enter pan, taking sand away on the opposite side.

Tom Forrest tilts his gold pan, allowing loose sand to wash over the edge. Techniques differ with individual.

great distance from the mother lode, although fine gold and minerals may be carried farther distances, especially in streams with steep grades and high velocities. In this way, glaciers wear away the rocks they pass over, carrying them along, until they melt and deposit the ground-up material in the moraines and windrows. These deposits then are carried by the streams stemming from the glaciers. From them, many rich placer beds are formed.

When sure of mineralization, sink to bedrock and check the cracks and crevices for rusty streaks in the gravel or dark lines of black sand or magnetite. The iron-bearing sands have a high, specific gravity and usually are associated with gold and other valuable minerals.

Rocks broken from the terrain become more rounded as they progress downstream to settle in a flat area and form a gravel bed. If gold has been transported along, it will be

Care is taken in allowing water to enter the pan. This technique works best where water is relatively calm.

Still working the pan, using a swirling action, water and some of the worthless sand begin to leave the pan.

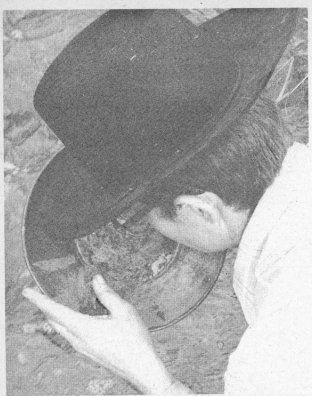

Forrest inspects the baffle in the bottom of metal pan for signs of gold. Today, many prospectors express a preference for pans made of the high-impact plastics.

deposited with the rounded chunks of gravel. Angular-shaped gravel rarely contains gold or valuable minerals, because it has not traveled far from its source. The feldspar portion of eroded rocks may be deposited and later covered up with alluvium. Gold can be transported along with the feldspar and disseminated in the clay bed.

Sometimes gold which has found its way into cracks and riffles during high water is left high and dry in the summer months. To test for this gold, use a whisk broom or brush to transport the dust into a gold pan. Take this to the water and pan it. You might be surprised at the amount of fine gold you can recover in this way.

In the last few years, gold nuggets have been picked up by the handful at construction sites, such as the Feather River project, the Castaic Dam project and various highway roadcuts. The fill dirt in the highway between Silverton and Durango, Colorado, was discovered to have gold. An Easterner moving into Central City, Colorado, heard that the railroad was going to tear up the track in the ravine just below town. He leased the area where the track had been torn up near the creek bed and found a rich placer that had been concealed for years.

For a note of humor, during the Korean War, Marine Corps engineers spotted a pile of gravel near a construction site and used it to build a badly needed road, according to legend. As it turned out, the gravel was gold ore which the United States Government later paid for in the amount of several million dollars!

A river can cross an ancient river channel that flowed in a different direction and redeposit the gold from this area. The ancient river channel therefore should be checked in either direction. Take samples at regular intervals in the tributaries to the main channel. If the samples look good, mark the location for future reference. If the concentrates don't show gold but your pocket megascope indicates minerals such as garnet, olivine, zirconium, topaz, quartz crystals, pyrites or black concentrates that are not magnetic, you have good reason for checking further upstream.

Know your concentrates before discarding them. The little black, brown, white or red grains that you see in the concentrates could be columbite, samarskite, tantalite, cobalite, asseterite, wolframite or bismuthnite.

When you come to a likely area for prospecting, proceed to a high vantage point with a camera and binoculars. (If possible, use a single-lens reflex camera with a wide-angle lens.) From this vantage point you can study the area, taking pictures for future reference. Try to determine how high the stream gets during the rainy season, check the tributaries that enter the stream or creek, study the curves and obstructions. Notice where the rapids are, as well as whirlpools, deep and shallow areas, sandbars, eddies, and the rounded rocks of an ancient, gold-bearing riverbed. Look for fault indications, large areas of riffles and for old workings in exposed bedrock. Mercury was used by early day operators for recovery work and much of it has washed down into creeks or rivers, attaching itself to gold nuggets or forming BB shot size balls. It can be recovered by dredging or with a mechanical gold pan.

The flakes of gold will show in the baffle at bottom of the pan — if there are any — as sand is washed away.

The pan is moved back and forth with a gentle movement so that gold doesn't wash out during final dirt removal.

Gold usually is found on the downstream side of obstructions, on the inside bend of curves where a draw meets the bedrock, on the downstream side where a tributary enters, in layers or streaks in sandbars, at the edges of whirlpools and at the tail of eddies. In the shallow areas it is usually of a fine nature and coarser in the deeper areas. Gold is usually plentiful downstream from the intersection of an ancient riverbed. The rougher the gold flakes or nuggets, the nearer you are to the source of the gold. When the nuggets or flakes are smooth and round, the gold has traveled a greater distance from the location of its origin. Quartz veins and mica-type rocks trap gold readily.

A diving suit will save you time. Walking or diving upstream, snipe for samples, taking crevicing tools and a gold pan. If you have a new gold pan, burn the grease off. Gold and oil don't mix.

As you progress upstream, keep in mind your observations from your vantage point. Check the crevices by digging them out, putting the gravel in your pan to look for colors. Check the inside curve of any bends in the stream and any suspicious looking topography.

Beginners should try their luck as near to bedrock as possible. Move upstream in a steady manner, picking out all of the lucrative areas and crevices in the exposed bedrock.

Before prospecting, obtain maps of the area in which you are interested. Check whether the land is open for prospecting by contacting the county land office or the assessor's office in the particular county in which you are interested. Maps to check are: government maps of placer occurrences of gold in the United States and Alaska, forestry maps, county maps, Department of Agriculture maps (aerial photos also available) and Geological Survey topographic maps. The U.S. National Forest district ranger will have maps showing sections of national forest land that are open for prospecting. The Bureau of Land Management can provide maps and information. Various state divisions of mines distribute geological maps. Federal geological maps also are available. The geological maps show what type of surface rocks are exposed, the definite area of their location and any known faults. The Automobile Club of Southern California, for example, has excellent maps of the southern half of California which include the do's and don'ts of desert travel. Sectional aeronautical maps from the FAA can be helpful. The Army Map service, 6509 Brooks Lane, Washington, D.C., can furnish maps and aerial photos of the section in which you are interested.

If you want to check out old mines, you may find old government survey maps in bookstores or from private collections. Along with old, abandoned mines, check out the dumps. Many of the oldtime operators unwittingly threw away fifty percent of the values. Investigate old placer locations. Over the years of seasonal runoff of rainwater, they may have been replenished with a new crop of gold or metallics from the surrounding terrain.

You can prospect on private property, provided the owner does not have surface rights. First obtain the owner's permission and agree to pay a predetermined cost per acre of damage to the terrain or fences. If he does not allow you to prospect, in some states the local sheriff will provide a bond for a fee. The sheriff can demand of the owner that you be allowed to prospect.

The California legal guide for miners and prospectors of 1962 states the following lands are open to prospecting: 1. Public mineral land within a national forest and unconfirmed Mexican grants, 2. Congressional grants to a railroad company that are unpatented, 3. Land within the limits of an unpatented townsite or a known lode within the limits of a placer mining claim (but you may not search for a vein on a placer claim without the owner's permission).

Land known to contain coal, petroleum, potash, oil shale, phosphate and sodium salts cannot be located under the lode or placer laws, but are obtainable under lease, subject to the regulations of the Secretary of the Interior. Mining locations cannot be made on land that belongs to the state, but prospecting permits can be issued under the rules of the state lands commission.

The railroad companies, when they built the transcontinental line, were awarded every other section along both sides of the right of way. These lands cannot be prospected. School sections — sections 16 and 36 of each township — cannot be prospected or filed for claim. Other restricted lands are national forest watersheds, or national parks, with the exemption of Death Valley.

Regulations forbid a stationary residence on a mining claim. Many people who have built living quarters on a mining claim have returned to find their home bulldozed and burned. The law states a claim must be used for mining purposes only.

The gold pan is the basic tool for prospecting. The best way to learn how to use the gold pan is from someone who is efficient in the art of panning. Written instructions cannot properly show the necessary physical motions

One continues the washing procedure until all of the sand has been washed away, taking care in each step.

With all of the sand removed by washing, pure gold is caught in the seam of the pan; it's barely visible here.

Virtually the same techniques are used today for panning gold as were used by prospectors of last century.

required. The methods of operation vary, for they depend on whether you have a pan of gravel with heavy material, a combination of light and heavy material or a mixture of coarse and fine. A time-saving method is to wash and screen your gravel, classifying it before panning. By working it down to the concentrates and putting it in a bucket for further concentration, you avoid the chore of spending three hours to get fifty cents in gold.

After you have a good supply of concentrates, remove the magnetites with a magnet or battery-operated magnetic separator. Check that you do not remove gold along with the magnetites. If you have a self-erasing magnet, use a plastic or aluminum pan. Pick up a load of magnetites, drop them, pick them up again and place in another part of the pan. Repeat this several times. The large gold flakes can be removed with tweezers, if there are any. The fine gold can be recovered later with mercury.

Gold must be clean to be amalgamated. First, wash the gold in a pan with water to remove any foreign matter. The clay that is left can be removed with a little lye and fresh stream water. Dry the concentrates in the sun or use a propane torch. Be sure there is no cinnabar or mercury in it, as the fumes are very dangerous.

Next, clean the pan with lye or baking soda. Coat the pan with a solution of silver, mercury and nitric acid, using an eye dropper. Put your concentrates into the pan and, when you add some mercury, the gold will sink to the bottom. The gold can be separated by immersing it in a fifty-fifty solution of nitric acid and water. Within several hours, any copper, silver and mercury will be dissolved. You will be left with about 900 fine or better gold. The liquid can be used over again for the next amalgam. The silver and mercury can be knocked back down with table salt.

Electrum is placer gold alloyed with silver about fifty-fifty. It is a silvery color and has a brassy tinge. Do not throw it away. It is valuable in this form or it can be refined to separate the silver from the gold.

The following is a summary of the equipment that is necessary for basic prospecting:

Steel gold pan; sizes are 16, 12, 10 and 8 inches.

Copper gold pan to use with quicksilver for removing gold from samples that have been ground up, or concentrates.

Tweezers for picking small flakes of gold or mineral from the pan.

Whiskbroom or brush for sweeping samples from dry crevices or rock.

Magnifier of pocket type for checking your concentrates.

Notebook to keep record of samples and where they were obtained.

Small aluminum pan for clean-up work, also for removing magnetite from concentrates.

Quicksilver for making gold amalgam and clean-up work.

Screens of various mesh sizes for classifying.

Sample bags or other containers for holding your samples.

Pry bar, pick and shovel.

Geologist's pick for prying out rocks.

Mortar and pestle; small size for grinding rock or concentrates.

Propane torch used for checking some types of samples.

A Geiger counter or scintillator can be used to find thorium, rare earths and uranium — heavy radioactive minerals that usually indicate the presence of gold, silver or platinum.

A dual-wave, ultraviolet light is an excellent piece of equipment for finding fluorescent minerals such as scheelite, an ore of tungsten. Scheelite fluoresces a brilliant blue under the short-wave light. If your sample shows blue under both the short and long wave, it is probably hydrozincite rather than scheelite. Impurities and dust can show up as blue under the ultraviolet light, so brush away the surface impurities. A willemite screen works in conjunction with the ultraviolet light in prospecting for cinnabar and ore of mercury (quicksilver).

To check for mercury, place the willemite screen eight or twelve inches from the ultraviolet light, preferably in a dark area. Put your sample in a metal or ceramic container between the light and the screen, then heat the sample with a propane torch. If it contains mercury, it will show up on the screen as a dark purple cloud of smoke. The darker the cloud, the richer the sample. Do not do this testing unless you are upwind from the smoke or have a fan blowing. Mercury vapor breathed into the lungs reconverts to metal and can cause serious illness and even death.

When — and if — you find a location of commercial value, you will want to lay out your claim and record it. In respect to state and Federal laws, a placer claim is less complex than a lode claim. Before filing a claim, check the Federal and state laws that apply to the state in which you are operating. When filing a claim on government land or public domain, contact the nearest office of the Bureau of Land Management or send your inquiry to the Bureau of Land Management, Department of the Interior, Washington, D.C. Also check with your state land office or with the county assessor in the county where your claim will be recorded.

Eight people staking a placer claim are allowed one hundred and sixty acres. If fewer than eight people, the law allows twenty acres for each individual. Filing as a group or association has the advantage in that only one annual assessment work is required and only one discovery shaft is needed.

In California, for example, a placer claim must conform to lines of public survey. If the land is unsurveyed, the claim should be laid out, if practicable, with East-West and North-South bounding lines. If possible, the claim should be rectangular and in a compact form. If the placer deposit lies within a gulch, an unnavigable stream or canyon, it may exclude the land not suitable for mining purposes. The notice of location must be posted, stating the name of the claim, date of location, name of the locator or locators, acreage claimed and include a description of the claim with reference to a natural object or permanent monument. The boundaries should be marked so they can be traced easily. In California, you can lose your claim unless you obey the state law which demands you record a true copy of the notice of location with the office of the local county recorder within ninety days of the date of location.

You can locate a mill site of five acres with your placer claim. When you abandon the placer claim, you automatically lose the mill site. You cannot locate a claim on the basis of discovery of gravel, sand, pumice, stone or cinders.

Mining claims in the eleven Western states are laid out and measured according to Spanish law. All boundary measurements are in a straight line. You would measure through the slope of a hill. In the other states, which are under English laws, you would measure up one side of a hill and down the other side. Approved forms of location notices can be obtained from stationery stores, stores in mining areas or mining supply houses.

Placer claims do not have rights to the lode claim, but a claim for the lode may be laid out over a placer claim

With four-wheel drives replacing the pack mule or burro, seeking gold is less demanding than in the past.

provided you obtain permission from the owner-locator of the placer claim. All lode or placer claims requiring assessment work of $100 per claim must be completed before noon September 1.

For prospecting or placering in California, one must obtain a permit for dredging and gold panning. If you are concerned with Arizona, write the state land commissioner in Phoenix. In Nevada, contact the state land registrar at Carson City; California, the State Division of Lands, Sacramento; Colorado, the State Board of Land Commissioners, Denver; New Mexico, commissioner of Public Lands, Santa Fe; Oregon, clerk of State Land Board, Salem; Utah, executive secretary, State Land Board, Salt Lake City; Texas, commissioner of State Land Office, Austin.

Black sands may contain rare earth minerals that, in some cases, can be more valuable than gold. If you run across blue clay, be on the lookout for diamonds. Tree trunks near streams with clay deposits should be checked. Sometimes gold nuggets are trapped in this clay. Rare earth minerals are used for a variety of things, such as tracer bullets, coloring mediums in the glass industry, lighter flints,

reducing agents, as the getter in the manufacture of steel, dyes for textiles and leather, in photography and antiseptics and in the manufacture of pyrophoric alloys and colored carbons.

Gold may bring a glisten to your eye, but it will never glisten under reflected light nor will it change color. Gold has an atomic weight of 197.0. It will not rust, but it will accept an alloy coating of another metal such as manganese, iron, copper or oxides of other metals. Sometimes gold will have a brassy-silver color due to the presence of silver. The specific gravity of gold is 19.3. A cubic foot of gold weighs almost 1200 pounds.

Hydrochloric, sulphuric, muriatic or nitric singular acid will not dissolve gold. If you want to dissolve gold and put it into solution, mix one part nitric acid and three parts hydrochloric acid. If you want to purify gold of any mercury, silver or copper, immerse it in nitric acid. This solution can be saved for cleaning and amalgamating a copper pan. The silver in the solution can be saved by precipitating the nitric. Gold is a malleable metal. Pure gold can be beaten to a thin flake with a hammer.

The fabulous area of Goldfield, Nevada, was founded on a gold pan. The oldtimers had found a placer gold but could not locate the lode, so an experienced gold panner from Alaska was hired. Panning systematically, he traced the gold to its source.

Panning involves shaking the heavy particles to the bottom and washing off the lighter particles from the top. Panning is not difficult. Fill your pan with your selected material and submerge it in water. With your fingers, break up any lumps, agitating the material while it is still under water. Give the pan a brisk back and forth, rotary motion. The coarse-grained lighter materials will come to the top where you can remove it with your fingers. Repeat this process several times. Agitate the pan gently while under water, applying the same rotary motion, gradually tilting the pan forward. The heavies on the bottom of the pan will concentrate in the side crease at the bottom. Tilt your pan forward, letting the lip get just below the surface.

Dip the pan in a forward, up and back motion so the water washes off the light portion that has accumulated on the top. Lightly brush off this material with your fingers, being careful not to brush out the heavies.

If you have a large amount of light material, keep doing the forward motion to cover the material with water. Raise the pan, letting the water gently flow off. It will take the lighter grains with it. Alternate the washing action with the rotary motion, until only the heavy material in the bottom of the pan is left. Use your thumb to scrape off any light grains that float to the top.

Put some fresh water in your pan and rotate it in a circle, tipping the pan toward you to make the swirling motion. This action will cause a tail at the upstream end of the rotating water. It is a good idea to do your panning in another larger pan or tub so that, in the event you lose some values, you can repan it.

It takes practice to pan quickly and skillfully. What really counts is being able to interpret and qualify what you have left in the pan. Sometimes a pan of material will seem to twirl about the pan in unison during the rotary motion, almost as if it were floating. If this is the case, it probably means it is all light material and you can disqualify it.

In lode prospecting, the prospector usually sells his find to a mining company. Unless the prospector finds small, rich deposits, he rarely becomes the miner. This is why prospecting and mining generally are separate trades. However, in placer, the prospector usually becomes the miner, for the two phases overlap. In dry placers — especially if the placer is a large, low-grade deposit — the prospector usually leases or sells to a mining company. The mining company has large, efficient equipment and, if the prospector mined on a small scale, he would lose money. If the prospector found a small, high-grade deposit, he would be well rewarded to work it himself.

If you have sizable amounts of amalgam that you want to separate, you can do so by squeezing it through a chamois skin. The gold will stay inside the chamois and the mercury will go through it. For separating small amounts of amalgam, cut a potato in half, hollow out the halves and insert the amalgam. Wire the potato together and roast it in a fire. The mercury will evaporate, leaving the gold. A small commercial retort can be used, such as the Lucky Mercury Retort manufactured by the Lucky Mining Company, Box 476, Lebec, California.

There is gold almost everywhere in the United States, but the question is whether it is economically plentiful.

gold seeker's encyclopedia

ACICULAR: Crystals in the shape of a needle, common in Antimony minerals.

AGGLOMERATE: A breccia formed mostly of fragments of volcanic rocks.

ALASKITE: An igneous rock that contains mostly quartz and alkali-feldspar.

ALBITE: Sodium feldspar.

ALKALI: A substance formed mostly of sodium, potassium, and calcium.

ALKALINE: Minerals that have the taste of soda.

ALLIACEOUS: Minerals having a garlic odor, such as arsenal pyrite.

ALLUVIAL: Gravel, mud and debris that have been deposited by water.

ALTERED: In geology it refers to a rock that has had its components altered.

ALUMINA: An oxide of aluminum. Ruby and sapphire, also corundum are pure crystalline types of alumina.

AMALGAM: An alloy of mercury with another metal, such as silver or gold.

AMORPHOUS: Means no definite structure, usually applied to rocks or minerals without a definite crystal structure.

AMIANTHUS: A silky variety of asbestos.

AMPHIBOLITE: Hornblende schist.

ANDALUSITE: Sometimes used as a precious stone, a silicate of alumina.

ANDESITE: A volcanic rock with porphyritic structure, resembling trachyte.

ANHYDROUS: Means without water.

ANTICLINE: A fold or arch in the earth's rock strata.

APATITE: A common mineral of igneous rocks, it is a lime phosphate and chloride.

APLITE: Muscovite (white mica) granite, occurring in dikes of fine crystalline structure.

AQUEOUS ROCKS: Sedimentary rocks.

ARENACEOUS: Means sandy.

ARCHEAN: Pertaining to ancient times — a geological period.

ARGENTIFEROUS: Means silver bearing.

ARGILLACEOUS: Clay-like material — example, slate and shale.

ARID: Very dry, hot and barren, with scarcity of vegetation.

AURIFEROUS: Means containing gold, usually referring to gold-bearing gravel.

ANCIENT PLACER: Buried by lava flows, or other kinds of strata.

BAR: A bank of sand or gravel at the mouth or a slack portion of a stream, that is gold bearing.

BASALT: Igneous rock of dark volcanic nature.

BASE: A compound that reacts with acids to form salts, this is opposite of acid.

BASE METALS: All useful metals except the precious or noble metals.

BASIC: Igneous rocks that have less than 55 percent silica.

BEDDED FORMATION: A formation of many layers of strata.

BEDROCK: Referring to solid rock, under gravel, that gold has settled on.

BITUMINOUS: Meaning coal.

BLACK SANDS: Consists of grains of magnetite, ilmenite, cassiterite, chromite, tourmaline, or any black heavy element or mineral in placer.

BLOW-OUT: A large outcrop with the vein underneath being much smaller.

BRECCIA: A formation of angular and fragmental rocks, caused by the grind-action of faults and eruptions, sometimes being cemented together.

BUTTE: A small mountain with steep slopes or sides.

CALC-SCHIST: A schist type of rock, containing calcite or dolomite.

CALCEROUS: Containing lime.

CAP ROCK: A barren layer of rock, usually sandstone, covering an ore formation.

CARBONACEOUS: Containing carbon or coal.

CARBONATE: A chemical compound of a metal, carbon and oxygen.

CARBONIFEROUS: A geological time period.

CHALCEDONY: A transparent crystalline type of quartz.

CHERT: A siliceous rock of chalcedonic silica, or opaline silica, sometimes both, occurs in limestone as flint.

CLASTIC: Formation of fragmental parts of other rocks.

CLAY: Hydrous silicate of alumina.

COMPACT: In reference to rock, it means fine, firm, solid, dense or heavy.

CONCHOIDAL: Rocks such as flint or obsidian, that break with both concave and convex surfaces.

CONCRETION: Usually a spheriodal build-up around a nucleus, which is sometimes a fossil. They form into many odd shapes.

CONFORMABLE: Strata that lie upon one another in correct order.

CONTACT: A place where two different rock formations meet, frequently ore-bodies are formed in contact zones.

CONTACT DEPOSIT: An ore deposit between two unlike formations.

CRETACEOUS: A geological time period.

CROSS-BEDDED: Formations of which the strata is cross-stratified.

DACITE: An igneous rock containing quartz and feldspar.

DETRITUS: Rocks, or sand and gravel collected in a common place, but not cemented together.

DIABASE: An igneous rock, composed of feldspar and iron-magnesium, it is usually intrusive and occurs in sheets.

DIKE: A mass of igneous rock, forming a dike, by entering fissures in a fluid condition, then cooling. A dike is a vertical formation.

DIORITE: A rock of the granite family, formed of hornblende and feldspar, on occasions it has quartz.

DOLERITE: A basaltic rock that is coarsely crystalline.

DUNITE: A serpentine rock containing iron-magnesium.

ELECTRUM: A natural alloy of gold and silver.

ELEMENTS: There are 92 elements in the crust of the earth of a definite composition.

ELUVIUM: Sand and gravel deposited in a common place by the wind.

EPIDOTE: A basic silicate rock of calcium, aluminum and iron. It is usually an alteration product of another rock.

ERUPTIVE: Igneous rocks that have been erupted through others in a molten condition, examples are rhyolite, basalt and andesite.

EXTRUSIVE: Igneous rocks that have cooled after reaching the surface.

FELDSPAR: A group of rock forming minerals containing silica, alumina, soda, lime or potash.

FELSITE: A quartz porphyry, very finely crystalline.

FERRUGINOUS: Iron-bearing rock.

FISSILE: Refers to a type of rock that can be easily split, such as slate.

FOSSILIFEROUS: Fossils imbedded in the structure of a rock.

FREE GOLD: Gold that can be obtained from ore without the use of chemicals or smeltering.

GABBRO: Any of the heavy, dark igneous rocks composed mainly of feldspar and pyroxene.

GEODE: A nodule with an inner cavity that is lined with crystals.

GLAUCONITE: A greenish rock or rocks containing silicate or iron magnesium.

GNEISS: A metamorphic rock that is coarse grained and resembles granite, it has alternating layers of feldspar, quartz, mica and hornblende. It has a banded appearance, and is usually wavy.

GRANITE PORPHYRY: A coarse crystalline rock of the granite group with large crystals of quartz.

GRANO-DIORITE: A type of rock in-between granite and quartz diorite.

GRAYWACKE: A shale type of sandstone.

GREENSTONE: Referring to the diabases and the diorites.

GYPSIFEROUS: Containing gypsum.

HORNBLENDE: A dark brown, black or blackish green silicate of calcium and magnesium, usually with iron manganese. It is commonly found in granite and other igneous rocks.

HORNFELS: A dense compact rock, usually occurring in a contact of granite intrusion with slate.

IGNEOUS: Rocks of volcanic origin and of great heat, solidifying from a molten state.

INTRUSION: A mass of igneous rock, forced into or between other rocks, while in a molten state.

LATITE: A type of rock that is in-between dacite and trachyte.

LAVA: Molten material that has been extruded from a volcano. Basalt is a lava flow material.

LEDGE: It is a horizontal layer or deposit. A vein or lode is not a ledge.

LENS: An ore body that is wide in the center, thinning out at the edges.

LITMUS PAPER: Used in testing. Acid turns the blue paper red and alkali turns the red paper blue.

LODE: An irregular vein without well-defined walls.

MAGMA: Molten liquid of which igneous rocks are formed, as it solidifies.

MICACEOUS: Implies that mica is contained in the rock.

MASSIVE: A rock of which the crystals are of large size, as in pegmatite.

NATIVE: Referring to an element occurring in nature, in the native state, such as gold, platinum, copper or silver.

OBSIDIAN: Extrusive volcanic rocks, quickly cooled without crystals, sometimes referred to as volcanic glass.

OOLITIC: Limestone containing many small grains of carbonate of lime, cemented together and looking like fish eggs.

ORE: Any rock containing a valuable element or mineral that can be mined at a profit.

ORTHOCLASE: A potash feldspar.

OXIDE: A compound of oxygen with any kind of metal.

OXIDIZED ZONE: The higher portion of an ore deposit that has been altered by oxygen, water and carbon dioxide to form oxides and carbonates.

PEGMATITE: (Massive Granite) A coarse, large-grained igneous rock, usually occurring in dikes, and is a source of many of the non-metallic ores. May contain valuable gem stones.

PHENOCRYST: A porphyritic crystal.

PHONOLITE: An igneous rock of extremely fine grain, containing feldspar, potash, sodium, silica, potassium, aluminum, calcium, iron and magnesium.

PLUTONIC: Entirely crystalline and coarse grained.

PIPE: An elongated formation of an orebody.

PISOLITIC: Limestone formed of pea-shaped pebbles.

PLACER: A gravel deposit containing gold or valuable minerals or elements.

PLUMBAGO: In ancient Rome a word meaning lead, in modern usuage it refers to graphite.

PRIMARY: Concerned with prospecting, it means virgin metals.

PUMICE: A porous lava that will float on water, used mostly as an abrasive.

QUARTZITE: A metamorphic sandstone with secondary silica deposit between the original grains. It is, therefore, harder and less porous than originally.

QUARTZOSE: A type of rock containing mostly quartz.

RHYOLITE: An igneous flow rock containing quartz and feldspar.

RUST GOLD: Free gold that is coated with an oxide of iron or manganese, and silica. It needs grinding before it can be amalgamated.

SANDSTONE: A sedimentary rock consisting of cemented sand.

SCHIST: A crystalline rock with a parallel structure — it can be easily split.

SCHISTOSE: Means schist-like.

SEDIMENTARY: Formed by erosion of grains or fragments of other rocks, one of three main classes of rock.

SILICEOUS: Has silica in its composition.

SLICKENSIDE: A smooth, sometimes glossy surface on vein walls, created by a rubbing motion during a fault process.

STRATIFIED: Sedimentary formations are formed of large sheets of sediments, sometimes the layers are of different materials.

SPODUMENE: A silicate of aluminum and lithium. Some varieties are used as gems, others for medicinal purpose.

SULPHIDE: A compound of sulphur and any metal.

SYENITE: A granite rock, composed of feldspar and mica, and small amount of quartz.

ULTRA BASIC: Igneous rocks containing less than 35 percent silica.

UNCOMFORMABLE: Example — Top formation has a horizontal strata, while the lower formation has vertical layers.

VEIN: A definite mineralized zone, with or without values.

BUILDING & USING A SLUICE

This Simple Device Can Save Hours Of Panning And Can Help Move A Lot More Dirt, Find A Lot More Gold — If It's There!

WHILE THERE ARE numerous miniature sluices on the market today of the type that can be packed into remote areas on your back, if necessary, it wasn't always this way. In the so-called old days, miners tended to use the materials at hand to build such an instrument for separating gold from sand and gravel.

A couple of years back, one of the treasure-oriented publications offered detailed instructions for building a mini sluice, using materials easily obtainable — although somewhat more modern in nature than those used by the Forty-Niners and others of their era. Even with the cost of today's high-priced lumber, the entire unit can be built for a few hours' labor and less than $10 in materials.

But before we get started with the actual instructions, we should assemble our materials, all of which are available at the local lumber yard or perhaps even in your scrap pile, if you have one.

Here is what you will need: one 1 x 10, four feet in

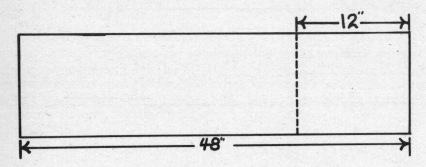

In first step, cut a 12-inch piece off the four-foot 1x10. This allows three feet for the main box, as well as a one-foot section for the holding tray.

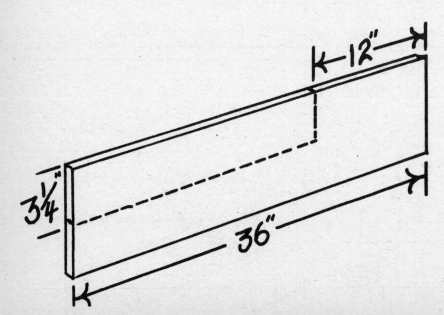

Using two pieces of three-foot long 1x8, make measurements cut as shown in the line illustration at left.

Chapter 14

length; two 1 x 8s, each measuring three feet; two 1 x 1s, twenty-two inches; one 2 x 4 of eleven inches; a dozen pieces of ¾ x ¼-inch molding, each measuring 9½ inches in length. Other necessities will be a piece of indoor-outdoor carpeting measuring 9½ x 22 inches and four 3/16-inch bolts, eight flat washers and four wing nuts. That's all, other than the hammer and a few nails out of your workshop, along with a saw and perhaps a plane, if you want to do a fashionable job.

Perhaps this is the logical time to advise that it is not a wise move to precut the pieces; experience has shown that finished lumber can vary in dimensions. This, in the end, means that precutting can throw off the whole project, resulting in a poor fit and defeating the whole purpose. Instead, cut and fit each piece, as you work. This should assure that you have a perfect fit of each piece, ending up with a piece of equipment that should give you service over many years.

This possibly is the moment at which to point out, too, that the most critical part of building the miniature sluice is in assembling the riffle tray. This section must be easily removable for washing, so be certain to allow a little extra room to compensate for the fact that wood tends to swell a trifle, when it absorbs water.

The first steps is to cut out a twelve-inch end off of the four foot 1 x 10. This gives one the three-foot piece needed for the bottom of the box, as well as a one-foot section to be used for the holding tray.

The next step involves the two pieces of 1 x 8. These are measured so that a cut is made twelve inches from the end, then a section 3¼ inches deep is cut out. A measurement nine inches long and 1½ inches deep is made on the narrow end and this angle then is cut out.

With this done, nail the two side pieces to the outer edge of the bottom section. Then fasten the eleven-inch 2 x 4 to the rear end of the unit. This piece of timber, when against

After the first cut has been made, measure the angle on the sides and cut both according to the diagram.

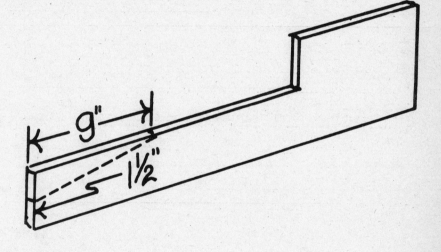

Although photos that follow show in better detail what must be done, the drawing at right shows the box when partially completed, using sections that have been cut and assembled.

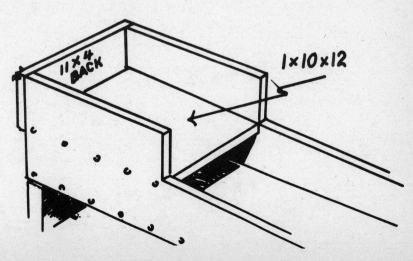

The materials and tools necessary for this project are simple, with wood costing only a few dollars at most.

As assurance that all measurements will fit correctly when parts are assembled, mark cuts with square.

A crosscut saw and patience should help to make the joints come out as they should. Power tools would be an aid, but using only hand tools, the project took less than two hours.

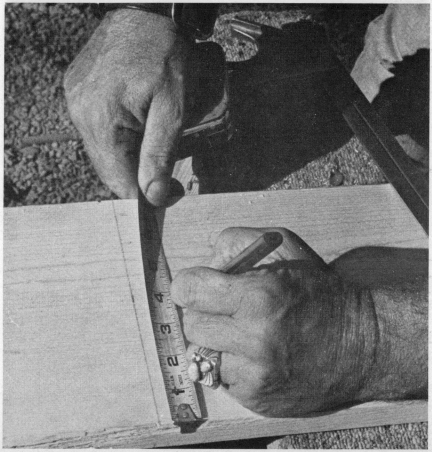

Take care in making your measurements accurately, using either a steel tape or carpenter's ruler made of wood.

The square is used again to measure the 3¼x24-inch section that must be cut out of two boards used for sides.

The end of the board is checked for squareness. In this age, not all of the lumber is cut squarely and this should be checked as accuracy factor.

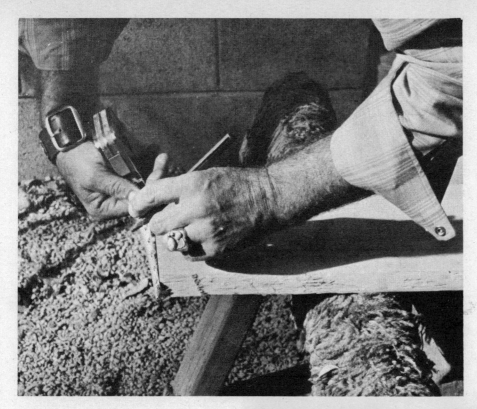

If the wood is not finished, added care must be taken to ascertain that all measurements and cuts are true.

The angle cut in each of the sides is nine inches long, 1½ inches deep. Be certain both cuts are identical.

In the absence of a rip saw, we used the crosscut saw for cutting slots on the sides, found that it sufficed.

the ground holds the sluice at the right angle for operation and, at the same time, should hold to anchor it in the bed of the stream you are working.

The holding tray is installed next, positioning the one-foot piece of 1 x 10 and nailing it in place. A piece of scrap lumber measuring eleven inches in length and four inches in width then is cut and nailed across the opening on the back to enclose the holding tray on three sides.

In constructing the riffle tray — the heart of the mechanism — the two twenty-two-inch 1 x 1s are posi-

tioned in the main box, taking care to leave a slight margin of room on each side to take care of water expansion, as mentioned earlier. The distance then is measured to the outside edges of the parallel pieces and two pieces of the molding are cut and nailed on each end of the 1 x 1s. Be certain to check the fit, again. If it is a sufficiently loose fit, remove the frame and install the other riffles, spacing them equal distance between the two on the end. If they are distributed about 1-1/8 inches apart, edge to edge, you shouldn't have any left over. *(continued on page 185)*

The angle cut in the side of sluice is easy to make, following the mark that was made earlier in measuring.

Two-inch nails are used in put the various sections of the sluice box together, thus assuring its strength.

After the sides are nailed to the bottom of the sluice box, an eleven-inch piece of 2x4 is attached to the bottom to give the box correct angle.

The holding tray section proved to be warped, resulting in tight fit. The side of another board was hit with the hammer, helping to force the misshapen piece into position.

After the holding tray is fitted into the box, a length of one-inch board, four inches in width, is cut and nailed to close back of tray.

For the base pieces of riffle tray, lengths of 1x1-inch wood were used. For the cross pieces, ¾x¼-inch molding was selected of white pine.

The molding is measured to the proper lengths, then cut. Don't use any of the hardwoods, as they tend to split.

Although not a necessity, white glue can be used to glue parts of the tray together for better fit, longer life.

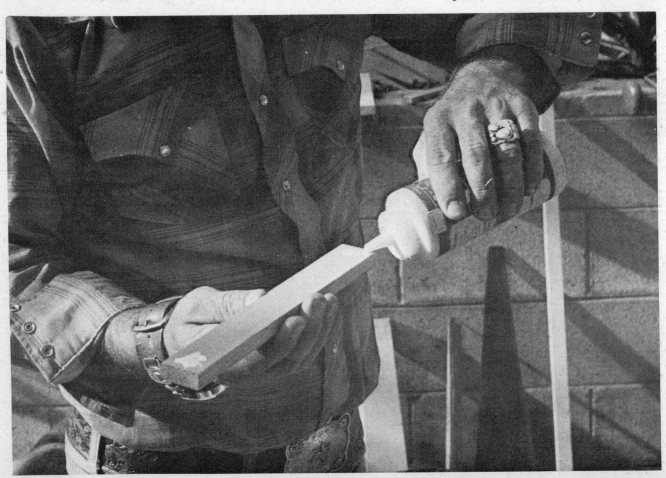

Before gluing and nailing down the cross pieces, all parts are squared to be certain final fit will be right.

Using the completed riffle tray as a guide, the section of indoor-outdoor carpet is cut to fit into the sluice.

Using the hand drill, quarter-inch holes were drilled in the rails of the riffle tray, two on each side.

With holes drilled through the rails, the carpeting and the bottom of the box, the 3/16-inch bolts are run all the way through, using washers and wing nuts to secure parts as a unit.

Richard Taylor of Modjeska Canyon, California, an avid treasure hunter, holds the completed sluice box, now ready to take out in search of gold!

Next, the section of indoor-outdoor carpet should be fitted into the bottom of the sluice box. Purpose of this, of course, is to trap the fine gold that you are going to find. One must think positively in these matters, of course!

The final step is to position the riffle tray in the sluice box over the carpet. Four holes of quarter-inch diameter are drilled through the 1 x 1s on the riffle tray, going through the carpeting and the bottom of the sluice box, itself. You then install the bolts and tighten them down with the wing nuts. This should insure that the riffles in the frame are held down tight against the section of indoor-outdoor carpeting.

The theory is that the gold will come up against the riffles. Being heavier than the sand and gravel, it will collect there, behind the riffles, hopefully adhering to the carpet, if everything has been done correctly. A final step that can be taken to help preserve the rig — as well as reduce water expansion — is to coat the entire mechanism with water-proof varnish.

About the only other thing one is likely to need is a large bucket, a sifter of some kind — and a friendly, inviting stream. Needless to say, gold-bearing terrain is a help, too.

Once you have located a likely area, set up the sluice — being careful to see that it is properly anchored so that it

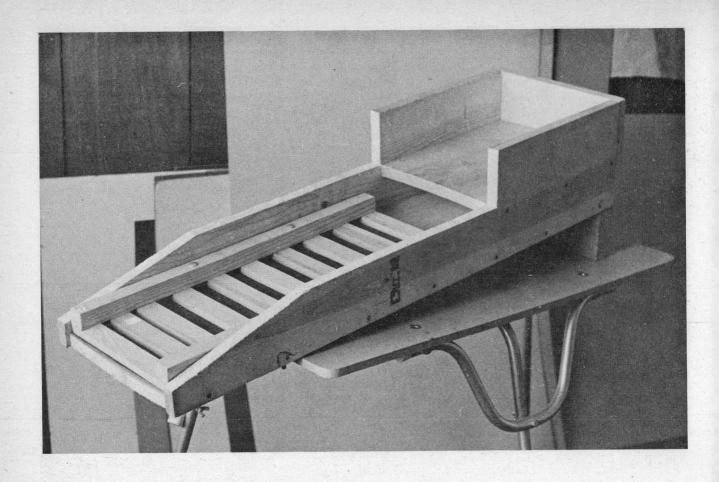

This three-quarter view of the completed sluice box shows simplicity of its construction. But a word of caution: If you intend to use scrap materials, do not use plywood as it tends to separate rapidly, when immersed in water. (Below) Seen from the top, the details of riffle tray are evident. If made too tight, it is hard to remove.

Above: The bottom view of the sluice box is rather sterile. However, for better holding of the ends of the riffle tray, one may want to space the bolts a bit farther apart. (Right) In this end view of the finished box, the simplicity of its construction is more evident.

doesn't go floating away downstream. Position the sluice so that water enters the opening below the tray. Sift the dirt into your bucket, thus getting rid of the large stones, rocks and foreign material. Then carry the bucket down to the stream and begin pouring the dirt and sand into the tray. It then is pushed slowly into the riffles, allowing the washing action of the water that enters the opening beneath the tray to trap the valuable yellow stuff against the riffles. It may take a little practice, but perfection comes in time.

Whether you're using this homemade version or one of the commercially built jobs of lightweight metal, there are some definite techniques to be used in sluicing for gold.

As suggested earlier, sluicing is probably the most widely used placer mining technique in existence. It consists of little more than using water to carry what hopefully are gold-bearing materials through an angled trough, going over a series of riffles.

Sluicing is said to have come into existence in the Sixteenth Century, a system used by the Spanish in their efforts to take as much gold as possible out of the New World. As mentioned earlier, these mechanisms — as well as those used by the Forty-Niners — were heavy, unwieldy creations usually built on the spot from the materials at hand.

The Forty-Niners often built what were called Long Toms. These sluices sometimes were as much as a quarter-

Using factory-built aluminum sluice box, Tom Forrest dismantles the unit to look for gold that might have been trapped in the baffles or carpeting.

mile in length, with up to twenty men shoveling sand, gravel and dirt into the box. According to Jerry Keene of Keene Engineering, a leading maker of prospecting and gold recovery equipment, there usually were two crews working such a rig. One group would bring the materials to the sluice site, while another crew was kept busy shoveling the materials into the sluice.

According to Keene, who has made an extensive study of such techniques and equipment, "The riffles in the old sluices were made of any material at hand, from railroad ties to cobblestone boulders. Anything causing a disruption in the water flow would work but, due to inefficiency, the gold loss was tremendous."

Today, many modern prospectors have made better than average wages simply by reworking the old piles of tailings, which often contain anywhere from $5 to $15 worth of gold per cubic yard. In fact, even in those days, the Chinese used to working hard for little — often worked over the tailing piles left behind by the Forty-Niners, after the latter had moved on to what they hoped would be richer gold grounds.

"While the general shape of the sluice box hasn't changed much over the years, the two notable improvements have been in the materials and in the efficiency of the riffle design," Keene contends. "Lightweight alloys such as aluminum have reduced the weight drastically, for example. Today's three-foot sluice can handle the same amount of work that it took a twelve-foot sluice to handle in the days of Forty-nine.

"A properly designed modern sluice should hold about ninety percent of the gold within the first four to six inches of the box," Keene says.

Because wood saturates with water so quickly, it either must be given plenty of time to dry out after each use or it eventually must be discarded and a new one built. A metal sluice, at the opposite extreme, weighs no more than ten pounds, as against up to thirty pounds for one of the same size of wood. As the latter becomes saturated with water, the weight increases, making packing a bit more difficult.

Rot and imperfections in the wood also create problems, as evidenced by some of the old sluices found in the nearly forgotten gold fields. In fact, many modern prospectors

Forrest gives the length of indoor-outdoor carpeting a minute inspection for any evidence of fine gold that might have been caught by the manufactured riffle tray.

Disappointed at not finding any evidence of gold in the black sand, Forrest washes out the carpet before he goes about reassembling. Panning separates this concentrate.

have disassembled old wooden sluices, panning the material that fell out of the cracks and joints, finding considerable gold. Others have burned the timbers, then panned the ashes to find gold that had been caught and missed by the original operators.

A word of caution, however: before disassembling or damaging such artifacts, be certain of the local laws and possible restrictions. In many areas, these have come to be considered historically significant and damage to such items can bring a healthy fine or even jail!

Whether using one of the modern metal sluices or one you build yourself, there are three important points to consider in setting up: the depth of the water should be no less than four inches; you should have proper incline; and it certainly helps if there is easy access to get the materials to the water's edge, where you have set up your sluice box.

Although the area in which you gather materials may be close to the water, as you work you will find yourself moving in an ever-widening circle. One should collect sand and gravel from areas that can be considered natural gold traps. This includes the bases of large boulders and outcroppings; faults, crevices and cracks in the bed or the stream or along

the adjoining bank; around the roots of old trees; in mossy areas; and adjoining bedrock formations. There are almost endless possibilities.

The ideal incline for a sluice box is about one inch per foot. In other words, if you have a three-foot metal sluice, the entry end should be three inches higher than the bottom.

"You can tell if the water is flowing at the proper speed by dropping a small shovelful of material into the box," Keene suggests. "It should disintegrate gradually — taking about thirty seconds or so — moving with the water flow, rather than being gushed out suddenly due to a flow that is too rapid."

The sluice box should be cleaned once or twice a day, unless one is in an area of extremely heavy black sand or gold. One picks out the larger nuggets — if lucky enough to find them — by hand, then dumps the rest of the washed and concentrated material into a gold pan, separating all of the sand from the gold with standard panning techniques.

In fact, there are even those who save the black sand, as it has several commercial uses and may sell for as much as $10 per pound!

The Montana Mud Mover

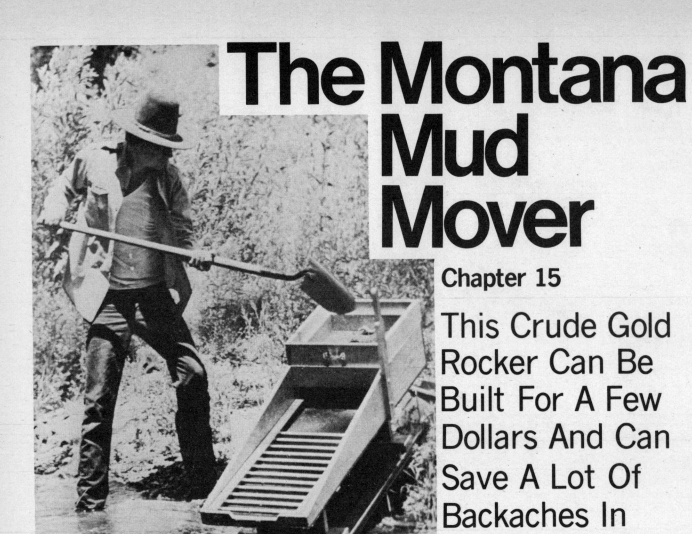

Chapter 15

This Crude Gold Rocker Can Be Built For A Few Dollars And Can Save A Lot Of Backaches In Gold Washing!

THE GOLD PAN is perhaps the simplest means of finding gold, but it also requires the most work for the least return. At the other extreme, if you want to work areas where the gold is thin, hydraulic mining is the answer, if you can get financing from Wall Street or some other enterprise with endless funds.

What it really comes down to is that one interested in gathering gold — once he has found gold in sufficient quantities to make it interesting — must plan on moving and inspecting the greatest amount of sand and gravel possible with the least investment in time and effort. Like everything else these days, unless gold mining is strictly a hobby, time is money and you must have a return on that investment that is better than you could make washing cars.

An incident that reflects this feeling, perhaps, took place during the days immediately following World War II. At that time, I was commanding officer of an establishment called Camp Robert H. Dunlap, which was located in the middle of the Colorado Desert not far from Southern California's Salton Sea. While the title may sound imposing, the fact that I was a second lieutenant at the time may give you a hint.

The camp actually was an abandoned artillery range; most of the gear — including all of the air conditioners — had been sold off as war surplus and our sole duty was to keep the local inhabitants from wrecking the structures and carting them away. Including myself, there were twenty-three men in the camp detachment. The evidence that our efforts were a failure — or those of our successors — is reflected in the fact that today, the only sign of the camp is a few sun-cracked concrete slabs where the buildings once stood.

Boredom was the order of the day, unless you enjoyed hunting jackrabbits with an M-1 rifle, a hobby that palled after a few evenings on the hot desert sands, where it rose to 130 degrees during the day and sometimes cooled down to the 90s after sunset.

An old desert prospector — a relic of the last century by appearance — would show up about twice a month to spend the night, water his burro and fill his canteens. Then he would disappear into the sand dunes once again.

One day he arrived with his burro weighted down, a tarp covering his load. One of the sentries, excited at the seeming load, wanted to know whether he finally had struck it rich. Several other Marines were in the area and crowded close as the old man shook his head.

"No, but I found somethin' out there I don't unnerstand. Figgered maybe you fellers might know what it is!" he explained, stripping back the canvas.

Suddenly he was alone with his burro. Marines had

1

Cut the 1x8 side pieces in conformation with the illustration at right. Each measures five feet by eighteen inches wide. However, measurements can be altered proportionately for larger, smaller unit.

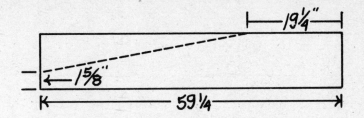

2

Once the sides, back and cross piece have been put together to form main box, they should look like this.

3

Using measurements shown on accompanying diagram, cut a 1x2-inch piece for front section of your box.

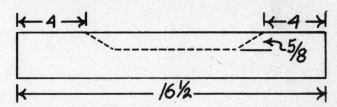

4

Once the 1x2 has been properly cut, it is installed in the main box as shown at right as the front section.

5

Position the 1x1, ten inches in length, side rails between the cross piece, angling them down towards the rear of the main box. Take care in installation.

6

In nailing the sifter frame together, allow the inner frame to protrude about one inch. The sifter box is slightly smaller than the main box, thus allowing for a certain amount of swelling when the wood gets wet.

7

The screening of wire mesh is stapled or tacked to the bottom of the sifter screen. Handle is a convenience.

8

Using the measurements shown, the riffles are spaced about two inches apart, but must be equally spaced. Make certain the overall dimensions are correct so that the mechanism will not bind and can be removed.

9

The 1x1 is nailed to the underside, back edges on both of the riffle frame's side rails. This will help to keep carpeting down and everything on even keel.

10

The outdoor carpeting is fitted in the main box, then tacked into place. A word of caution: Don't use glue. Don't use carpeting with rubber backing; it will rot.

11

The riffles are positioned in the main box, then two holes drilled through both of the riffles from frame side rails, carpeting and the bottom of the main box. The carriage bolts are inserted through the four holes, tightened down with wing nuts on the underside.

12

Using same type outdoor carpeting, cover the large baffle after the 1x1 piece has been nailed into position. Here, use contact cement to hold in place.

13

The large baffle is held in place by drilling a hole through each side of it, as well as the runners that are underneath, then sticking nail through each hole.

14

The base of the rocker is assembled in the fashion shown by the photo at right, taking care in fitting.

15

Drill a 3/8-inch hole in both the front and back 2x4s, allowing approximately one inch of unthreaded portion of the bolt to protrude. It is possible one may have to cut off the bolt to obtain desired length.

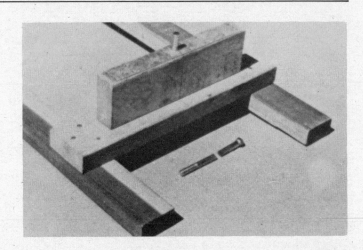

16

Using the dimensions shown in the illustration at right cut two rockers from eighteen-inch lengths of 2x4.

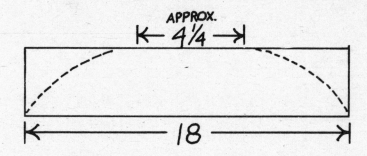

17

Locate the exact center of the rocker and drill a 3/8-inch hole about 1¼ inches deep. Covering rockers with a thin strip of metal will reduce amount of wear.

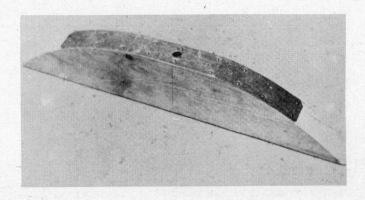

18

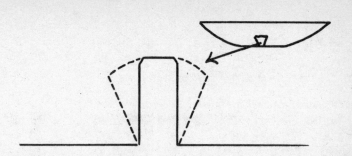

Using a chisel or even a screw driver, widen the holes
in the rockers as shown in drawing so that there is
no binding on the steel pins and they will rock freely.

19

To install the rocker, put the front one in place,
making certain mounting screw heads don't fall under
a riffle, as this will prevent all the riffles from
seating flat on the carpeting. Screw heads should be
positioned between riffles. Front rocker tightened
in place, line up rear rocker and secure with screws.

found instant foxholes all over the area, for the burro was
weighted down with two unexploded 155mm artillery
duds. They finally were unloaded from the burro with great
care and detonated for him to see. The resulting explosion
turned the old man pale and scared hell out of his burro, as
well. We thought he would be thankful that we had relieved
him of his find before it had made him and his pack animal
a permanent part of the desert, but he seemed to resent the
help.

However, he got even some weeks later. One of our men
had found gold in the sands along the All-American Canal,
which cut through the desert camp. More to relieve
boredom than for any other reason, we had gone out with
G.I. wash pans and started to pan out the yellow flakes. But
our supply seemed to grow with great slowness. Finally,
when the old prospector returned, he was told about the
gold, being invited to join the strike. Instead, he simply
shook his head and spit some tobacco juice at a scorpion
that was basking in the sun.

"There's gold in all this sand," he verified, "and it makes
good exercise, since it runs about fifty cents worth to every
ton of dirt you pan!"

We knew from experience that we could make better
off-duty wages shooting wild burros for their hides!

The gold pan has been the beginning of many fortunes
over the centuries, admittedly, but it's larger equipment
that makes gold mining profitable; as a result, serious gold
seekers, once they have located gold with a pan or by other
means, invariably build a sluice box or utilize a gold dredge,
if the gold is in water. Both can be expensive, but there is a
design known as the Montana gold rocker that can be constructed and put into operation for less than $50 worth of
materials and a bit of carpentry.

Ken Doe, publisher of Treasure Magazine, says, "The best
way to describe the unit would be to say it fits somewhere
between a gold pan and a dredge. It doesn't have the luxury
and convenience of a dredge's motorized power unit for
delivering gold-bearing sand and gravel, but the gold rocker
does require a supply of sand and gravel, if you expect to
recover any gold. To accomplish this, all that is needed is a
good pair of hands and a shovel. The Montana gold rocker
really does work."

To date, no one is manufacturing a machine of this
particular design so, if you want one, you are stuck with
building it yourself.

The instructions included in this chapter should be self-
explanatory, but there are several points that should be
made. The carpeting material to be used in the unit should
be the indoor/outdoor type, but definitely without rubber
backing.

The rubber-backed variety of carpet may be less expensive, but it will rot in a relatively short period of time,
requiring replacement. Also, this rubber cushion acts as a
sponge, absorbing a good deal of water. This makes it tough
to move the unit.

It also is suggested that brass bolts be used for assembly,
as they will not rust or corrode. As a result, the unit will
last longer. To reduce further wear and repair, it is
suggested that one use fiberglass screening on the bottom of
the sifter box rather than the steel type.

Finally, since the parts must fit well for the best result,
it is suggested that — in following the instructions for construction — the parts not be pre-cut. Instead, they should
be cut as the unit is built, thus assuring proper fit.

Use of the Montana gold rocker may require a bit of
experimentation before one learns to use it properly. But,
actually, there is little to it other than shoveling sand and
gravel into the box, then running water through it, as the
unit is rocked.

Chapter 16

A MATTER OF DREDGING

This Underwater Technique Is Returning Riches To Countless Gold Seekers Even Today!

The size of the engine used, as well as that of the hoses is directly proportional to amount of material that can be moved in a given amount of time. The larger the equipment, of course, the more expensive it becomes.

PERHAPS THE ULTIMATE in gold-recovering equipment is the gold dredge. This is a reasonably modern piece of equipment that has gained a good deal of favor in recent years, in view of the number of stories — some of them true — about the amount of coarse gold that has been recovered with them in such far-flung locations as Alaska, British Columbia, Latin America and California.

In Northern California, as an example, gold dredgers have done well in recent years, since underwater dredging equipment has been developed to its present efficiency. In 1971, a group recovered more than two hundred ounces of coarse jewelry gold from the slow-moving Yuba River. The following summer, they took another forty ounces from exactly the same spot!

Also in 1971, another dredging team recovered 137 ounces at another location on the same river, then went back to take another two hundred ounces in the Summer of 1972. There also is adequate proof that one California diver has taken as high as $500 a day from a river that was by passed as unproductive by the Forty-Niners!

All this, of course, is enough to make some of us want to shuck the demands of a workaday world, buy a gold dredge and start bringing up gold immediately. It's a most noble ambition, but somewhat more complicated than that. First, one should know how a dredge works, then know something about selecting the right one for the job he intends.

Back in the early days of this century, a dredge was a giant floating rig that was used to scoop up silt from the bottom of rivers and lakes, often being used to build harbors or to move dirt for build-up of real property. Some of these still are in existence, but the term, dredge, has come to mean something else entirely for the gold seeker.

Today's modern gold dredges are, for the most part, small and compact and work on the Venturi suction principle. Water from a river or stream is drawn into the intake of a centrifugal pump. The pump is driven by a small motor such as those used on lawn mowers or washing machines, requiring only a few horsepower for operation.

The action sends water out of the pump discharge at a high rate of speed and resultantly under high pressure. A high-pressure hose — usually with an inside diameter ranging from one to three inches — is attached to the pump discharge by means of a strong coupling. The end of this hose, in turn, is attached to a suction nozzle or a jet, the choice depending upon the type of dredge you are using.

On many gold dredges, the pump output goes underwater via the pressure hose to a curved tube arrangement called a suction nozzle. Here the water coming from the pump is sent through a small aperture in the bend of the tube. This small opening called the orifice is directed toward the back end of the curved tube.

The pump output, when passing through this orifice, creates a tremendous suction that results in rocks, gravel and water being drawn into the front end of the attached

The suction nozzle used for gold dredging consists of a bent section of steel tubing with orifice welded to bend.

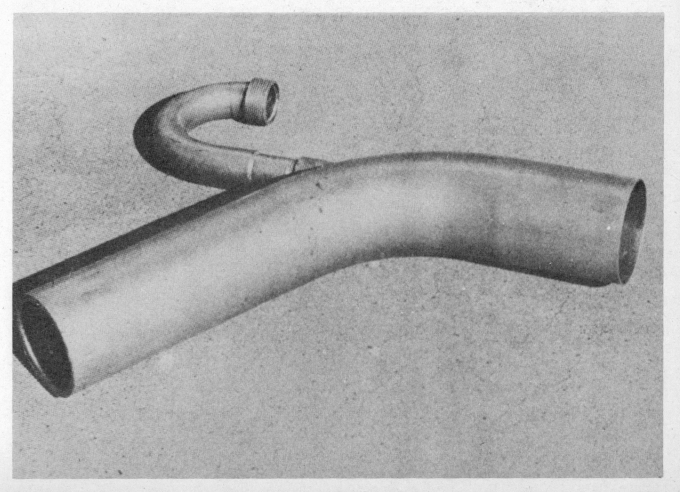

197

suction nozzle. The water acts as the carrying agent, causing the gravel and rock to move past the orifice and into a suction hose, usually of vinyl, that is attached to the back of the suction nozzle. This suction hose carries the gravel up into the sluice box that is floating on the surface of the river or stream.

In the sluice, the rocks and gravel are set through a baffle box, which is arranged much in the fashion of the more common sluice discussed earlier in another chapter. This action causes the solid material to settle, dropping out of the moving water. Among the material that settles would be gold — if there is any. It settles in the riffles of the sluice box, where the water action is less violent.

There are any number of dredges available of the suction-nozzle type, but one of the most modern and most effective is one built by Keene Engineering of North Hollywood, California. This firm, headed by Jim Keene, has developed a new method of creating suction that uses an orifice welded into the side of a straight metal tube called the Power Jet.

In the Keene Power Jet, water from the pump passes through the orifice, then into this metal tube, one end of which is attached to the back of the sluice box.

The other end of the tube has the suction hose attached to it. This goes down to an intake nozzle at the bottom of the river or stream. According to Jim Keene, the only difference between a suction nozzle and his invention is in the fact that the Power Jet pulls the gravel and rocks up the suction hose to the surface, while the standard suction

nozzle pushes the gold-bearing materials to the surface from the depths.

Knowing which type of dredge best suits your needs and the waters in which you will be working can mean the difference between finding gold and going home with a bad cold, according to Keene, who has devoted a good share of his life toward development and use of such equipment.

He advises that one first should buy a dredge from a reputable manufacturer who specializes in such underwater prospecting gear. There are exceptions, since gold is being taken with them, but most home-concocted rigs are decidedly inferior to those that have been engineered and designed specifically for this type of work.

There are numerous questions one should ask himself before he selects a dredge: Are you going to be satisfied with dredging the waters adjoining a public campground, will you be working the small crevices and cracks at the edge of your river, or are you serious about finding gold and intend to work in thirty feet of water at the bottom of a major river? To determine the need and what will do the job, one first must understand what underwater prospectors term the dredge's inch-rating.

For example, when one discusses a 1½-inch dredge, this reference is to the inside diameter of the suction hose that leads up the sluice box. It is not to be confused with the diameter of the rig's suction nozzle. The diameter of the suction nozzle, incidentally, can range from a quarter to a full inch less than the inside diameter of this suction hose.

A small underwater dredge such as this one can be used to clean out gold-bearing gravel from behind obstructing boulder. Experienced gold dredgers realize that many times the precious metal is trapped behind such objects.

As a result, rocks of the same diameter as the inside of the hose don't pass through the nozzle to continually clog it. In other words, if one is using a 1½-inch dredge, the diameter of the suction nozzle probably would be about 1¼ inches.

According to Keene, the inside diameter of the suction hose has a direct relationship to the amount of gravel that can be moved per hour with the dredge. "A general rule of thumb," he says, "is that, if you double the inside diameter of the suction hose, you increase the capacity of the dredge by a factor of four."

To clarify this, let us use a 1½-inch dredge as an example, using a one-horsepower engine for power. With this, one should be able to move about one cubic yard of gravel per hour. But if you doubled the diameter of the hose to three inches — necessarily adding a larger power plant to handle the added load — one should be able to move about four cubic yards of material an hour. If this then was doubled again to six inches — requiring an even larger engine and pump unit, of course — the amount of material that could be moved in that hour's time would be upped to sixteen cubic yards.

According to Keene, "If you are thinking only in terms of amateur searching around a campground, the 2½-inch model should be more than adequate, since it will move as much as four yards of gravel per hour, yet will not be too expensive and will be a light enough unit that it will be easily portable."

Units such as this usually use an engine of three to four horsepower. This, in turn, means that you get more dredging time for each gallon of gasoline used. The ten feet of suction hose that usually is a standard part of the equipment with a unit such as this "still should be able to reach the areas at the bottom that usually are too deep for the snorkel searchers," according to Keene.

For the hardy individual who intends to pack into an area that cannot be reached by vehicle, there are several so-called mini-dredges being marketed today. According to Keene, these miniature models always are built in the 1½-inch size and are equipped with suction hose measuring from seven to fifteen feet.

"The small nozzle of the 1½-inch dredge makes it almost ideal for working cracks and crevices in shallower bedrock areas of small streams that often are rich in gold," he contends.

But for those who want to go after serious gold, be prepared to spend something over $2000 for the necessary equipment. "Going after the big nuggets that invariably lie at the bottom of some of the mean, fast-moving mountain streams is real work," Keene explains. "For this type of professional approach, one needs a dredge that has a minimum six-inch measurement and you will need from fifteen to thirty feet of suction and pressure hose. An engine with a minimum of twelve horsepower is required here. Other requirements will be a wet suit, an air compressor for an oxygen supply while working underwater, as well as weight belts, regulators and even boulder-moving equipment. But

This four-inch surface dredge is an example of the type of equipment used to search streams that might bear gold.

FIGURE 1

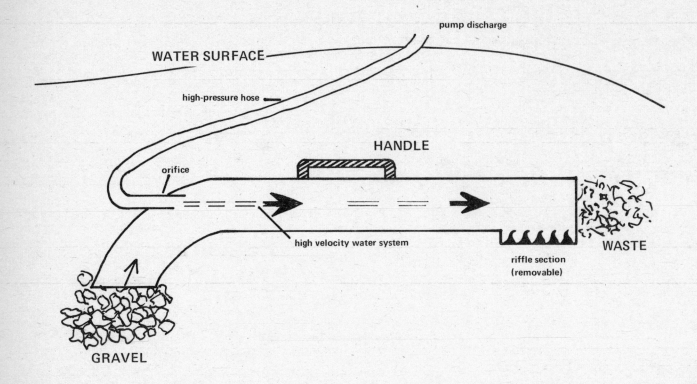

pump discharge

WATER SURFACE

high-pressure hose

HANDLE

orifice

high velocity water system

riffle section
(removable)

WASTE

GRAVEL

Figure 1 *is an underwater dredge with a small riffle section at the back. This makes it less efficient for recovery of fine gold than some of the surface types.* **Figure 2** *uses a sluice box as well as a Power Jet that must be airtight for the unit to function properly.* **Figure 3** *utilizes a suction nozzle to attain the vacuum needed to deliver the gravel from the bottom of the river to the surface-type sluice box. This is one of the more common types used.*

the most important piece of equipment will be what is called an underwater dredge."

Until now, we have been discussing surface dredges, the type of device that sends the gravel from the river bottom up to a floating sluice box on the water's surface. The underwater dredge is submerged completely and operated beneath the water's surface. It is equipped with a suction nozzle that features a long metal tube with the necessary riffles welded onto the rear end in the spot where a suction hose ordinarily would be attached.

"The underwater dredge still works off the high-pressure hose from the pump outlet," Keene explains, "but in this instance, the gravel is not sent to the surface through the long suction hose. Because of this added mobility, the underwater type of dredge can be used to move large amounts of overburden." Incidentally, overburden is the prospector's term for the loose gravel that invariably covers the bedrock of a river or stream.

Keene advises that "if you plan to go down really deep to explore a section of a river that you feel has not been searched before, I recommend a six-inch underwater unit. This can move from sixteen to twenty cubic yards of gravel per hour. This unit also makes an ideal companion for a four-inch surface model. Between these two, you should be able to take on almost any type of river or stream."

But before one takes off for the gold fields, it's an excel-

lent idea to check out the equipment. There is nothing quite so discouraging as to arrive on a site, ready to collect the yellow nuggets, only to discover that you're out of business due to some oversight.

The engine, of course, can be the greatest problem in the field, when you may be miles from civilization. So make certain the recoil spring on the starter works properly. Also, if the engine is the type that is started with a rope be certain you not only have the rope, but that it will not break on you. If it looks frayed or worn, replace it before you leave on your treasure trek!

Most of the small engines used in the smaller dredges are designed to be used only a few hours a week. Dredging on a more or less continuous basis can create a lot of wear and tear, so it is recommended that you not only start with fresh oil, but be prepared to change the oil every four or five days.

In this check-out, inspect the spark plug, then be certain to take along a spare or two, as well as the tools necessary for cleaning the plug and resetting the spark gap. Also, check the air filter and the throttle for any potential problems.

That done, be certain to check the suction and pressure hoses for possible leaks, going over every foot for worn spots that could blow under pressure.

If the pressure hose shows any signs of weakness, it

FIGURE 2

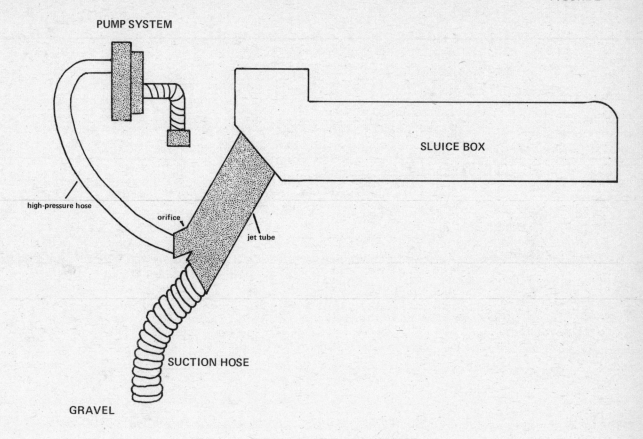

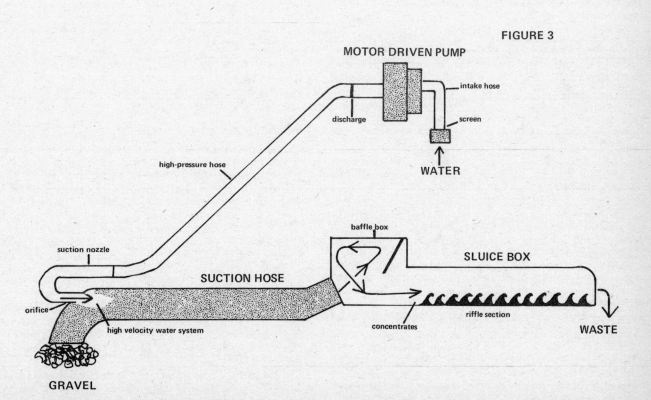

FIGURE 3

201

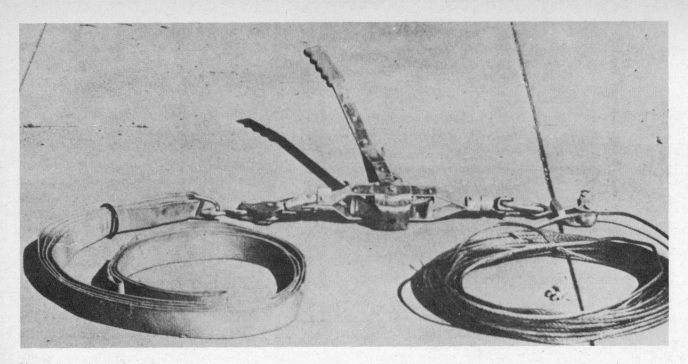

Since big boulders often cover nuggets, a rig for moving the underwater obstructions is necessary for the serious gold hunter. This rig consists of heavy nylon webbing to encompass the boulder, length of quarter-inch cable that goes to the nearest tree and a winch device for moving the boulder out of the way. It's simple but effective.

would be an excellent idea to replace it immediately, although this certainly shouldn't be a problem with a new rig. Also, it is a good idea to check the inner tubes or whatever flotation unit you intend to use to float the dredge in the water. One always should carry a patching kit and some kind of an air pump. In fact, if using inner tubes, it is easier and more practical to carry them in their deflated state, using a bicycle or tire pump to inflate them once the site has been reached.

"Also be certain to go over the foot valve and priming hose," Keene advises, "for if either of these is faulty, chances are that your entire trip is shot. At least, you're not going to find gold with your dredge!"

In addition to checking your camping and diving gear, determine what type of gasoline is necessary for the engine. If you are using more than one engine, it is possible that each will require a different grade of fuel.

Once in the river, with your pump, engine and sluice unit all properly set up, check that the pump is primed. The gold seeker, new to this type of operation, often thinks that all he has to do is drop the hose in the water, start the engine and start pumping gold. But it's more complicated than that.

The pump must be primed manually. This means one must move the priming hose up and down with a rapid motion to force water up into the pump. The priming hose boasts a small valve in the end that goes into the water, forcing the water up into the hose with each downward movement.

If, when starting the engine, the pressure hose becomes hard immediately, this means the pump has been primed and that water is being expelled into the pressure hose. However, if the hose doesn't become hard and stiff, stop the engine immediately. Chances are, if you run the pump for more than a few seconds without it being primed properly, you will break the seal and require a major overhaul. Also, it is a good idea to carry along a spare seal.

With the unit working properly, you're ready to start finding gold, putting the suction nozzle beneath the water. If the pressure hose fittings are correctly installed, one should feel a powerful suction when he places his hand over the end of the nozzle.

For dredges equipped with the Power Jet, it is a bit more complicated to get started. For the dredge to achieve suction, the air in the Power Jet and the suction hose must be exhausted totally. In short, the entire hose and vacuum assembly must be filled completely with water from the intake nozzle at the bottom of the stream to a point just above the Power Jet's orifice.

According to Keene, "If your dredge has the Power Jet beneath the water, the orifice should be well below the water line. Slowly dip your suction hose into the water, the nozzle end first. When the entire hose is beneath the surface, air will be exuded and the free end of the hose can be hooked onto the orifice end of the jet to start dredging."

However, if the Power Jet tube is above the level of the water, the suction hose will not be filled completely with water. The rest of the hose will be filled with air. That means that the suction hose will have to be relieved of air manually.

This is accomplished by placing the nozzle of the hose in the water, the free end attached to the back of Power Jet. Start the engine, but run it only at half speed; then hold the Power Jet in the left hand, using the right palm as a cup to block the end of the jet that connects to the sluice box.

"The water going through the Power Jet will hit the right hand and start flowing backwards through the suction hose," Keene explains. "This will blow the air out the end of the hose that is underwater.

"When you no longer see bubbles coming from the nozzle end of the suction hose, that means the air has been evacuated. All one has to do is hook the Power Jet to the back of the sluice, start the engine at full speed and begin dredging operations."

Keene suggests that, if the overburden is deep, one should start with a small area, cleaning the material away down to bedrock, then switching to the suction nozzle or Power Jet. This will send the gravel up to the sluice box for final separation and, hopefully, recovery of the gold.

In using this type of unit, however, one must keep in mind that, due to the small riffle section and the great amount of gravel being processed, gold recovery with an underwater dredge is less efficient than with a full-size sluice box.

For this reason, the professionals make constant checks of the gravel for gold content. The idea is that they can switch back to the surface sluice box, when the gold in the concentrate begins to accumulate.

Geologists, gold miners and professionals assure us that there still is more gold waiting to be taken from streams and rivers than has been taken to date. It is simply a job of getting to the right spot with the right equipment.

Power Jet is an innovation patented by Keene Engineering. It uses an orifice welded onto the side of the straight metal tube. The inventor claims that this development results in increased suction to move more materials.

TECHNIQUES FOR DRY WASHING

This Method For Finding Gold Is Hard Work, But Is The Answer In The Waterless Wastelands!

Chapter 17

THE EASIEST — AND usually the most prosperous — method for prospecting for gold involves the use of water, but when one finds yellow dust or nuggets in the middle of an arid desert, he suddenly is confronted with a whole new set of problems.

The obvious answer here is the use of a dry washer.

The dry washer is a mechanism that operates in much the same manner as a sluice — but without water. As with a sluice, the dirt, sand or gravel is made to flow over a series of riffles. But instead of water being used to agitate the sand and separate the gold, the riffle tray is set at a steeper angle and air is used to force the movement of the gold-bearing materials.

In using a dry washer, dry dirt — and it has to be quite dry for proper and productive operation — is thrown onto the slanted screen. Usually, a wire net is used, as the size of

This dry washer was home-built. Tom Forrest prepares to start engine that powers the unit and supplies the stream of air that activates the material moving over riffles.

the screen determines the size of the gravel permitted to fall through and into the operating mechanism.

The dirt passes through the screen, falling into the bin, which is built to control a continuing flow of the material onto the riffle tray, the rate of fall being constant.

It is in this step that the gold and black sands are separated from the valueless materials. The force of gravity simply causes the dirt to flow over the tray. At this point, a flow of air is created at the bottom of the tray by means of a bellows that is operated by a small gasoline engine.

The flow of air forced up through the riffle tray not only helps to agitate the dirt and gravel, but blows away much of the accompanying dust. At the same time, this action causes the gold and other heavy materials to fall out and collect in the angles of the riffles.

The riffle tray usually is built so the bottom is of some porous material that will allow the air to pass through, yet is woven finely enough that the gold and black sand cannot slip through.

As the riffle tray is agitated and the air blows through the bottom, actuated by the motor-driven bellows, most of the dirt is thrown off the end of the tray. The heavier materials that remain in the tray are trapped in the riffles. This usually consists of some of the gravel, black sand and, if you are sufficiently lucky, gold.

Incidentally, if you are digging up large nuggets, they

The sand and gravel move over riffles in constant stream, being fed from the screen-covered bin above.

The gold — hopefully — and heavier materials fall to bottom through action over the riffles, rest of the sand and gravel being dropped off end of tray. The concentrate left is taken for panning later. (Below) Forrest takes a closer look at the riffles for any sign of yellow dust that might mean he has made significant find.

usually will be caught by the screen on top through which the material originally was sifted. So don't throw away the rocks and pebbles that gather there without at least making a quick inspection.

After the dry washer has been run for an hour or so, the riffle tray should be removed and the contents dumped into a container of some sort. The resulting concentrate then can be carried out of the dry area and can be panned in the usual fashion with running water under more normal conditions.

Keep in mind, however, that use of a dry washer can be hard work. The continual revolutions of the gasoline engine can cause the machine to eat up a lot of dirt, gravel and sand. This means that one should set up in an area where he can use a shovel to dump materials directly onto the screen rather than having to dig, fill a bucket, then carry it for any distance. It just becomes unfeasible to do so.

This brings us to the next question. If one is going to go to all the work of building or acquiring a dry washer and there are all these miles upon miles of open desert just waiting to be dry washed, how does one learn to choose the more productive spots?

The answer here is relatively simple: One goes to an area that has a history of gold production. Oddly enough, today's dry washers will recover a minimum of ninety percent of the gold in an area, if it is there at all. One obvious source is the old dumps, where the Forty-Niners and later prospectors dumped the tailings after the gold had been extracted.

With the equipment used in the so-called old days, miners usually recovered no more than fifty percent of the gold that was in the ground. That means that there is almost that amount still waiting to be taken.

Chances are that you aren't going to find any big nuggets, since these were what the oldtime miners were after, but you should be able to find smaller nuggets and the dust that they overlooked.

If you find evidence of gold in an area that is damp, there are ways of handling this, but again, it is hard work and slows down your production considerably.

The technique here is simply to take the wet material and spread it out on a tarp or plastic sheet, letting the sun dry it, then running it through the dry washer. But while waiting for it to dry, you can play a lot of solitaire, if you brought along a deck of cards.

All too often, of course, the amateur gold miner isn't certain he will recognize gold, even if he finds it. Perhaps the most simple determination is what oldtime miners called the hammer test.

Gold can be pounded down to a thin sheet, a layer that is no thicker than a sheet of tissue paper; in fact, this is the means by which gold leaf is made. However, iron and copper pyrite both tend to shatter or crumble, when hit with a hammer.

Another means of determining the difference between gold and pyrite — the scientifically oriented name for fool's gold — is the fact that real gold will retain its luster and sparkle in sunlight or in shadow, whereas the fool's gold may shine and sparkle in the direct rays of the sun, but appears much more dull in color, when removed from direct light.

Another bit of advice has to do with the heat factor. If dry washing for gold in the desert in Summer, be certain to take along an adequate supply of water for your own consumption as well as salt tablets. This can be tough work, feeding a machine that seems to have an endless appetite, and dehydration can take place in a matter of hours!

This single nugget caught in the riffles of the dry washer would indicate there is gold in the area and this usually is enough to make the casual weekend treasure hunter renew his efforts in search of sands.

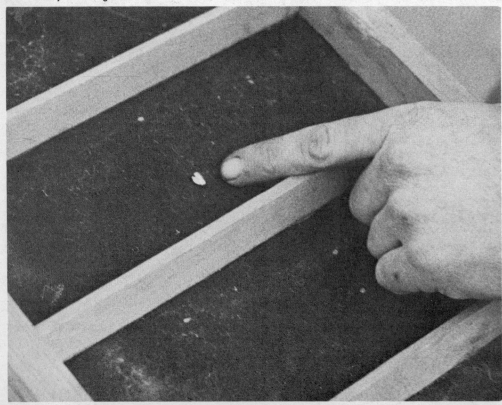

One should not neglect inspecting the screen through which material is sifted. It might yield a large nugget!

Chapter 18
RECOVERING FINE GOLD

Using Mercury Can Be Dangerous, But With Care, Here's How To Increase Your Take Of Dust!

LET'S SUPPOSE YOU have discovered a pretty good thing. You have found a running water stream and spotted color in it. Out comes your gold pan and you start panning.

The only problem is that the flakes are minute, even smaller than the grains of sand themselves. How are you going to be able to separate the gold from the worthless sand that surrounds it? Sure, you can sit there with your tweezers and pick it out one grain at a time, but you'll find that your efforts are making you less money on an hourly basis than a paper route does your son. Much less.

But before you toss the whole mess back into the stream and see whether your gold pan will float downstream, take a look at a process that has been used for years by the serious goldseekers. It is called "amalgamation."

Using mercury, the amalgamation takes place with the gold mixing with the liquid metal in one of the oldest methods of recovering the precious metal that is known to man. Mercury, in its liquid state, tends to assimilate heavier metals such as platinum and gold, but, at the same time, passes over lighter materials such as sand and gravel, seeming to reject them.

However, there are some minor problems before the amalgamation can take place and this requires an additional step. Inasmuch as gold — including the small flakes or powdered dust — tends to pick up iron and sulfides, these make amalgamation difficult.

The obvious answer is to clean the gold before the process begins. If you wonder whether this is really necessary, think of it in terms of greed. If the gold is not cleaned of its impurities, as much as thirty percent can be lost during amalgamation.

There are any number of methods for cleaning gold, but one of the more simple ways is with nitric acid, but the cleaning must be done in a plastic gold pan or any other container that will not be eaten by this powerful acid.

One covers the concentrated gold-bearing gravel with half an inch of water, then adds a small amount of the acid, until what appears to be a slight boiling action is visibly evident.

This action, incidentally, begins when the ratio is one part acid to thirty parts water. However, if you want to avoid what could be a dangerous and serious incident, add the acid to the water rather than the other way around. The acid has a tendency to boil over — or even explode — if one pours water into the concentrated acid.

Once the proper measurement has been attained, swirl the mixed liquids around the pan, making certain that all of the concentrates are covered. The solution then can be washed away by allowing stream water to flow through the pan. If you are doing this at home, water from a tap run into the pan in a continuous flow will accomplish the same thing.

When the concentrate is free of acid, pour off the rest of the water. You now are ready for the amalgamation process.

It requires little mercury — only a few drops — to gather the powdered gold. In fact, those with experience rarely have more than a quarter-pound bottle of mercury, as this will literally recover pounds of gold, if the liquid material is cared for and used properly.

To accomplish the amalgamation process, place a small quantity of mercury — no more than a few drops — in the pan to cover the concentrates, then agitate these contents of your pan under water.

The mercury should be worked through the sand, thus making complete contact with all of the sand and gravel in the pan. In the end, the globules of mercury will appear rough on their outer surfaces; this is sure evidence that the gold has been gathered, for it is the more precious metal that is giving the rough appearance, adhering as it does to the mercury.

The residue — namely the sand and gravel — should be panned out just as in normal gold panning, leaving only the mercury amalgam globule in the bottom. Care, of course, should be taken not to wash away or pour out any of the gold-bearing mercury drops. They will run together, as they are worked, to make a single larger ball.

The ball of mercury now holds all of the powdered gold that might otherwise have been impossible to recover, but keep in mind that the chemical action of the mercury tends to turn the gold a gray color and to make it brittle.

Now that you have the gold separated from the sand and gravel, there comes the problem of separating the gold from the ball of mercury.

The method used most commonly for this is simple. The

As illustrated in the drawing at left, hydraulic mining moved a great amount of sand, dirt and gravel in the search for gold, but much of it was missed. (Below) For recovery of fine gold, a plastic goldpan, mercury and nitric acid are used for the amalgamation process. However, be aware of the dangers involved in the system.

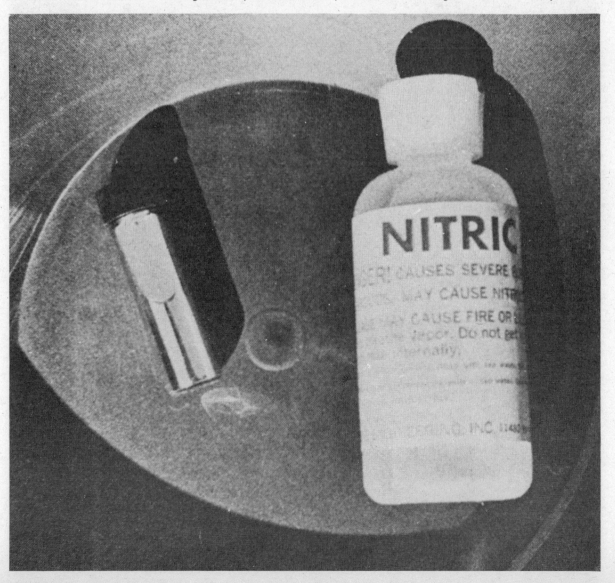

first step here is to wash the amalgam — the combination of gold and mercury — then strain the gold-impregnated mass through a piece of chamois, buckskin or even tightly woven canvas. This allows one to recover the greater part of the mercury, as it will squeeze through the pores in the hides or between the woven threads. That material — namely the gold — remaining still will be impregnated in some mercury.

The straining material then is burned, either by fire or strong acid to remove the rest of the mercury, leaving only the raw gold. This does waste a small amount of mercury, however.

Another simple method of separating the gold from the mercury is the so-called baked potato method, which is practical enough for the weekend prospector who cannot afford great amounts of professional equipment. Another method, the use of a retort requires a good deal of complicated equipment, as well as available high temperature.

This simple potato method involves simply cutting a small cavity in half of a good-sized potato. The amalgam is poured into this depression, then the two halves of the potato are fitted back together, being fastened together with wire or some material that won't burn or melt readily. The potato is wrapped well in aluminum foil and placed in a fire.

Within an hour — depending, of course, upon the size of the potato and the amount of amalgam in the cavity — the heat will vaporize the mercury, driving it into the potato.

This leaves the remaining gold standing alone in the cavity.

The gold is removed, then the cooked potato can be mashed up, the mercury being panned out as one would gold. The remains of the potato are washed away, while the recondensed mercury remains in the bottom of the pan.

There are, however, a couple of cautions to be exercised here. First, try not to cook the potato too rapidly or it may explode. If that happens, you could have potato and gold-bearing amalgam all over your camp.

Even more important, do not attempt to eat the potato, as the mercury in its condensed state is deadly poison.

The more professional gold hunters may end up with respectable amounts of powder gold that needs processing. A retort may be used. This is usually a cast-iron pot with a tight-fitting lid. The pot is connected to a condenser by means of a tube. It is the condenser that actually does the job of recovering the mercury from the gold.

The amalgam of mercury and gold is put into the cast-iron pot and heated. The temperature must reach 675F, the temperature at which the mercury will turn to a gas. In this state, the vapor escapes through the tube to the condenser, which is nothing more than a water-jacket wrapping around the tube.

The water cools the vapor as it passes through the tube, thus condensing it back to its original liquid mercury form. After all of the mercury has been removed and reformed as

The gold-bearing amalgam can be recovered with hollowed-out potato baked in a fire.

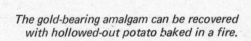

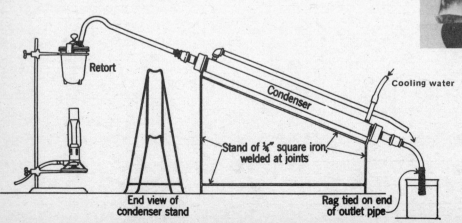

Retort

Condenser

Cooling water

Stand of ¼″ square iron; welded at joints

End view of condenser stand

Rag tied on end of outlet pipe

Diagram outlines construction of a typical retort for gold recovery.

Apparatus for retorting amalgam and quicksilver.

*Using nitric acid that has been diluted with water,
one can boil away the mercury, leaving only the gold.
However, be careful not to breathe the poisonous fumes.*

liquid, the iron pot should be allowed to cool. When the lid finally is removed from the pot, there should remain in the bottom a mass of what is called sponge gold, gold in its purest state. If the pot is tapped hard, the gold will be loosened to fall out.

In working with the retort or in boiling mercury with nitric acid, stay clear of the fumes, as they are highly toxic. Breathing these fumes can result in mercury poisoning and enough of this can lead to death.

Recovered mercury can be used over and over, but in time, dirt of one kind or another will begin to permeate the substance and discolor it. Eventually, this will cause the mercury to break into small drops or particles, making amalgamation difficult and even impossible.

When this happens, go back to the thirty-to-one solution of water and nitric acid mentioned earlier — again, taking the precautions outlined in mixing the two. Boiling your mercury in this substance will remove all of the dirt and debris, giving you pure mercury again, once the nitric acid has been washed out.

As for source, both mercury and nitric acid can be obtained from most chemical supply houses, some pharmacies or a store specializing in prospecting supplies. In some states, it may be necessary to sign for the nitric acid, because of its deadly qualities.

But with these simple needs, a great deal of gold that might otherwise be lost can be recovered, adding to your potential as a gold miner.

*Clean, pure mercury will form into a ball or puddle, but when it
becomes contaminated, it breaks up, making amalgamation impossible.*

NOT ALL OF the waiting treasures are ledges of gold and silver discovered — and lost — by prospectors, packets of bills hidden in the wall of a house by a miser or raw gold at the bottom of the sea amid the wreckage of ships.

Gem hunting is gaining in popularity in this country, as the hills and streambeds are literally filled with semiprecious and even precious stones. Not all of the diamonds are in Africa's Kimberly Mines. Indeed, our own state of Arkansas has its known diamond fields and there is one specimen from that location, valued at $25,000, that was discovered by a tourist.

Agreed, most of the diamonds found in Arkansas are not of gem quality and are better used in tools to make saws and bits, but they still are diamonds and — because they are scarce — bring some money for use in tool manufacture.

The number of amateur lapidarists has multiplied manyfold in the past two decades. As a result, there is an everincreasing demand for gems — including the semi-precious varieties — from which they can make rings, necklaces and similar items. The result has been numerous gem hunting clubs across the nation, some of which organize safaris into the wilds in search of nature's jewels.

While searching for gold and silver may be a good deal more romantic, both are becoming more difficult to find each year, as there are hordes of part-time prospectors searching the hills and rocks in search of the precious metals. However, the gem stones and even minerals that can be used for industrial purposes are endless and often can mean varying degrees of wealth for the finder. For example, there are all sorts of abrasives — including the industrial quality diamonds mentioned earlier. This category includes those items that can be used in cutting, cleaning, polishing, grinding, ad infinitum. Such abrasives may range from extremely hard surfaces to fine compounds that can be used for buffing. Common in almost any locality, this category includes quartz, garnet, corundum, sandstone, perlite and diatomacous earth.

Insulating materials are in great demand today and can be found in natural surroundings, if the prospector knows what it is he seeks. Perhaps the best known is asbestos, which is used for insulating and countless other purposes, including linings for such friction-bearing surfaces as clutches and brakes in vehicles and machinery. Gypsum, perlite and diatomacous earth also are used in insulating materials.

A broad spectrum of rocks and minerals is in demand for building materials. The list is lengthy, of course, but there always is a market for new finds of things as common as

Gems & Minerals

Look Closely; That Rock In The Way Of Your Prospecting May Be More Than Just A Rock!

Chapter 19

sand and gravel, especially if the supply is clean and relatively free of clays. Other items in this category of discovery include gypsum, lime, pigments and the various types of building stone such as granite.

Clays, lime, lithium, quartz, sand and feldspar also are in demand for use in the manufacture of ceramics and glass, but one must know the qualities required for each of these manufacturing processes. For example, not just any type of clay can be used in quality pottery. A good deal of study may be required to know to what use a specific find may be put.

There are more than 1500 types of minerals known today and, of these, roughly a hundred are classified as gems. A gem is separated from other minerals by the fact that it must be hard and durable; as a result, the harder a stone, the greater its value. The diamond is an excellent example.

There are scales of hardness which are used by rockhounds and lapidary buffs to evaluate any stone that might by found. For example, talc is one that can be scratched with the fingernail, while gypsum is in that category that can be cut easily with a knife. Calcite can be cut with a knife, but it is a bit more difficult. Flourite can be cut with difficulty, as can apatite. A departure from the scale is feldspar, which can be scratched, but cannot be cut with a knife.

One often hears that, to determine whether a diamond is real, he should try to scratch glass with it. This is not strictly true, as quartz will scratch glass; topaz will scratch quartz, a sapphire will scratch topaz — and a diamond will scratch the sapphire.

Knowing what you are seeking can be important. For example, there is the story of a Colorado woman who was digging for beryl. Instead, she found a deposit of pitch-

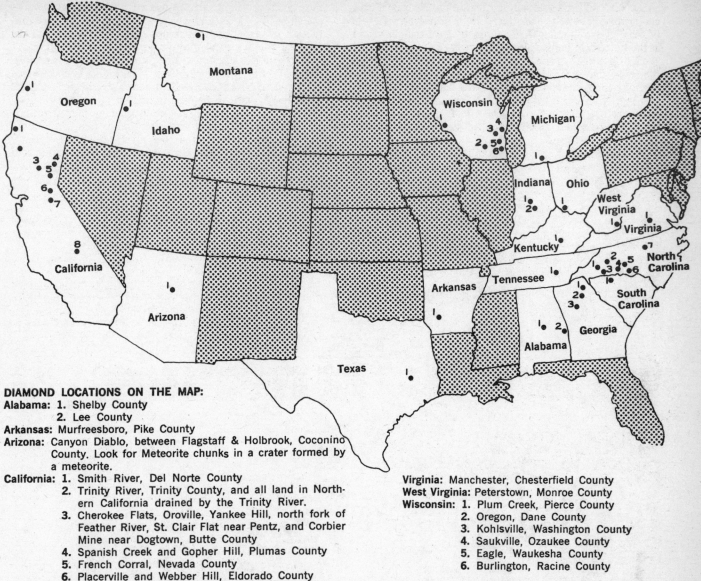

DIAMOND LOCATIONS ON THE MAP:

Alabama: 1. Shelby County
2. Lee County
Arkansas: Murfreesboro, Pike County
Arizona: Canyon Diablo, between Flagstaff & Holbrook, Coconino County. Look for Meteorite chunks in a crater formed by a meteorite.
California: 1. Smith River, Del Norte County
2. Trinity River, Trinity County, and all land in Northern California drained by the Trinity River.
3. Cherokee Flats, Oroville, Yankee Hill, north fork of Feather River, St. Clair Flat near Pentz, and Corbier Mine near Dogtown, Butte County
4. Spanish Creek and Gopher Hill, Plumas County
5. French Corral, Nevada County
6. Placerville and Webber Hill, Eldorado County
7. Indian Gulch, Jackass Gulch and Volcano, Amador County
8. Alpine Creek, Tulare County
Georgia: 1. Harshaw Mine, Acooche Valley, White County
2. Gainesville, Hall County
3. Morrow Station, Clayton County
Idaho: Diamond Basin, Ada County
Indiana: 1. Martinsville, Morgan County
2. Lick Creek near Morgantown, Brown County
Kentucky: Cabin Fork Creek, Russell County
Michigan: Dowagiac, Cass County
Montana: Nelson Hill near Blackfoot, Glacier County
North Carolina: 1. Headwaters of Muddy Creek, Dysortville, McDowell County
2. Brindletown Creek Ford, Burke County
3. Twetty's Mine, Rutherford County
4. King's Mountain, Cleveland County
5. Cottage Home, Lincoln County
6. Todd Branch, Mecklenburg County
7. Portis Mine, Franklin County

Ohio: Milford near Cincinnati, Clermont County
Oregon: Coos Bay Area, Coos County
South Carolina: Spartanburg County
Tennessee: Huntsville, Walker County
Texas: Clinch River near Union Crossroads, Roane County

Virginia: Manchester, Chesterfield County
West Virginia: Peterstown, Monroe County
Wisconsin: 1. Plum Creek, Pierce County
2. Oregon, Dane County
3. Kohlsville, Washington County
4. Saukville, Ozaukee County
5. Eagle, Waukesha County
6. Burlington, Racine County

blende, the material from which uranium is derived. Another gem hunter found a material he didn't recognize. He polished his find to a high luster only to learn that he had discovered the teeth of a prehistoric three-toed horse. In their original state, the teeth would have been worth a small fortune. However, in their polished state, they were worth considerably less!

Twenty-odd years ago, while serving with the Marines in Korea, the author found a number of rough blue stones in a streambed. I brought a number of pieces back to the States strictly as souvenirs of an unpleasant thirteen-plus months only to learn that they were high quality jade!

If one has no experience in hunting for gems and has no idea of normal appearance in their rough state, the best source of information is the minerals section of a museum or perhaps a visit to a local college. An excellent reference found in most libraries, incidentally, is "Handbook of Gem Identification" by Richard T. Liddicoat, Jr.

From the descriptions and photos in Liddicoat's book, one can get an excellent idea of what the various gems look like in their natural state. Included are methods for testing the various gems and minerals to determine whether they

Tom Forrest uses prospector's hammer to break a rock found in San Gabriel Canyon area of Southern California. Gems often are found imbedded within rocks washed down from the mountains.

are what you hope they might be. There are numerous other books available on the subject, but we consider this the best we have come across.

Other than museums and libraries, another good bet is local rockhound and gem collecting clubs. The tips one can gain from members, as well as opportunities to inspect their collections for familiarity, are endless.

The first question the neophyte usually asks is where to look. Actually, gem stones are all around us. They are found in cliffs, canyons, ravines and in fields among boulders left from the Ice Ages. Many gems have been found in road cuts, where earth has been removed to make way for concrete; they have been found in old quarries and in the tailings of mines. According to the experts, lakes, riverbeds and ocean beaches are excellent searching grounds. As evidence, the best ruby and sapphire mines usually are located in dried riverbeds.

Emeralds have been found in quantity in Alexander County, North Carolina, while sapphires have been located

in both Idaho and Montana. Rubies are found frequently in Georgia and North Carolina.

Florida's Tampa Bay is considered prime territory for gem hunters, with agates and opals in the area, as well as chalcedony coral. Some gem hunters have found centuries-old shark teeth and even those of dinosaurs in this locality.

While one tends to think of Africa's famed Kimberly Mines as the source of the world's diamond supply, this isn't necessarily true. Diamonds have been found frequently in Wisconsin, for example, located for the most part in glacial drift. The first diamond found in this specific Great Lakes region, for example, weighed fifteen carats. It was discovered by workmen in 1883, near Waukesha, where they were digging a well.

According to experts, these diamonds probably were brought southward out of Canada by the glacial movement of rocks and boulders during one of the Ice Ages. It also is assumed that somewhere — between this Great Lakes region and Hudson's Bay — a major diamond field is awaiting dis-

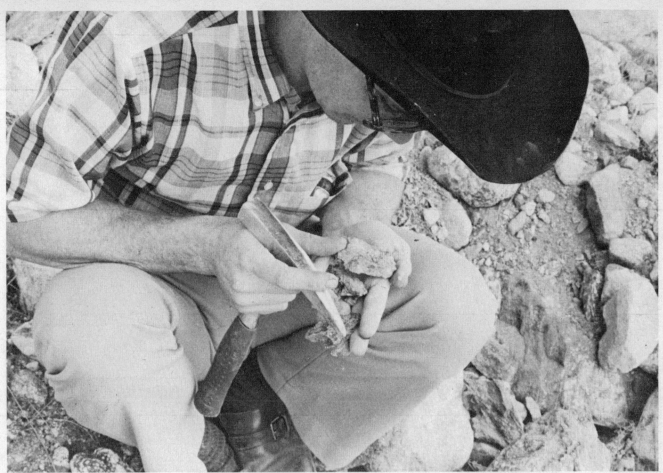

Forrest takes a look at small gems he found in the interior of the rock. Too small to be commercially valuable, they were tested and found to be amethist.

If all one needed were rocks to become rich, Tom Forrest would have found a real bonanza, but knowing what type of material you are looking for is help.

covery. However, anyone who has ever visited this country realizes how vast it is and how great a search would be involved. Chances are, if it ever is discovered, the diamond field will be located by accident rather than design!

Arkansas has been the site of numerous diamond mines and near Murfreesboro is a mine open to the public, where one can search for a daily fee. Incidentally, this is where the $25,000 diamond was discovered by a tourist!

Diamonds have been found with some frequency in North Carolina, while gems of the same brilliance and quality have been discovered in such unlikely places as Indiana, Kentucky and Missouri. One especially good area is in the Smoky Mountains, along the Blue Ridge Parkway. There is easy access because of the highway, but there also are plenty of lookers.

California has been the scene of enough diamond finds that legends have grown out of these discoveries. One such story revolves about Michael J. Cooney, who become known as the King of Diamonds. His story — in America — began early in this century, but actually had its foundation as early as 1866, when a miner, Mike Maher, rode into the town of Oroville, still a relatively small community in the Sacramento Valley, shouting that he had found diamonds!

At first, the town was pretty unimpressed, having been through several false gold rushes since the days of Forty-nine. However, shortly after the miner walked into the nearest bar to display a large blue stone, some two hundred men and women headed for the tailings of the Cherokee

If one doesn't recognize gems in their raw state, it often is possible for the amateur to overlook something of value. (Left) Forrest makes a minute inspection of a section of the boulder that he has chipped away from the main body.

Flat Mine, where Maher claimed to have found the stone. He said he had found the diamond, while searching the nearby cliffs for gold-bearing gravel.

No one found a diamond that day and the townspeople felt they had been hoodwinked despite the miner's claims. Lethargy again set in over the town.

However, the following year, a well known Oroville businessman found a 1.5-carat diamond in almost the same spot where Maher had found the original. In 1868, John Moore, also a local resident, unearthed a six-carat diamond at the entrance to an old mine shaft.

As news of the diamond finds spread, prospectors moved in from all over the West, some of them jumping existing gold-mining claims. The favorite spots were at Thompson's Flat, adjoining the Feather River, and lands next to the Spring Valley Mine. A number of small, poor diamonds were discovered and it wasn't long before the prospectors had moved on.

Over the next half century, numerous diamonds were found in the immediate area, but none were really of cutting quality and most of them went for less than $100 each.

Finally, in 1907 — by design or circumstance — four wealthy miners arrived in Oroville at almost the same time Michael J. Cooney stepped down from the stagecoach and checked into the Union Hotel, the community's leading hostelry.

Cooney has been described as something of a dude, with his derby hat, his gold-rimmed glasses and his closely trimmed goatee. But whatever his appearance, this was the man who had been the actual developer of the Kimberly Mines in South Africa!

The four miners, who had struck it rich in Nevada silver and gold, have been identified as Charlie Ross, Al Christie, John McMullen and A. G. Lorbeer. The four immediately latched onto Cooney and it wasn't long before they – plus a number of small investors – had incorporated the United States Diamond Mine Company. They bought forty acres of land virtually on the outskirts of Oroville. When the owners found who was after it, the price suddenly tripled, but Cooney was nonchalant about it.

"We're going to be millionaires in a year or two," he told investors. "We can't lose."

Cooney's enthusiasm was catching. After all, he had been checked out by some of Oroville's leading bankers, as well as the four miners with whom he had formed the diamond mining company. He had explained that, while working for Kimberly, he had heard of the Oroville

diamond discoveries and had felt the area showed great promise.

He spent days in the hills surrounding Oroville, seeking likely looking areas. At 60 years of age, he outworked many men much younger than himself. He insisted there was endless promise, as the soil around Oroville was almost identical to that of the Kimberly area of South Africa.

"You have a lot of blue rock around here," Cooney explained to his backers. "It's what we refer to as Kimberlite and it's the kind of clay that harbors diamonds." He also told them that the black volcanic rock in the area was another good sign.

"I've found round stones in the hydraulic washings," he added, referring to old gold diggings he had inspected. "That's also a good omen, as diamonds tend to appear with such stones."

The expert dug two small stones out his pocket to display them to the group. "They are small but valuable stones I found on the ground. This is real diamond country."

Meantime, Cooney's words and his enthusiasm for the area had reached San Francisco's Montgomery Street, even

The fire agates at right were found in Mexico. The four at top have been separated from the material surrounding them.

This agate, which has been cut with a lapidary saw, was discovered in a mine in Brazil. Note the heavy jacket.

then the heart of the thriving financial district. Diamond merchants in Holland were contacted for a further check on the doughty little Irishman's credentials and he was given the highest marks. Based upon this, the financiers wanted a piece of the action and it wasn't long before Cooney and his four mining partners had sold more than $2,500,000 worth of public issue stock.

Cooney spent the better part of two years sinking shafts with no sign of diamonds. Meantime, there were those who were pointing out that such cartels as DeBeers never would allow California diamonds to reach the world market, as they controlled it.

It was in the Spring of 1909, in a partially flooded shaft, that Lorbeer was feeling in the mud to determine the depth of the water, when he found a mass of rough stones. He rinsed away the mud, then shouted his glee.

Rushing back to the hotel room in Oroville, Lorbeer showed them to Cooney, who tossed the pebbles aside, saying they were nothing but quartz; that they were worthless.

But Lorbeer wasn't so sure. Instead of taking Cooney's word for it, he returned to the mine shaft, where some

of his men picked up more than two hundred similar stones out of the mud, washed them, then took them to a jeweler in Oroville.

That professional declared they were diamonds rather than quartz, but suggested they be taken to a diamond analyst in San Francisco for an opinion. Instead, Lorbeer and his partners returned to Cooney's room, where he was waiting for them. Again, he insisted the stones were not diamonds. At the same time, he resigned as chief officer and engineer of the company, ordering that the entrances to the shafts be covered. His reason was that he did not want the investors to lose any more money.

Late that night, Cooney left for San Francisco, returning two days later. Upon his return, he called the stockholders together, stating that since he had talked them into investing in a losing thing, he considered himself responsible. He bought up all of the outstanding shares.

The four miners who had gone into partnership with Cooney found themselves so close to broke that they had no other alternative except to allow Cooney to close the mine, board up the entrance and sell off the equipment.

Rumor was, of course, that Cooney had gone to San

This amethyst geode, which is a deep purple in color, was discovered in Mexico. Again, note that, without cutting, it would simply have looked like a rock; note round shape. This usually is a hint to investigate.

This gem-like creation of nature was discovered in Oregon. Again, the roundness was enough to make the experienced rock hound feel it was worth cutting into with a lapidary saw.

221

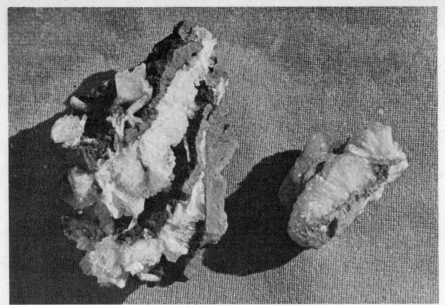

These examples of adamite were found in Mexico and are composed of white and yellow crystals. The crystals are formed from raw zinc arsenate.

Francisco for the express purpose of selling out to the DeBeers interests, thus preserving the international diamond market.

Cooney remained in Oroville for a time, then moved to nearby Grass Valley, but if he had been paid off by the African diamond interests, it didn't show, for he continued to live in the same conservative, almost frugal manner for which he had become known.

In time, he moved to Salem, Oregon, where he died in 1929 at the age of 90. When his safe deposit box was opened, those who recalled his exploits — or exploitations — expected it to be packed with cash. Instead, it was empty.

Because of the iridescent quality, these ore samples are called peacock copper and were collected in Arizona.

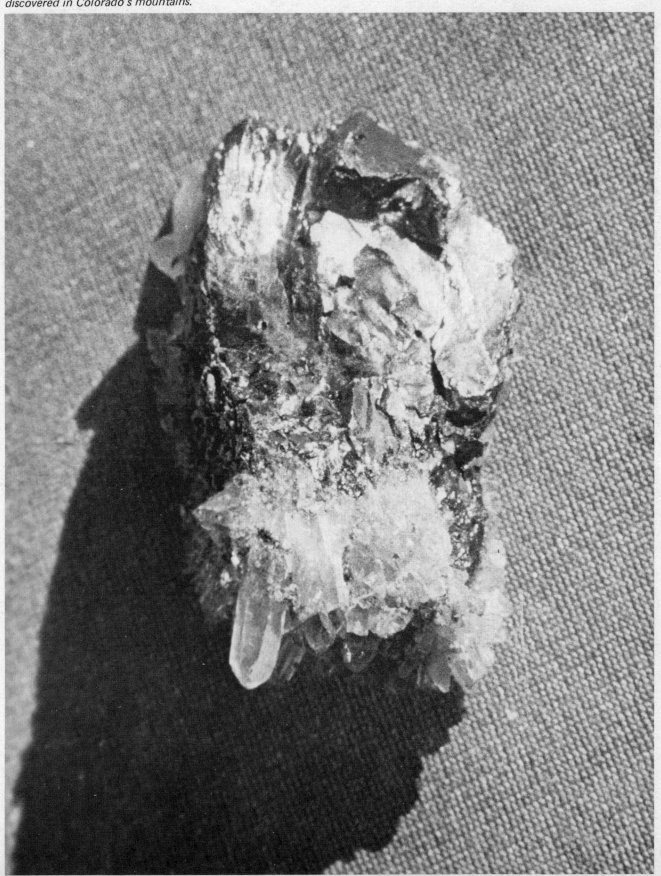

These calcite crystals, carried in a rock formation called pynte, were discovered in Colorado's mountains.

This type of mineral, called galena, is found in the areas covered by Missouri, Kansas and Oklahoma. At the present-day market value of lead, discovery of large quantities could mean wealth; it actually is lead ore.

Unless he had buried his money somewhere, Cooney died virtually destitute!

Investigation indicates that Cooney had gone to San Francisco to draw his personal fortune out of several banks, then had used these funds to pay off the investors in the diamond mines.

However, in the past seventy years, more than four hundred diamonds have been found in the vicinity of Oroville. The catch, of course, is that they were of such poor quality that they won't bring high prices in jewelry stores.

Oddly enough, the Oroville area now is big in turkey raising and some of the best stones have been found in the innards of these birds, when they were killed and cleaned. The turkeys apparently have picked them up as they would feed or gravel, swallowing them.

That, however, does not mean gem-quality diamonds are not there. One of the greatest problems is the fact that the Oroville Dam — the largest earthen dam in the world — now holds back the Feather River. The resulting lake covers thousands of acres of what once was considered prime diamond country.

While it isn't likely that the average neophyte is going to locate his own personal diamond field overnight, there are many ways of finding gems. They often are stuck in larger sections of rock and must be chipped out or the rock broken apart. They are found in lava formations. Some gem hunters even dig up anthills, seeking gems in the soft sand after finding that the insects have brought bits of tourmaline to the surface.

Equipment for the beginning gem hunter is simple enough. He needs only a few items, including a mineral hammer or a prospector's pick. This particular pick should have a flat, blunt end on one side for breaking off rock, while a sharp end on the other side will be excellent for trimming excess rock away from the gems once found. The beginner also should have a screen pan for washing gravel free of sand and silt; a cold chisel for splitting open rocks, some kind of a magnifying glass for inspection of gems that are encased in rocks.

Excellent though perhaps unnecessary aids include a notebook for recording data on a find, as well as a knapsack for carrying all of this equipment — and any gems or mineral samples one might find.

The material in the right-hand side of this broken
piece of granite is gold ore from British Columbia.
When one finds a deposit as large as this, it can
be considered a valuable find; there should be more.

A few years ago, turquoise was not
considered valuable. Today, some of
it sells for as much as $400 per
pound. This particular variety is
called seafoam turquoise. This was
found in Mexico, is a light blue.

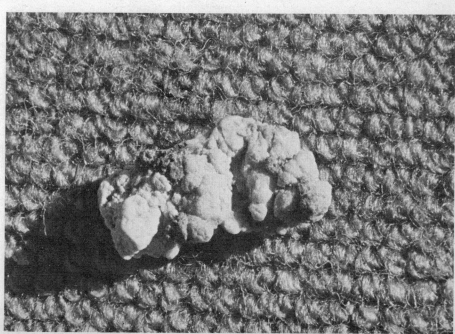

A Matter Of Indians

There Are Plenty Of Collectors Waiting To Buy Those Artifacts You May Find In A Burial Mound, An Old Campsite, Even An Open Field!

Chapter 20

DISCOVERING AND COLLECTING Indian relics can be profitable and provide one with a strong historical and archaeological knowledge. Relics are bits of history and scientific evidence from a limited, nonrenewable source. By collecting such relics, you also help insure that this source is not diminished.

Before starting a collection, contact your state archaeological society and find out your state and local laws governing archaeological finds. Most states prohibit digging on any archaeological site, except by trained personnel. Some state societies may inform you of good areas in which to search or you should be able to purchase state land maps from them. There are books, pamphlets and atlases available which detail the location of Indian villages, ceremonial sites and battlegrounds.

Locating a probable site is not difficult nor is there need to travel great distances from your home. David Austin of Oklahoma has collected over 1000 Indian artifacts, many of them found in a single quarter-acre site near his hometown.

If you live near a river or creek, you may be able to locate a rich site. A description given in an 1880 journal about the Plains Indian reveals their village was "located on the high ground within a quarter-mile from the river...the reason for this being to escape the flooding each year." With the possible exception of the desert tribes, the Indians almost always built their permanent camps in situations similar to this description.

If you do not live near a river, you may want to obtain land maps from your state geological society; from these

Left: Grinding stones used to pulverize corn are found in a wide variety of shapes and sizes. This one, now in the collection at California's Knott's Berry Farm, was turned up at site of an old Indian village in Colorado. (Below) Indians used the materials at hand to develop their crude tools and jewelry as this array illustrates.

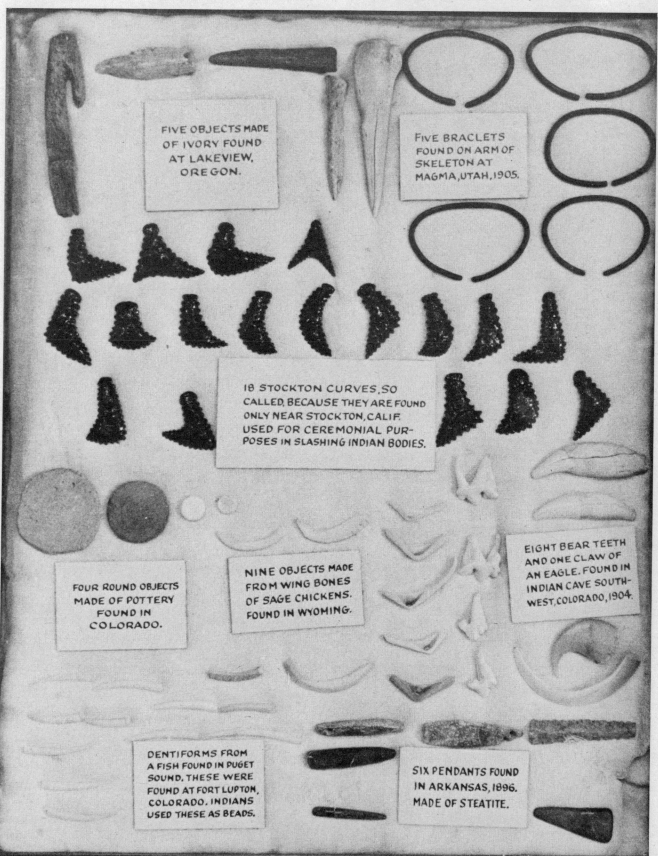

FIVE OBJECTS MADE OF IVORY FOUND AT LAKEVIEW, OREGON.

FIVE BRACLETS FOUND ON ARM OF SKELETON AT MAGMA, UTAH, 1905.

18 STOCKTON CURVES, SO CALLED, BECAUSE THEY ARE FOUND ONLY NEAR STOCKTON, CALIF. USED FOR CEREMONIAL PURPOSES IN SLASHING INDIAN BODIES.

EIGHT BEAR TEETH AND ONE CLAW OF AN EAGLE. FOUND IN INDIAN CAVE SOUTHWEST, COLORADO, 1904.

FOUR ROUND OBJECTS MADE OF POTTERY FOUND IN COLORADO.

NINE OBJECTS MADE FROM WING BONES OF SAGE CHICKENS. FOUND IN WYOMING.

DENTIFORMS FROM A FISH FOUND IN PUGET SOUND. THESE WERE FOUND AT FORT LUPTON, COLORADO. INDIANS USED THESE AS BEADS.

SIX PENDANTS FOUND IN ARKANSAS, 1896. MADE OF STEATITE.

Above: These finely chipped arrowheads were used to kill small game; weigh from 0.4 to 3.5 grams. (Below) Keeping an accurate record of the place, date of find can be important to archeological record. (Below) This unusual cog stone, as an example, was discovered in an area of Orange County, California, now being covered with houses.

WHAT WE KNOW AS "COG STONES" FOUND IN ORANGE COUNTY, CALIF. AND IN NO OTHER PLACE IN THE WORLD.

you should be able to locate several good areas. Remember, the area you are looking for should provide natural protection and plenty of water.

If the area you have selected was a well-used campsite, the first thing you will notice are many flakes of flint. Although these may seem numerous and insignificant, they should be saved; by examining them, you may be able to determine much about the tribes that occupied the area.

For instance, if there are a more or less equal number of small and large flakes, one may assume the relics were manufactured on the spot. However, if there are only small flakes, it is almost certain that these Indians traded for what is called preformed "blank." In other words, points were made into a rough shape by another tribe, then reworked into a fine shape by the tribe at this site. Examine the edges of the larger flakes. If you find there have been small flakes taken out, it is almost certain that these were used as knives or tools.

Keep accurate records as to where each relic is found, and, if possible, what type it is. As your collection grows, you will find it helpful to devise your own personal numbering system for later reference and work. If your digging is accompanied by photographs, drawings and notes, you will be helping to preserve a small part of man's last 20,000 years. If you can, work with or observe a trained archaeologist; otherwise in your digging you may be destroying more than you save.

Two of the best times to hunt are in the Winter and

Cheryl Lynn of Knott's Berry Farm displays a set of woven baskets by the Papago Indians of Arizona.

Searching for clay bowls at an old Indian campsite such as these is best accomplished after annual rains.

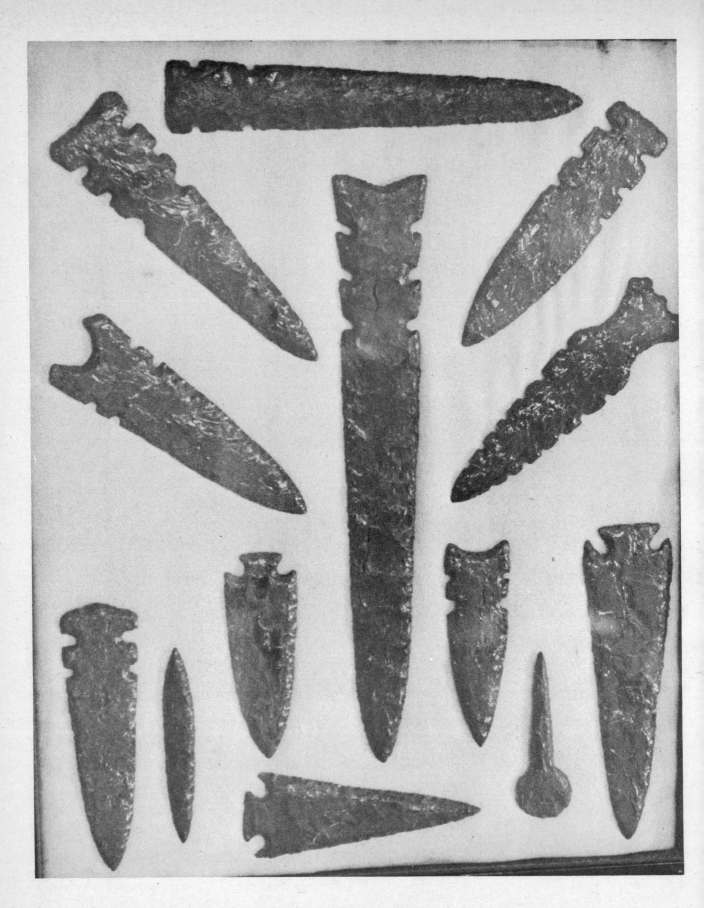

Indian spearheads discovered in California range from a minimum of three inches to eight inches overall length.

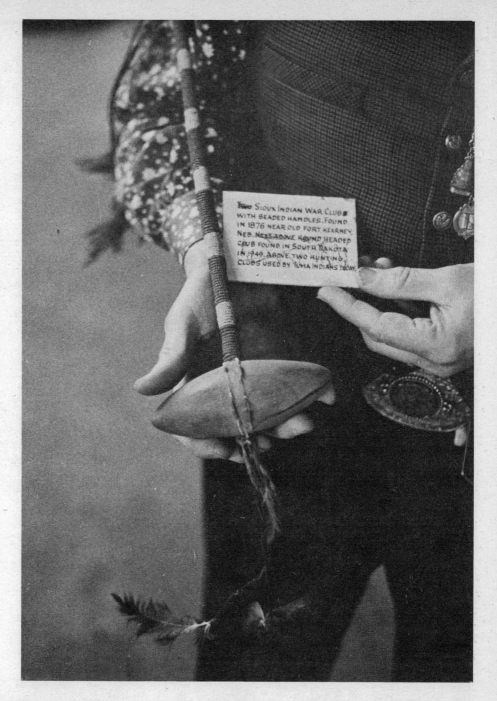

Sioux war club was discovered in nearly perfect condition. As card indicates, finder kept an accurate record of date and place of find.

Spring after a heavy rain. During these times, grass is almost gone and rains will wash away much of the topsoil.

Examine every rock at your site. Even if other collectors have been there before, you still may find many interesting artifacts such as choppers, scrapers, grinding stones, knife blades and celts.

There is basically little difference between scrapers and choppers except for size. Both were manufactured by percussion flaking. A hide scraper is long and fairly narrow, while choppers are thick and oval. Knives, like scrapers and choppers, will have had large flakes removed and additional smaller flakes cut along the edges where they have been sharpened.

Arrowheads come in many shapes and sizes. The true arrowheads will have small points which were hafted to an arrow. The bigger ones are dart and spear points which were hurled with an atlatl or spear thrower. The size of the point was not related to the size of the game hunted. If you might wonder how this is possible, here is the answer: The weight and momentum of the shaft is the real killer and the point only served to make an opening for the shaft. Many bison kill sites have yielded only small points.

Research has determined that the true arrowheads are the small, finely chipped points with an average weight of 1.1 grams and a weight range of 0.4 to 3.5 grams. Any point weighing more than 4.5 grams should be considered a dart or spear point.

A blunt is a point which has a rounded or flat tip. Most of the time, these will be about one-half-inch in length, but do range up to two inches. They were used to stun game such as birds, squirrel and rabbits and there is also a possibility they were used as a small tool. Unlike most stone tools, many times these were not manufactured deliberately, but were made from other points that had been broken.

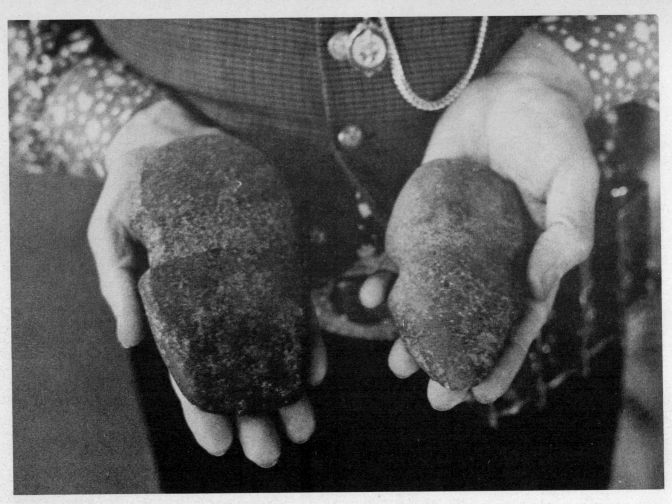

Hand-made stone axe heads such as these are common finds at old Indian campsites across North American continent. (Below) Enlarged several times its actual size, arrowhead indicates the hours of patient hand work that went into making each item. Note how individual chips were removed. This arrowhead is part of Knott's Berry Farm's collection.

This grinding stone was discovered in Arizona. Imagine the amount of work required to make a single loaf of bread using such crude equipment!

The tips of these broken points usually were made into small knife blades, while the base was reworked into a blunt.

Pricing relics, as with all collectibles, is determined by the condition of the artifact and by the law of supply and demand. If you have a relic you want to buy or sell, you need to know how much to ask or how much to pay for it. Although it varies greatly, the following price guide was drawn up with the help of several dealers.

Scrapers .... 50cents-$2

Choppers .... 75cents-$3

Knives
   a. Triangular .... $1-$5
   b. Tang .... $10-$35

Axes .... $5-$35

Bannerstones .... $25-$150

Celts .... $3-$10

Boatstones .... $10-$25

Arrowheads
   a. Common .... 35cents-$5
   b. Rare .... $5-$35

Pottery .... $10-$125

The price quoted for arrowheads includes two categories: common and rare. The rare points would be those such as Cumberland, Ohio fluted, Folsom and the various Yuma types. As a general rule, common type points are those which are found in great abundance such as the Gary, Washita and Ellis. The pottery price is quoted for a complete pot, with the main factors being size and shape.

Should you buy some of the more unusual relics, use caution. You may encounter dealers trying to sell fakes as genuine artifacts.

Never buy relics sight unseen, such as those from a mail

This display of arrowheads indicates the fact that some craftsmen tended to be experimental in their designs.

This rare rabbit stick was found by Russell Knott in the Joshua Tree National Monument grounds near Twenty-Nine Palms, California. Used much in the fashion of a boomerang, Indians threw it at small game to stun or kill the animal.

order house. Of course, many mail order dealers are honest, but due to the fact that the names of relics vary nationwide, it is possible to become confused.

The key factors in buying points are workmanship and general appearance. Most modern-made points are well shaped but poorly made. There will be a variety of large and small flakes all over the point or no flakes at all. On authentic points, large flakes will be found mainly on the body and small flaking along the edges. Points with no flake marks or a waxy sheen are obvious fakes. Any shine an authentic point once may have had should be long gone by the time it turns up in someone's shop.

It is harder to determine the authenticity of pottery. There are only two rules to help the inexperienced buyer. First, there is no such thing as glazed pottery of early Indian origin, for the Indian did not know of this technique. The other rule is to watch for charred clay pots. Most of the cooking was done by dropping round, red-hot stones into the pot with the food, so charring should be absent. Faked implements and tools usually can be recognized by being too well made and showing no signs of use or wear.

The American Indian has left a unique archeological history in the form of discarded relics such as flint arrowheads, chipped thunderbirds and smooth-ground tomahawk heads. These relics are available to the treasure hunter who exercises a little foresight and care.

Indians usually camped en masse along the large streams. Camps were built on large, flat, treeless spaces just above a high river bank for maximum visibility and protection from the sudden rising water of a flash flood.

Due to the passage of time, these areas now may be located in a grove of trees or under a grassy pasture. A good sign of a buried campsite is a fire-burned rock. Some limestone retains a reddish tint long after it has been burned and many stones will show coloration change from the surrounding rocks. Flint chips or obsidian chips are good markers of campsites, especially in areas where arrowhead materials are not natural minerals or rocks. Piles of sun-bleached, broken mussel shells on the river bank could be the remains of an Indian's lunch. Worked chips are an excellent sign. The Indians usually made arrowheads while in camp, but occasionally gathered on an isolated island in a creek or on a hillside away from the main camp to make their arrow points. The artifact hunter keeps a watch for tributary streams, animal trails or any time-worn path leading from a high bank to the water's edge.

Fortunately, the Indians weren't great housekeepers, so trash and used items were cast out the door and forgotten. A little digging around the burned rocks, piles of shells or flint chips could produce an exciting find. Use a hand trowel or an old spoon to scrape the layers of dirt off the artifacts. A reckless plunge of a spoon could shatter a string of bone beads. A small sifter comes in handy to separate the smaller artifacts from the dirt, especially in a lucrative area. Crumble the clods. They could hold a perfect point.

Besides the large campsites, explore the surrounding hills. Sometimes lookouts were posted or a few teepees might have been built beyond the edge of camp. The small camps will be found farther from the edge of the stream bank. If you locate a round, flat-topped mound of earth about fifteen feet in diameter, search the mound thoroughly. Teepees were built on these mounds as an added protection against the flash floods. The small streams had a tendency to overflow their banks, covering a greater surface area than the large rivers.

Hunting parties camped on little mesa-topped hills or on heights with naturally terraced slopes. These sites can hold rich finds.

Caves can be artifact gold mines. The Indians often occupied caves with wide mouths and a ceiling of six feet or more. When the floor of a cave became littered, the Indians carried dirt into these homes and covered the refuse. Layer upon layer of artifacts were piled-up for generations.

Arrowheads can be located anywhere. The many Indian battles left the ground strewn with relics. The Indians hunted for food, played games and lost their possessions just like any other people.

When you find a good location, don't be afraid of getting dirty and crawling on all fours; when the eyes are far from the ground they miss a lot. Crawl the small washes through the campsites, where running water has carried numerous artifacts into miniature gullies.

There are recent re-interpretations of U.S. Forest Service regulations concerning casual collection of Indian arrowheads and other artifacts on Forest Service lands. Under terms of an "emergency directive" placed in force in January, 1974, artifacts and "objects of antiquity" were redefined to include such items as Indian arrow points and beads. On the basis of the directive, government attorneys have advised the Forest Service that collection of such articles can be accomplished legally only under terms of special permits issued to museums, universities and similar institutions. Necessary permits for collecting arrowheads on national forest lands are issued by the Secretary of Agriculture. Violators are subject to $500 fines and ninety-day jail terms. The basic Antiquities Act applies to all public lands, including that under Bureau of Land Management jurisdiction.

Indian jewelry, before they learned uses of silver and gem stones such as turquoise often was crude, made of nothing more than a smooth stone that was tediously drilled for a hole, then worn about the neck on a thong.

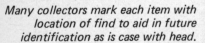

Many collectors mark each item with location of find to aid in future identification as is case with head.

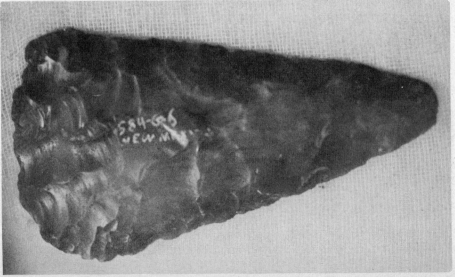

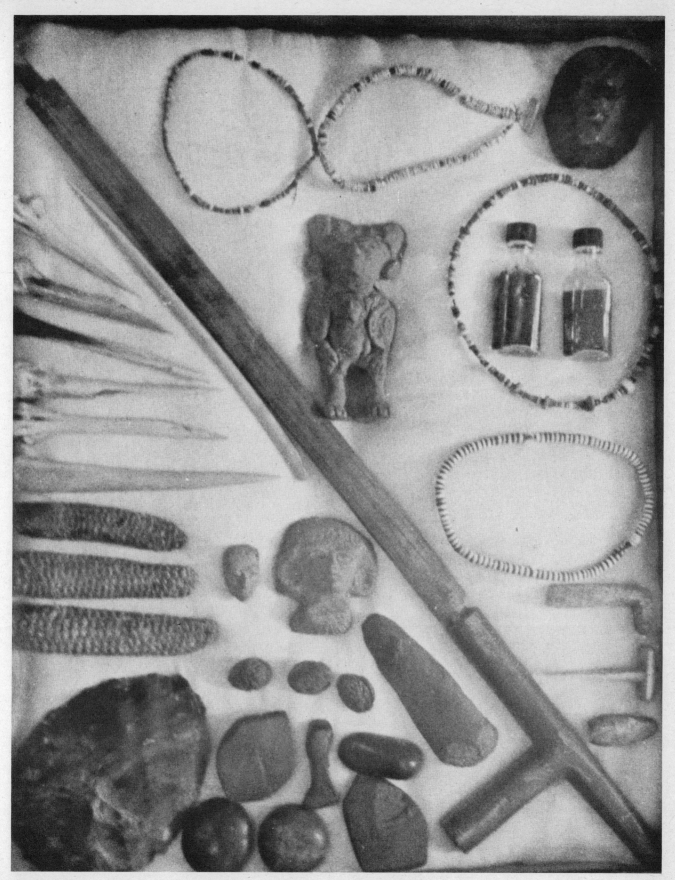

Pipe, tools, figures, et al., in this unique display all were found in South Dakota. Before starting to dig at any site, check with local officials to make certain that the law does not prohibit such investigations of Indian ruins.

Finding, Cleaning & Selling Coins

Chapter 21

Easily Found And More Easily Lost, Coins Can Be Of Incredible Value, Providing You Know What To Look For And What To Do With Them!

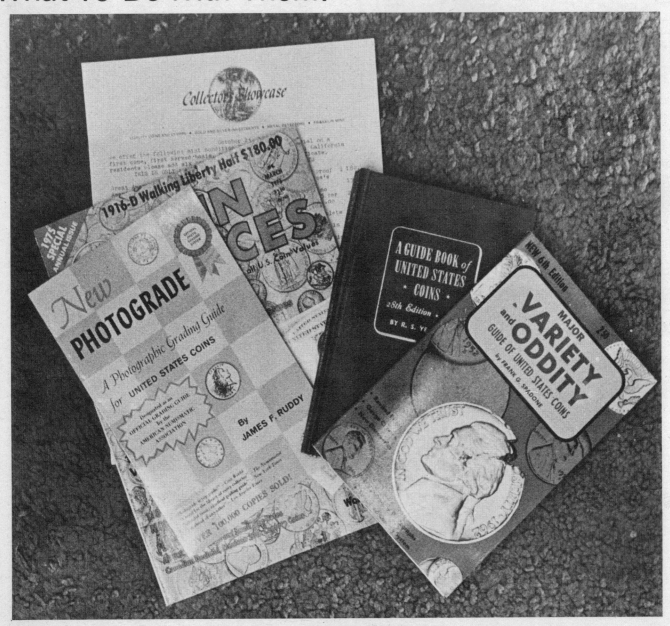

Before rushing out to a garage sale to stock up on rare and valuable coins, it is best to know what you might be buying with your hard-earned cash. Books such as these can do much to help the neophyte in buying, selling coins.

This 1874-S in uncirculated condition will bring about $350. A trade dollar, it is larger than standard size.

C OINS ARE SCATTERED everywhere about the country, hiding in singles, pairs and clumps. Coins like to hide in sand, soil and clay; on the bottom of lakes, rivers and ponds; behind fireplace stones and under building corners. Every day treasure hunters with metal detectors find coins that exceed their face value, some by as much as 100 times.

Few coins are buried deep enough to escape detection by an electronic metal locator, except where fill dirt may cover them at considerable depth. With these exceptions, a metal detector is supposed to sense every buried coin, even those resting on edge. Single coins lost for thirty years and more around parks and similar places seldom go deeper than five inches into the earth. In the North, where frost works the ground, coins lost for thirty years or so may stabilize around two inches under the surface, depending upon the type of soil.

A large number of rare U.S. coins are worth a considerable amount to collectors. Many are valued at several thousand dollars; an 1804 silver dollar, for example, has an estimated value of $30,000. Many of the coins circulated during the mid-1800s today are considered highly desirable collector items.

The key to determining the value of a coin first is to establish the degree of wear. A coin in nearly new condition may be worth several hundred dollars, while the same coin in poor condition would be of little or no value as a collector's item. However, most coins will clean beautifully. Those lost to heavy corrosion, if in demand, can be sold to a collector for use as a "filler," filling out his collection.

This 1802 Liberty, while circulated and worn, still is worth $6500 on today's collector market. Note the thick plastic cover, which is used to avoid further wear on the coin.

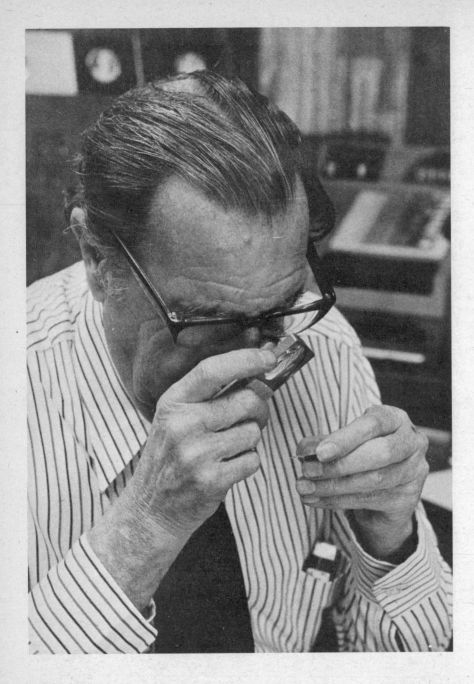

Jim Burnett of Collector's Showcase in Orange, California, offers close inspection to a rare gold coin as a part of appraisal. This particular coin turned out to be counterfeit.

The inclination of many oldtimers to hoard their money rather than carry it with them increases the likelihood of finding coins which are not worn excessively.

In addition to grade (condition of the coins) and date (rarity), the price of a coin is also determined by popularity. For example, a Lincoln cent, one of the most popular types of coins with collectors today, with a mintage of less than one-half million would be worth about $125 in average condition. A "seated Liberty dime," which is not as popular but with about the same mintage, would be worth only $4 as of this writing.

The history of American coinage reflects the history of America, itself. The first American mint was established on May 27, 1652, in Boston. Although the next few years provided some interesting history for American coins, those that are the prime target of treasure hunters belong to a much later period. The decimal system of coinage was adopted by Congress in 1792. In that same year, a mint was set up in Philadelphia and the basic denominations were established in copper, silver and gold. The first copper coins were issued in 1793. These included a one-cent and half-cent coin. The rarest of these coins is a 1796 half-cent piece that has an estimated value of over $2,000 in average condition. The 1793 one-cent coin follows closely behind with an estimated value of $1400, in average condition.

The second part of the Nineteenth Century produced several new coin types. These included: two-cent coins, three-cent coins, the five-cent nickel, twenty-cent coins and two new gold pieces, a three-dollar gold coin and a four-dollar piece. The rarest two-cent piece, minted in 1854 at the Denver mint, has an estimated value of $1800, in average condition. Oddly, of all the new coins issued during this period, the nickel was the only one to remain in public favor and live to the present time. The rarest of these early nickels was minted in 1871 and has an average value of $50 today.

Although coins of an odd type, like the two-cent piece, are considered collector's items, many more common coins

This 1860-O silver dollar is one of 515,000 minted, but still is worth $575 when in uncirculated condition.

Proof sets are an excellent way for the new collector to get started at minimum expense, although certainly not as exciting as discovering ghost town gold. This set sells today at $11, when it is purchased from bona fide dealer.

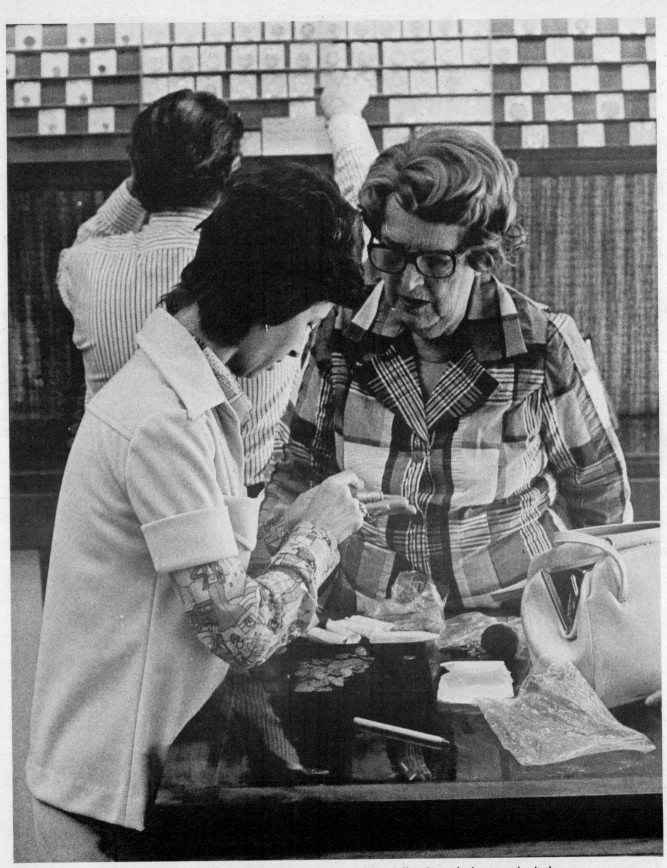

The appraiser on the left carefully inspects a sack of dimes and old silver dollars brought into a coin dealer by a collector. Although some of the coins were quite old they were of little value on the collector market, as they had been circulated. Instead, they were purchased for their silver content alone rather than coin value.

These uncirculated 50 peso Mexican coins are of solid gold. Weight is 1.20 ounces, making them worth more than $200 each at current gold rate.

also have rare dates which mean high value. As an example, the 1873cc dime in average condition has an extimated value of approximately $600. A dime with an 1894s date is considered a real find and has an estimated value of approximately $12,000.

Silver dollars first were issued in 1794. The U.S. Mint continued to turn out silver dollars until 1804, when silver dollar production ceased for a period of 36 years. There are a number of rare silver dollars, many of which prove a real treasure for the finder. An 1804 silver dollar is probably the rarest of all American coins and has been valued at up to $30,000. An 1895 silver dollar, although not worth a fortune, would make a nice find with an estimated value of $4,500. Even an 1873cc silver dollar would raise a little joy around most treasure hunting camps as it has an estimated value of upward of $850.

Gold coins were first issued in the United States in 1795 and circulated freely until 1933. Most of the available supply of gold coinage was melted under the Gold Redemption Act of 1933 and now rests in bullion in our treasury vaults at Fort Knox, Kentucky. For this reason, gold coins are scarce today and command high prices as collector items.

Contrary to popular belief, it is legal to own gold coins as part of your collection, provided they are dated before 1933.

Many gold coins that are of great value today, circulated

Those old coins that grandmother used to hoard for grocery money can be of value simply for their silver content.

These U.S. coin proof sets have original face value of only 91 cents each. The 1954 set at top now sells for $24.50; the 1956 set is worth $11; the 1963 set, $5.50. A 1974 set is worth $11, simply on the basis of the fact that the total number of coins minted in the United States was a great deal lower that year, thus increasing rarity.

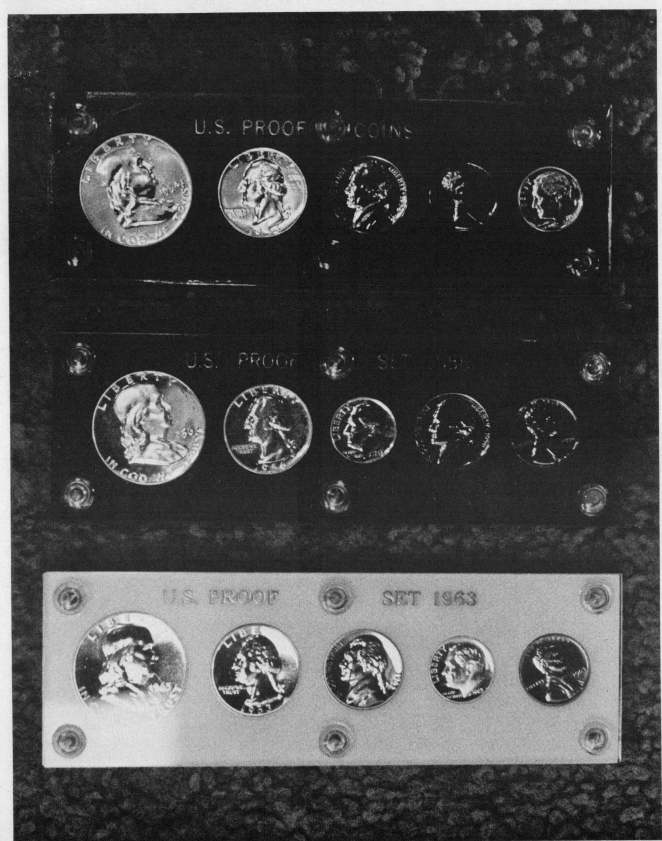

Left: Value of 1868 shield nickels is $75-$275; the 1883-C, $40-$350; 1938-D is worth $20-$650; 1943-D is a common variety. Value depends upon rarity, condition. Above: Closed circuit teletype advises gold values.

freely during pioneer days and most are unaccounted for. In addition to the official United States issues, private or territorial gold coins were struck to provide a local medium of exchange, particularly in the Western states.

Private gold coinage was struck in both coin and ingot form. These coins range in value from a few hundred to several thousand dollars each on today's market. Regular issues of U.S. gold coins also were used in the mid-Nineteenth Century and the smaller denominations generally prove the best bet for rare finds.

As an example, a five-dollar gold piece with an 1879cc date is worth approximately $700, in average condition. These five-dollar gold pieces were minted between 1839 and 1908 and are considered as collector's items, regardless of the dates. The $20 gold piece is the rarest of this type and is valued up to $6500. Another rare gold piece of a later date is the 1931d. One of these coins in average condition will bring upward of $1600.

The system used to separate coins into value groups can be helpful to know. A coin's condition, date and mint mark determine its numismatic value, no matter how slight or how great. The grading formulas are:

About Good or Fair (AG-F): A badly worn coin; parts of the design are missing; the date still is legible, though almost worn off.

Good (G): A worn coin with all details smooth but unmistakable.

Very Good (VG): It shows lots of wear, but some detail points not worn smooth.

Fine (F): Wear shows on all high points, but all features clear; the design and lettering are clean.

Very Fine (VF): With noticeable wear, portions of the original new luster still are visible and details are crisp.

Extremely Fine (XF): Only highest points of detailing show wear.

About Uncirculated: Those coins which have not known circulation, but which have been mishandled or jostled in the bag; coins have a fresh-from-the-mint luster, but may have some scratches.

Uncirculated: New coins intended for circulation, these may have a tarnish from long-term storage or may have slight scratches; coins close to being without flaw.

Proof: These special-issue coins sold by a mint to collectors have flawless mirror surfaces.

Mint marks are usually placed away from easy notice on the reverse or back sides. They are as follows:

p: Philadelphia, Pennsylvania
 (not used except on 1942-43 war nickels)
s: San Francisco, California
d: Denver, Colorado
d: Dahlonega, Georgia
 (gold only)
c: Charlotte, North Carolina
 (gold only)
cc: Carson City, Nevada
o: New Orleans, Louisiana

To determine the date and mint mark, look closely with a magnifying glass at each coin discovered. Collecting this data sometimes will require removal of soil, sand and corrosion from the coin face. Do not chemically brighten coins with commercial cleansers. Most collectors prefer the naturally aged surface of old metal — something that, once removed, cannot be restored. Don't remove anything more than grime.

Clean the coins from each day's search immediately after returning to your base of operations. This practice will prevent corrosion from continuing or perhaps even starting. Coins often remain in the ground for many years without any sign of corrosion, while exposure to the air will start the process.

Light corrosion can be handled by soaking the coins in pure olive oil for several days. Soak the coin in the oil until the corrosion can be rubbed off with a paper towel.

This is going to sound a little strange, but moderately corroded coins can be cleaned by soaking them in Worcestershire sauce. This method may take a few days of soaking and a light scrubbing with a light brass wire brush to get the coin cleaned. After the corrosion has been removed, give the coin a light coat of olive oil to preserve the surface. For heavy corrosion, imbed the coin in a potato, as the starch in the potato has a dissolving effect on corrosion. After a few days, when heavy corrosion has been removed, follow this by using the methods for light and moderate corrosion, thus completing the cleaning.

EARLIER IN THIS tome, we made passing mention of relics, artifacts and — what the treasure hunters call — collectibles.

Bill Mahan, the old pro out of Garland, Texas, opines that "relics and artifacts are the incidentals, the by-products of treasure hunting," but often these are worth their weight in the gold you may not find.

"Relic hunting is something you don't have to make an effort to do," Mahan says. "Just go ahead with your usual treasure hunting activities and, if you don't find monetary treasure, the chances are good that you will, at least, come home with some kind of relics."

The state of Texas, where Mahan headquarters, is sprinkled with old battlefields of forgotten wars and Indian actions, abandoned forts, old missions, ghost towns and countless other places that can offer various types of relics. The search, of course, usually is simplified with the use of a good metal detector.

"To most people, treasure is one thing — money or riches," Mahan offers, then adds his own philosophy. "To me, treasure means many things: antiques, relics, artifacts, old musty books, maps and manuscripts.

"To the person interested in these things, not for the intrinsic values, but for the monetary reward alone, they should not worry. Literally anything you find can be converted into cash. The markets are many for anything that is old."

Because of his stature and long standing in the field, Mahan has in his files letters from collectors, antique dealers and museums throughout the country.

"Actually, with almost anything I dig up, I have a ready market waiting for me to let them know what I have," he says.

Modern archeologists, when on a dig, first check out the story completely with all the known records of history, then carefully search until they find the correct area. Even

Chapter 22
RELICS & ARTIFACTS
While You're Looking For The End Of The Rainbow, There Are Residual Benefits Worth Lots Of Loot!

The answer to every treasure hunter's dream is lost gold, such as this cache discovered by Bill Mahan, but he is quick to insist residual finds can be rewarding, too.

"I always select what I think will be a productive spot and lay out a straight line across the area, much the same as the archeologist does to dig his ditch. Then, starting at one side, I proceed carefully across the selected spot. If nothing is detected on this strip, I then select another angle and again make the straight line and again literally explore underground across the given area," Mahan explains. "When I detect some bit of metal, regardless of how small an indication, (I have found old .45/70 lead bullets at depths down to twelve inches) I then start to explore the complete area." When on a location known to contain either treasures or artifacts and relics, he usually lays the area off into lanes with cord tied to nails driven into the ground. These trails are five or six feet wide and up to one hundred feet long where space permits. By carefully working down each lane slowly, you are assured of complete success. You can recover each and every piece of metal in the entire area.

On one trip, Mahan was searching for the site of the first settlement by white men in Texas, the site of Fort St. Louis. Here were the first religious ceremonies, the first marriage and the first birth of a white man in Texas. This was the settlement for Rene Robert Cavalier Sieur de La Salle founded on the shores of Texas in 1685 near what is today known as Matagorda Bay.

Having first been lost in a severe storm at sea, he had supposedly mistaken the Paso Cavallo for the mouth of the Mississippi, the spot where he had intended to found his colony. The Paso Cavallo is where Matagorda Bay empties into the Gulf of Mexico and was named Paso Cavallo (Horse Pass) by the early Spanish explorers of Texas who used this point to swim the horses ashore from their ships when they first brought them from Spain.

After landing and building a temporary fort, La Salle had decided that he was not at the Mississippi and started

when reasonably sure of the area, they must first "trench" it to see if they do find the many bits of metal, pieces of glass, old nails, charred wood or scorched pieces of stone that indicate the presence of houses or settlements. To do this, they usually dig a trench twelve to eighteen inches wide and possibly eighteen inches deep. They may have to dig for dozens or even hundreds of feet in length to prove or disprove the area before starting a complete dig.

It is easier to take your detector and literally dig the area without so much as ever turning over one shovel of dirt.

With the aid of one of his D-Tex metal detectors, Mahan and friends discovered this hoard of artifacts at an old military campsite. Collectors provide a ready market for such items. Mahan boasts a market for almost every find.

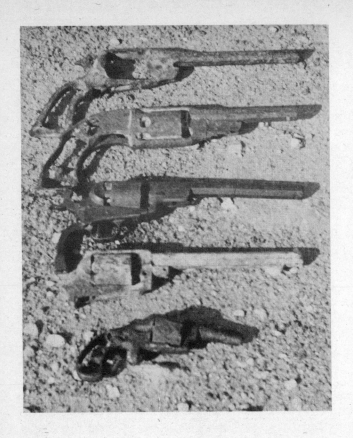

exploration trips eastward, trying to locate the intended spot for the French colony. During one of these exploration trips, he was assassinated by one of his own men. During his absence the Karanka Indians, noted for their cruel treachery, had tricked the people still in the fort into giving them entry and a massacre followed with all being killed except for a few of the children who were taken as prisoners.

The Spanish authorities in Mexico, hearing the French had a fortification on Texas soil, then known as New Spain, sent a detachment of soldiers under Captain Alonzo de Leon in 1689 to find and destroy La Salle's fort.

He found only the crumbling ruins and a few skeletons scattered about on the prairie. According to the report of de Leon's chronicler of the expedition, "The fort was in ruins, with the guns (cannon) turned over, broken harquebuses were all about and the chests of the settlers had been broken open and their personal belongings scattered and blown about by the winds."

La Salle had landed eight cannon and later, when the Spanish returned to establish a fort near the same spot, they remounted the cannon for their own use. Here, they first established what is still known as La Bahia Mission. Later, the mission was moved to another spot, now called Mission Valley. Still later the mission was again moved and located at the present site near Goliad. The existing records show that the cannon were again moved also.

Upper left: These rusted old guns were found at a river crossing at Red River Station in North Texas. (Below) The Goliad mission has been restored and now is under guard.

At left are some of the military items discovered with aid of a metal detector at old fort. (Above) Artifacts unearthed at scene of long-forgotten Civil War battle.

Later, during the Texas-Mexican War, La Bahia Mission was captured by the Texans and these same cannon were used by the Texans against the Mexicans. When Sam Houston gave the order to Colonel James Walker Fannin to bury or hide his cannon and retreat, he apparently failed to do so quickly enough and consequently, during the ensuing battle, was captured, along with the remainder of his men and, on March 27, 1836, was executed by the order of Santa Ana. The bodies were burned and all were buried in a common grave. This is today a shrine for thousands of Texans who visit the spot each year.

One of the cannons was later found in the ruins of the walls of the old mission and for years was on display in the court house in Goliad. It was marked Louis XIV on the breach. It is now on display in the Espirito Santo Mission just across the San Antonio River from the La Bahia Mission. The whole area is rich in history and legend as well as the many tales of buried Spanish gold. Across town and about four miles West are also the ruins of the mission Neustra Senores Del Rosario established in 1754 for the Cujans Nation by the Franciscan monks. Today, it stands a crumbling mass of shadowy ruins, an ideal habitat for large Texas rattlers.

"In starting my search for the old Fort St. Louis, I was hoping to be able to trail down the cannons and possibly some of the other small arms and relics. We camped near the suspected site and spent the night fighting off the large mosquitos. I had to sleep in my down-filled sleeping bag in 98-degree heat to get away from them," Mahan recounts.

"The next morning we got an early start and before long were on the site that most nearly fitted the description."

It was "located on a flat plain, on a high bluff over-looking the river and situated about two leagues above where the river fed into Matagorda Bay and back about two crossbow shots from the river."

Mahan at once started searching through the heavy underbrush, all the while keeping eyes and ears open for rattlesnakes. He and his party were soon getting indications on their D-Tex detectors and the digging, which was difficult in the hard, sun-baked soil, commenced. They found small bits and pieces of old copper, green with age and possibly pieces of cooking and eating utensils. Other pieces of rusted and tarnished metal had the appearance of possibly being parts of the mechanism of old guns.

The best find was an old bronze, hard-hammered handle from some type of trunk or chest. This today is one of Mahan's most prized possessions. The area that was once a barren plain is now grown over with heavy brush, prickly pear cactus and high weeds. As the members of the expedition only had a short time to stay, it was agreed it would be better to leave and come back in the Fall or Winter after all the vegetation had died and possibly the rains had softened the sun-baked soil.

"We were anxious to get over to Goliad to the old La Bahia Mission as we felt certain we would have all sorts of good luck on the battlefield and expecially around the crumbling walls of the old mission where most of the fighting took place.

"We soon arrived at La Bahia Mission and a sad surprise was in store for us. The University of Texas Archeological Department was conducting a complete dig of the mission area and hunting was not allowed in the area. We were

Bill Mahan, Jr., displays an ancient cap-and-ball pistol discovered at the ruins of an old Texas military fort.

told by the watchman that we could search all we pleased outside of the immediate mission area.

"Our time was short, as we only had the balance of the day to hunt in before returning to Dallas the next morning. We immediately started walking over the entire area to familiarize ourselves with it before starting hunting. We found some old stone ruins between the mission and the river, also learned that part of the old town had been located there."

There are also stories that the old-timers remember that, while swimming in the river below the old mission when they were boys, when the river was low they could stand on the round, smooth barrel of an old cannon and stick their feet in the mouth.

Searching across the road from the mission and in the area where some of the fighting took place, the D-Tex detectors kept the searchers busy digging up all sorts of old relics. For a good beginning, one man located and dug up

Bill Mahan, Jr., poses with some of the artifacts discovered near ruins of an old Spanish mission in Texas.

the remains of a gold-plated sword hilt. It had evidently been lost in the battle as it was all twisted and broken. Later, Mahan came up with the remains of an old broken sword blade. The blade appears to have been hand made and is assumed to be Texan. The hilt had the eagle insignia engraved on it.

Other interesting finds were pieces of old guns, knives, a brass butt plate from an old rifle, piece of a muzzleloader lock, several pieces of copper and one hand-hammered concho, possibly from some decorated saddle.

Another of the old forts of Texas that should be a happy hunting ground is old Fort Griffin. One of the later forts to be built in Texas, it was to protect the settlers, travelers and hunters on the far frontier. It was built in 1867 and immediately became the headquarters for the many buffalo hunters. The civilian settlement was located just North of the fort and quickly became a last outpost for the outfitters

for the buffalo hunters and in 1877 was one of the largest centers for this activity with over 1500 crews operating from there.

A buffalo hunting crew usually consisted of three men — one hunter and two skinners. The equipment usually was about the same with all outfits and was about as follows: At least one wagon with either mules or oxen. The big Sharps rifle was standard equipment (the old reliable of the plains) — this was usually the .50 caliber, with plenty of ammunition, skinning knives, whetstones and possibly a saddle horse or two for scouting.

The accepted way of hunting was to scout till the grazing herds were located. They then would either sneak up within range or hunt from a stand. One hunter could usually kill enough in a few hours to keep two skinners busy all day. A day's kill was usually thirty to forty head and the hunters usually received about twenty-five cents per hide delivered to the trading post.

At Fort Griffin, the first big firm of hide traders, the Mooar Brothers, established their headquarters. There the hunters outfitted themselves and from there thousands of hides were shipped East each year.

"This should be a good area for some serious treasure hunting. I have not as yet had the opportunity to give it a good search. I was there only one time, a hot August day when the thermometer was at about 110 degrees in the shade and no shade," Mahan recalls. "My friend and fellow hunter, Jim Koethy, and I were returning from a search a little farther West and decided to stop and look it over for future hunting. We did drive to the old fort area and immediately upon turning on his D-Tex, Jim had a good indication. Digging down about six inches, he was rewarded with an old army spoon, possibly lost many years ago. When we return, we intend to go to the site of the old civilian settlement to do our hunting."

It was wild and deadly as only a frontier outpost could be and killings occurred almost nightly. Many a buffalo hunter, in town to deliver a load of hides and collect his gold, never lived to spend it. What the outlaws, crooked gamblers, saloon operators and dance hall girls didn't get, the prostitutes of the civilian settlement did. You may feel certain that there are several good caches still hidden around the old town site.

Another of the many good spots in Texas for the relic hunter is what is called Tenth Cavalry Creek. This is located northwest of Wichita Falls and is named after a company of the Tenth Cavalry that was massacred there. The story from the son of one of the army scouts was that a company of Negro cavalry from Fort Sill, Oklahoma, was on a scouting action against the Indians of the area. They had camped for the night and next morning, before daylight, the scout had left camp to scout ahead the intended route for the day. He had been gone from camp for some time when he heard shots and yells coming from the direction of the camp. He

Bob Shelton, a noted Texas hunter of relics, displays some of religious artifacts discovered in old mission in Mexico. However, caution should be exercised, with understanding of the laws, in searching foreign ground.

immediately assumed that a large body of Indians was attacking while most of the camp was still in their bedrolls. Realizing what had happened, he quickly rode for help.

By the time they got back to camp, the Indians were through with their grisly work. The battle ranged over a wide area and all the soldiers were killed. They were all buried in a common grave.

This spot should not be hard to find and the relic hunter should have a field day here. You should be able to find old guns, pieces of guns, bayonets, uniform buttons, possibly even a few scattered coins and plenty of old ammunition as well as some Indian artifacts.

One enthusiastic treasure hunter has had quite a bit of accidental luck in relics. Even though he has only started recently, his finds have been extremely interesting.

This is Dave Zimmerman of Garland, Texas, who started out to try to locate all old ghost towns and forts in his vicinity. He has developed the habit of searching all old, abandoned houses that he happens to find. In one of these he had searched all around the yard and the lower floor of and old, fallen-down two story pre-Civil War home and headed up the stairs. As he came out on the landing at the head of the stairs, he thought he had a faint indication. Re-tuning his D-Tex and turning on the senstive meter, he found he had a good indication.

He immediately started prying around on that section of the floor and found a secret compartment that came open when he pulled on the edge of the top stair tread. He did not find a miser's hoard of gold or silver. Instead, he saw a large book and lying on top of it was an old style ladies broach which had attracted his detector. The book turned out to be a good find after all. It was a first edition of Webster's dictionary, published in 1845; Another relic virtually worth its weight in gold.

Another of his finds was at an old stage station near Sherman, Texas. Here he found the remains of an old revolver and several pieces of metal scroll work used to decorate the coaches. In his hunting, he has learned more history and more about the country than ever before. He has found one old town site — the town of Eureka — and in searching around it, among other things, found the remains of an old grist mill. The lower stone with the axle was still in place. It was about twenty-four inches below the surface and was driven by a water wheel. Where the old mill pond once stood he located a large area that gives a terrific reading on his metal detector. He probed it and says it is a large metal plate or the top of an old safe or chest that, when probed, gives off a hollow sound. He intends to dig it out sometime when the weather is cool and the soil soft from winter rains.

Another successful treasure hunter is Don (Doc) Laster of Dallas, Texas. He spends his time searching out stories and tracing them out. Naturally, he does not find something every time he goes out, but treasure hunting is like selling. It is the law of averages that pays off. And, as the salesman says, "You gotta make calls to get results."

The Mahans, father and son, display some of their finds, which comprise a literal fortune in artifacts and relics. The senior Mahan was a successful treasure hunter before he began manufacturing electronic treasure hunting gear.

Abandoned houses such as this may be found in virtually any area, especially in the rural sections. Such ancient structures usually can yield untold quantities of relics, if one exercises care in searching, knows where to look.

This cache of Confederate bills was discovered in a tin box in foundation of an old Texas house.

Laster has been known to get on a location and work all day, all night and well into the next day without stopping to eat or rest. He is a firm believer that the secret to successful treasure hunting is good stories and lots of complete research. Then it is only a matter of lots of hard work. He has proved his theory correct many times over.

"Doc and I had been in Arkansas and decided to drop by Arkadelphia to visit another of my many treasure hunting friends, Keith Tudor," Mahan says. "We spent the night camped outside of town and early next morning went in to see Keith. He immediately proposed a small hunt in the area to check out an old story of gold supposedly buried during one of the battles of the Civil War that was fought nearby. The party burying the gold was killed next day and never had the opportunity to tell his family where it was buried."

The area was covered with high weeds and almost impassable, but the trio finally managed to cover the suspected spot fairly well. All they found was an old wall-mounting coffee grinder, a few spoons and a couple of pieces of old knives. They decided that either it was not the correct area or someone had beat them to it.

"Having about three hours left on our hands, we decided to search the area we thought was the old battlefield. Keith had been told that after the battle the ground throughout the orchard was covered with the dead. The Southern boys were buried in the cemetery, but the Yankees were buried where they fell.

"Starting across the area, I was the first to find anything. I had a faint indication and getting to my knees I used my hunting knife to dig the sandy soil. At about nine inches deep I found a lone rifle slug — .45/70 — all white with lead oxide. It had been in the earth for over one hundred years"

Above: John Messina and Bill Mahan inspect relics found at the site of Fernandina French fort and trading post. (Below) Closer view of the finds made at Fernandina site.

With the aid of a modern detector unit, this cache of coins was discovered in the foundation of an old building. The value as collector items was much greater than the actual face value.

Altogether, Mahan found fourteen rifle slugs. Some were only a few inches below the surface, others were as deep as twelve inches. He also found parts of an old Springfield rifle, broken horseshoes, an old axe, an eye hoe and other pieces of unknown metal devices. Doc's finds were about the same. Keith, who was just a beginner and had not as yet mastered his detector, found only one of the old bullets, but still he did find the prizes of the day. These were a Confederate bayonet about ten inches deep and the nose of an explosive shell. He also found some metal parts from an old cannon.

Texas is full of good places for the relic hunter. At this writing, Mahan is checking a good one. In reading the records of the La Salle expedition, the Texan was surprised and impressed with the report of one of La Salle's trips in search of the Mississippi. He had traveled northeasterly from St. Louis on Matagorda Bay and, after crossing several rivers, came to the villages of the Cenis Indians. They were friendly and invited them to stay a few days in their villages.

To quote the record of this visit, "We were surprised to see the treasures of the Spaniards on every hand. Piles of gold and silver coins, silver utensils, spoons, lamps, harquebuses, pieces of armor, swords and other equipment apparently taken from the Spanish in some former raids."

Reading this was enough to get Mahan on the trail of the Cenis. He had inquired of everyone he knew from that area and had searched out all ancient maps available with no great luck, when he purchased an old book with rotting leather bindings and crisp brown pages.

"Imagine my surprise when, later, looking it over, I found an original ancient map that showed all the things for which I had been searching — villages of the Cenis, locations and areas. I now had the area I was interested in pinned down, so all I had to do was get more information from some of the residents of that region.

"I was having no luck at all when suddenly I have now hit the jackpot. An elderly lady tells me she was born and lived for the greater part of her life in the Piney woods. That is exactly where I was thinking of looking and,

Graniteware utensils such as those popular at the turn of century have become sought after by today's collectors.

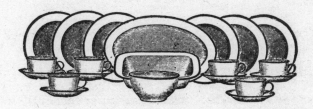

Almost any type of antique pottery or tableware can be turned to cash on today's antique market. Of course, the better the condition, the better the price to the finder.

While kitchen utensils may seem rather commonplace to the neophyte, there is a broad variety of antique cooking tools that may be discovered and turned to liquid assets.

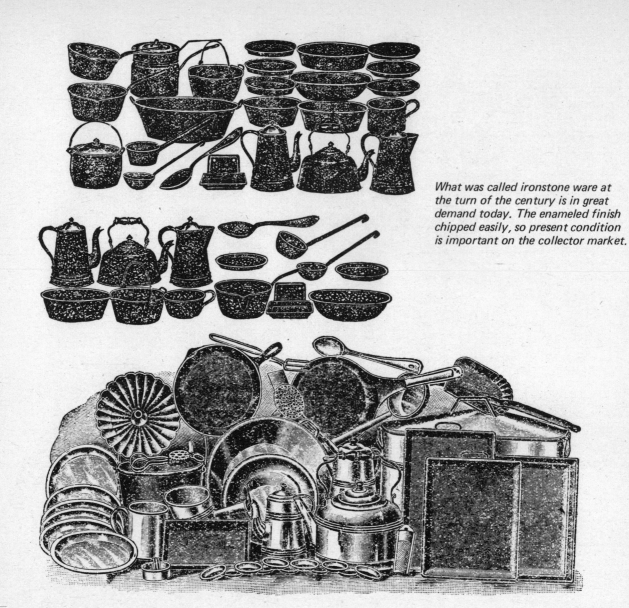

What was called ironstone ware at the turn of the century is in great demand today. The enameled finish chipped easily, so present condition is important on the collector market.

according to the map, would be right on the edge of the Cenis country.

"She told me that, as a young girl, she had little to do and was in the habit of going into the woods and playing around what they called The Mounds. One day, when idly digging into one of the mounds, she found a large amount of old-looking money. Quickly digging out all she could carry in her hands, she immediately rushed home to show her mother. Her mother, upon seeing the money and learning where it came from, was horrified and made her return to the ancient grave and take back all the money to the hole where she had dug it out. After covering it back up, she was told by her mother that it was haunted money and belonged to the dead. She made her promise never to go near the spot again and never to tell about it."

The women kept her promise not to tell for over seventy years. Mahan was the fortunate one she finally told. Now, with the detailed map and directions she gave him, he is prepared to go in search of this treasure.

But one doesn't have to find the pot of gold at the end of a dubious rainbow to make his treasure hunting efforts pay for themselves, as was indicated earlier.

For example, there is great interest among collectors in early American kitchen utensils, pantry accessories and similar items. Old graniteware also is at a premium, with the prices on such relics of a bygone age increasing almost daily. Also of great interest to collectors is agateware, which featured a mottled coating over the metal.

When the finish was chipped, the utensil usually was discarded. The pieces that are not chipped or otherwise damaged are almost priceless today, but even an item that shows some damage may prove to be of value to an individual who is trying to fill out a collection!

These utensils usually came in mottled shades of blue and gray, but there were more exotic shades, too, and these bring more money. If you find an old agateware pan that is rose-colored, tan, aqua or a pastel green, it might be well to have it appraised by an antique dealer — or even several of them — before putting it on the market. Perhaps the most rare of all is that utensil that has a vivid yellow finish!

There also are types of glassware that once were considered cheap and no great care was taken to preserve them. Among these is a type of glassware, usually in a transparent pink color, called "carnival glass." These were cheap dishes and bowls that were offered as prizes in the first three decades of this century at carnivals, fairs and similar

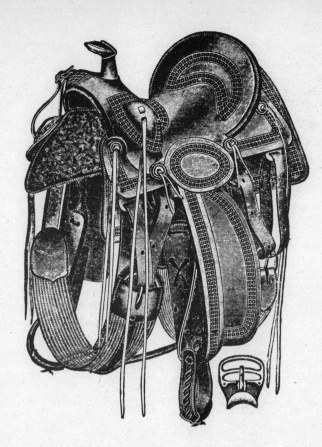

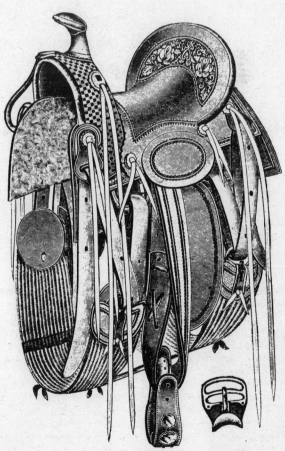

Among the collectors of memorabilia, such items as early saddles bring high prices. This Washington model stock saddle sold by Sears, Roebuck in 1906 was priced at only $30.59 then, but is worth several times that now.

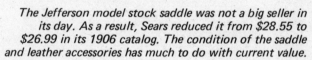

The Jefferson model stock saddle was not a big seller in its day. As a result, Sears reduced it from $28.55 to $26.99 in its 1906 catalog. The condition of the saddle and leather accessories has much to do with current value.

celebrations. They were worth only a few pennies at the time and their designs usually can be considered nothing short of grotesque. However, because no importance was placed on their value at the time and few survived, these items now are eagerly sought by collectors.

Even more important is what has been termed "goofus" or "hooligan" glass. This was the original carnival glass and was produced, at the time, by such leading houses as LaBelle, Crescent, Imperial and Northwood, as well as other leading glass houses that were well known at the turn of the century.

These items of pressed glass usually were gaudily painted, with golds, reds, greens and even orange shades being used to turn it into a splashy prize that cost little.

It now has been more than twenty years since the official occupation of Japan ended. In recent years, import items from that island country marked with the legend

While one is not likely to find many items as rare as this Hawley target air pistol, now in the Daisy museum, there is nonetheless a ready market for early air rifles and pistols. Many a collector item may be stashed in old attics.

"Made in Occupied Japan" have found a ready market among collectors.

Frankly, the Japanese people were working diligently to rebuild an economy and numerous toys and other metal items were stamped out of GI beer cans; but it is the rarity of these artifacts that now give them their value.

Oddly enough, it is the Japanese government that today is doing all it can to recover such items, as the nation's officials now consider the demand that their goods carry such a legend during the occupation an affront to their national dignity. That can only mean that the goods produced during the occupation period will become more rare and more valuable!

Literally hundreds of books have been written on the subject of arms collecting and it is a field all its own. Today, however, almost any firearm or edged weapon of a historical nature — and it becomes historical simply by being old — has value that usually is several times it original cost.

As the rare Winchester, Sharps and Volcanic firearms, not to mention Colts, Smith & Wessons and Remingtons, have been gobbled up by established collectors, those entering the field have had to concentrate on firearms or weaponry with less expensive asking prices.

That, perhaps, is the reason that early air rifles from the twenty-year period beginning about 1905 suddenly have become first-rate among some of the gun collecting fraternity.

Inasmuch as an air rifle rarely lasted more than a generation before becoming either inoperable or its owner advanced to cartridge firearms, early models are difficult to find. As an example, it is my understanding that not even the Daisy museum has all of the models which the firm has made over the years. The individual who owns a Daisy bearing the names of such early movie cowboys as Buzz Barton or Buck Jones has a collector item, indeed!

As time goes on, more and more items will become of interest to collectors, which brings us back to Mahan's earlier premise that virtually everything he finds has a market somewhere. What was commonplace ten years ago already may be a rarity. Some of the items we consider everyday now may be collectibles in two decades.

Anyone who searches for treasure should keep this philosophy in mind; it certainly doesn't cost anything beyond a bit of storage space.

The engraving on this antique firearm makes it even more valuable than were it plain metal. Condition of engraving also has a great deal to do with the value to the avid firearms collector. The amount of original bluing on the firearm also determines value. (Below) Early air guns from many parts of the world are displayed at Daisy's museum.

A MATTER OF DANGER

Knowing The Conditions You May Face And Being Prepared To Cope With Them Could Save Your Life!

Chapter 23

WITH THE BACKGROUND to which you have been exposed thus far concerning the various facets of treasure hunting, perhaps it is time to take a look at the manner in which a real pro goes about it. I have quoted Bill Mahan numerous times in this tome, but there is an obvious reason for it: Mahan is one of the nation's best known treasure hunters and the equipment and techniques he has perfected over the years have become a pattern for others to follow.

One of his favorite treasure hunting spots is Padre Island, which he terms "an enchanting, mysterious and provocative isle of treasure" lying just off the Texas coast. The island is 116 miles long and extends from Corpus Christi to Brownsville in a narrow crescent of shifting dunes and snow white sands.

Padre Island means many things: solitude and quiet; stark natural beauty, for the most part unchanged through the centuries; wild things, night creatures, birds of many descriptions; and over all the constant overtones of surf breaking on the sand. In her bosom she holds the secrets of fabulous treasures — gold, silver (bars and coins), precious jewels and religious artifacts from wrecks of the Spanish Flota.

Battered and tossed by the rushing winds and crashing surf, the ancient mariner often got lost in the black of a storm, with sails torn away, masts broken, only half afloat and blown ahead in the hurricane hell of the Gulf of Mexico. Swept relentlessly onward, he wrecked on the bar off Padre or was swept onto the Island by the mountainous waves.

"The thrill of finding a single coin amid the shells of the beach, a lone silver bar worn almost to nothingness by the

Left: Bill Mahan and Jim Koethey (right) huddle over a campfire, sipping sand-infiltrated coffee, while they wait out their Padre Island ordeal. (Above) A typical treasure hunter's camp built of wreckage on the island.

constant action of sea and sand, the chance of suddenly finding jewels and treasures — these are the things that keep calling me back to Padre," Mahan says.

"I have been on the Island many times, walked for miles in the dunes and on the beaches. I have camped for days in her solitude. Several times I have been her full length in a four-wheel-drive vehicle. Riding is smoother in the middle of the island, but there is danger of exploding one of the many aerial practice bombs. The Navy uses the center of the island as a bombing range."

When walking, one has to be ever watchful for the rattle-snakes that thrive there. There are no trees on the island, only low shrubs, weeds and grasses. It is under and around these that the rattlers like to hide.

Mahan has been there both summer and winter; it is mysterious, regardless of the season. At one moment a friendly, happy warm and pleasant place, without warning it is changed. With magic suddenness, the island becomes a wild, blowing hell of sand. Visibility is cut to a few feet and there is no place to escape the vicious wind. Rolling waves of the surf are suddenly transformed into a vengeful monster.

It is as if a curse is on the island, placed there by the suffering, dying Spaniards of over four hundred years ago, resentful of all who search for and find their lost treasures. These Spaniards, shipwrecked and cast upon the island by storms, carried with them in the holds of their ships tons of silver plate, bars and newly minted coins from the province of New Spain.

Even if you do not consider the hundreds of other wrecks, or the wealth buried by pirates and others known to history, the treasures of the 1553 wrecks alone are enough to fill the sands with fortunes.

"Jim Koethey, a feature writer for the Dallas *Times Herald,* had expressed a desire many times for me to take him to Padre. Jim has researched and written newspaper stories for years about the many fabulous treasures supposedly buried and hidden in Texas, but actually hunting for them himself was a new experience. He finally convinced me that he would be an asset on a treasure hunt and we made preparations for a week's trip.

"Our destination was a spot where I had been three times by land, coming down the island for seventy miles in a four-wheel-drive vehicle. On an earlier trip to this same area, made in the Spring with Bob Nesmith of Rye, New York, we had had poor luck and were almost blown into the Gulf. We had to leave suddenly because of foul weather and before we actually had time to start our search."

This is one place in which you certainly do not want to get trapped. In a severe storm or when there are unusually high tides, this section of the island is completely under water for miles.

"Only a skilled driver and one familiar with the island should attempt this trip, and Bob and I had such a driver — Louis Rawalt, a resident of Padre since 1923. He is a treasure hunter who has had many and varied finds, from bootleg booze to ancient idols and loads of raw rubber. Louis now has a bait and tackle shop on the island and is a

The ideal way to tour Padre Island in search of treasure is by four-wheel-drive vehicle, but one must take care to dodge the dud bombs dropped by Naval fighter planes.

good man to listen to for advice and the latest information."

Mahan and Koethey had decided to approach the hunt a little differently this time, and headed for Port Mansfield. This is primarily a port for sport fishermen and comfortable quarters are available. The Red Fish has a marina where boats can be rented. A forty-foot diesel fishing boat, *Lady Luck*, skippered by the competent Jimmie Reed with Lee Halbaur for mate, is also available. These men are familiar with the coastal waters and the pair contracted to have the boatmen take them out to the island, then come back at a pre-arranged time for pick up.

"We pulled up to the dock and loaded our gear aboard, being careful not to take more than we could carry. Actually, we did have a surplus of food and water, but we had decided we could set up a base camp to leave the surplus in, carry enough for about three days with us and then return for more as needed."

The water was calm and there was just a slight breeze stirring. Skipper Reed made the remark that it was a nice day, but he wondered what happened to the normal winds. When Mahan and Koethey arrived at the jetties, they unloaded all the gear and grub and carried the surplus back in the dunes.

"I have a large Bavarian leather pack and can carry a good-sized load. Jim had just bought a new pack with sleeping bag built in. As it turned out, they were both too small and the sleeping bag too thin. He carried along an air mattress and was anticipating sleeping in comfort. It punctured the first night and he had to sleep next to the ground with only a thin layer between him and the damp sand," Mahan recalls.

Finally, with packs bulging, they started out, intending to set up a camp about three miles up the beach, then work both ways up and down the island.

"As we headed North, we were both carrying our detectors and made frequent side trips searching in the dunes. By the time Jim and I had hiked two miles up the beach, plus all the side trips we had made, we were both tired out. I had about ninety pounds in my pack and it was getting heavier with each step."

The remains of a frame of some fisherman's shack seemed like a good place for a camp. The old frame was attached to the two-mile marker and Mahan made a joking remark, but half serious, that at least they shouldn't blow away if their lean-to was attached to it. With its back to the wind and blankets attached to either side for windbreaks, the framework tent was real comfortable. Koethey had found a large packing crate back in the dunes and had rolled it into camp and set it up as a cooking table. Inside the crate were stored extra food and equipment.

A 12x12-foot piece of transparent plastic sheeting had been brought along for the shelter, "so when we turned in, we lay looking up at the moon and observed that it was becoming a little cloudy.

"It seemed we had just dozed off, but in reality it was 3 a.m., when we were awakened by a stiffening breeze and rain. This was no problem, as we were set up with our back

Bill Mahan (right), looking like an ancient pirate, and another treasure hunting compatriot relax in their own version of the Padre Island Hilton during lull in search.

This battered sea chest was among the items discovered on one of his trips to Padre Island by Bill Mahan.

to the wind, so we just lay awake for some time listening to the surf — and what turned into a regular tropical downpour. We were about fifty yards from the surf and up on a slight knoll so had no fear of rising tides."

It had stopped raining the next morning but was still cloudy and windy. The two treasure hunters wandered about a mile into the dunes and began to find pieces of old beeswax on the surface. This was used by the Spaniards to make candles, and to treat caulking materials and the thread used in making and patching the sails. Mahan always watches for it when searching near the beach. Walking along beside Jim, Mahan was telling him how the beeswax was a sure sign of a wreck somewhere in the vicinity, when suddenly his detector let out a shrill scream. Koethey gave a start and asked, "What is that?"

Mahan replied, "That, ole buddy, is the tune we came to hear!"

"Dropping to my knees, I took my sheath knife and began to dig in the sand. At about five inches the blade scraped on metal. I continued to dig gently, but with my fingers. A nice large four reales coin, a part of the treasure of the 1553 wrecks, was soon brought to the surface."

Jim, taking the coin and turning it in his hand, looked it over, then remarked quietly, "Well, looks like it is time to start to work." Within a few minutes he, also, had come up with one. So it went and within an hour Mahan had found four of the valuable Spanish coins and also a 1944 U.S. fifty-cent piece. It was oxidized and black from being a long time in the salt water. It probably had been in a wreck at sea, also.

Mahan noted that the sky was getting darker and the wind suddenly hit with a roar. It seemed the whole beach just rose up in the air and started moving. Soon it was blowing so hard the two could hardly stand. They tried to huddle in the lee of a small dune and this, if anything, was worse. The blowing sand came over the dune with the velocity of an arrow.

The two decided they had better try to make it back to camp and make it secure before it was too late. That meant going head-on into the storm, for it had come directly out

The low vegetation is adequate to hide a healthy annual crop of the treasure hunter's best recognized natural enemy: the rattlesnake.

This oil drilling crew, which was on the island during one search, had the ideal rig for battling the sand, using a dune buggy with wide tires.

Holding one of the metal detectors he manufactures and uses, Mahan displays Padre Island coin take.

of the South. With heads bent low and with plastic bags over the detectors the pair started back to the supposed shelter of the camp. It was a hard mile.

"The handkerchiefs which had been tied over our faces to keep out the sand only seemed to trap it in. There was nothing to do but take them off and go the rest of the way with bare faces.

"When we finally did reach camp, we were too late. It was a complete wreck. The lean-to had blown down and was half covered with sand. The large box we had placed all the equipment and food in was filled also. Right beside our camp was a nice dune that had not been there before. By the next morning it was over four feet high."

Despite the wind which kept up its steady blowing, some driftwood boards were arranged into a low wall with others placed across to form a sort of roof. The plastic sheet had been torn in half, but the part that was found was stretched over the top and weighted down by more boards. It made, at least, a half shelter, but nothing stopped the sand from blowing and whipping right into their faces.

"Finally we just gave up and crawled into our sleeping bags, which were also full of sand. We realized it would be impossible to cook and eat. It was a long and uncomfortable night."

Sometime near morning the wind lay down and all was quiet. The aroma of a wood fire blended with the early morning air, and the old black pot made coffee that was pure nectar.

"I decided it was the most beautiful morning I had ever witnessed. Jim was awake and told me to go ahead, that he would join me later."

Mahan already had found several coins before Jim caught up to report he had not been able to find anything to eat but a can of cold beans. Even the loaves of bread were full of sand and no good. The unopened cigarette packs, wrapped in a paper bag, had sand inside the cellophane covering.

"I had started out about where we had stopped the day before and we were soon finding coins with regularity. So it went all day. We passed noon with no thought of being

The D-Tex Professional model metal detector is the most popular model made by the firm and the one used primarily by Mahan in his searches. (Below) On one trip, Mahan favored this carry-all vehicle to tour isle.

Above: Mahan and friend relax over a drink following a tough day of searching for Padre Island wealth. (Below) Some of coins taken include one, two, four and eight reales, all relics of wrecked Spanish vessels.

Mahan, head sheltered from the sun by a straw hat, pauses to inspect some of Padre Island coins, relics.

Back at his home base in Garland, Texas, the old pro, Bill Mahan, sorts out some of the relics, artifacts and coins taken with metal detector on Padre Island foray.

hungry. We were having lots of luck; first Jim would let out a yell and hold up a coin for me to see, then I would come up with another. Finally, about 2:30 p.m., we were both tired and hot. The temperature had been around 90 degrees all day. Jim, unaccustomed to being out in the sun, was as red as a lobster and, as he said, twice as raw and sore. We decided to head back and try to prepare some food. In our two days on Padre, we had actually had only one meal. As we reached camp, I observed that it was certainly getting still. Even the surf seemed to be quieter."

While eating eggs and de-sanded bacon, the two noticed that low, dark and rolling clouds were rapidly approaching from the North. They had barely finished their food when it hit. It seemed the winds of hell had hit; the gusts were so strong the two men could hardly stand. The surf started raising a frothy head and the roar of the breakers got louder. Waves that just moments before had been rolling smoothly and quietly along were suddenly ten feet high and crashing closer and closer to the crude camp.

"I shouted to Jim that we had better take just what we could and try to get out fast. We started throwing things back into our knapsacks. The wind picked our shelter straight up and the last we saw, it was still gaining altitude and headed south. Our sleeping bags were swelling and writhing and almost impossible to roll up. If the blowing sand seemed bad previously, it was doubly thick and stinging now. We were almost completely blinded by it. A roll of paper towels took off, unwinding and writhing in the

Suggesting the wide range of items available due to series of shipwrecks off Padre Island are a silver bar, old bullets, hand-forged bronze spikes and gold and silver coins ranging from modern to 300 years old.

air like some wild thing that was alive," according to Mahan's recollections.

He had thrown all the canned food in a knapsack, plus all the cooking utensils, and with skillets and coffee pot tied on, they were ready to travel.

"My load was so heavy I had to get help from Jim to get it on my back. He said he thought I must have about 150 pounds. It felt twice as heavy to me. Slinging my camera case over my head and grabbing my detector and the Coleman stove, we lit out. By this time, the clouds were so low and the sand so thick, nothing but the frothing surf was visible."

The campsite was washed right out from under their feet while the two made ready to go.

"I realized what could easily happen to us on our way back to the cut. The area that we had to cross was low-lying and when the tides are excessively high, breakers roll all the way across the Island with the force of a locomotive. If this happened before we could get back to the jetties, we had about as much chance as a snowball on a hot day."

Mahan took the lead. It was so dark the pair dared not get too far away from the edge of the breakers. On the back side of the island there is nothing but tide flats, with mud so deep in places a man with a load on his back could sink out of sight very quickly. The island is only a couple of hundred yards or less wide, so Mahan tried to stay in the edge of the surf for a guide.

"One moment we would be searching for the edge; the next moment the surf would be swirling to our knees, as we staggered on with our heavy loads. I considered ditching everything but realized that, if we were marooned for some time, that was all the food we would have. It is impossible to know how long these sudden storms will last.

"We kept on without a stop for rest and were both reeling with exhaustion when suddenly, straight ahead, were the jetties. This was the most welcome sight we had seen in some time. Climbing up on the rough stone, Jim and I searched for a place where we would be sheltered from the blowing sand and wind. Finally we just had to give up and, unloading, collapsed where we were."

The initial encampment set up by Mahan and Koethey on their near ill-fated adventure seemed secure enough at inception, but most of it blew away in high wind.

The only way to get any protection was to crawl inside the sleeping bags and attempt to close them up as much as possible. The heavy coats were packed in the bottoms of the packs since up to then the weather had been warm and pleasant.

So began another endless night. Mahan has no idea what time it was when he awoke, feeling completely numb with cold. The wind had not slowed down and now was like ice; this was a real Texas norther. He used a sheath knife to prop up the side of his bag and turned on the flashlight to learn he was two inches deep in sand which had blown in during the night.

"I lay back and lit a cigarette; the warmth of the smoke sure felt good to my frozen hands. Then I managed to find a candle I was carrying and lit it inside the bag for a while — anything just to get a little heat. I must have lain there for two hours before I stuck my head out. It was still about an hour until dawn but I could stand it no longer."

The change and ferocity of the weather spectrum on the island is reflected in this photo showing sandstorm.

Shaking and shivering and with teeth chattering, Mahan located his knapsack half-buried with sand. Inside was a heavy coat and an old, ragged Navy blanket. With both wrapped around him, he felt that he might live through it after all. A spot back near the dunes where the wind was not blowing so wildly seemed the most likely spot to build a fire.

"It had started to drizzle a little occasionally and the temperature was down to 35 degrees. I knew Jim was about frozen also, so when I got up I placed my sleeping bag on him. He later told me that he was awake at the time but so cold he couldn't move or talk."

Some large pieces of driftwood made a nice roaring fire. Mahan went back in the dunes, found the base camp and dug out a jug of water. The old black coffee pot was soon going again.

This was the beginning of a long and unforgettable day. The wind wouldn't die and occasional showers kept the victims of misery chilled to the bone. If they got close enough to the fire to keep warm, both got thoroughly smoked. Back out of the smoke, they were instantly freezing again. So it went for the whole long dreary day.

"We were wondering what had happened to the boat. I had told the skipper that, if the weather got bad, we would come back to the jetties and he should come get us. As we learned later, they had come out for us during the first part of the storm, even though it was a rough and dangerous trip, and had cruised up and down the channel with the spotlight playing over the area searching for us, but had decided we had not made it. All the while we were lying just a short distance away down behind some low dunes.

"Toward sundown, Jim and I were beginning to worry. We knew that the seven miles to the mainland could and often did, get too rough even for the forty-foot boat. It was too easy to get washed onto a hidden sand bar or reef.

"We had about resigned ourselves to spend another night

when out of the gathering darkness we heard the beautiful sound of that old diesel purring along. Quickly gathering up our blankets and the coffee pot we rushed down to the cut to let them know where we were. They were able to put the *Lady Luck's* bow to within six feet of shore. Several trips through the icy water were necessary to get everything aboard. Stowing our gear on the rear deck took several more trips and, by the time we were ready to get underway, we were about frozen."

The skipper ordered the two below in the cabin. It seemed like the first real warmth in days. They had gasoline lanterns sitting around for heating purposes and one was under the table. Bill Mahan quickly slid in at the table and his partner joined him.

"But I am not discouraged. I will go back, again and again. Once you get Padre in your blood it is like something contagious — and incurable. Next time, I want to take a crew of experienced divers with me and try to find the carcasses of the treasure fleet that perished in a hurricane off the Island shores four hundred years ago. The silver may be mostly ruined by oxidation, but the gold and some of the old relics and artifacts should remain.

"What about the spot where we were working? I believe I will let the spirits of the long dead Spaniards keep what is left. We had good luck once and were fortunate enough to get out alive with all our equipment and our finds. Besides, I don't believe we left very much in that particular spot!"

But actually, there is a moral to all this, Mahan is an experienced treasure hunter and outdoorsman. Because of his past experiences, he knows the need for being able to evaluate weather conditions and be prepared for any eventuality.

In almost any type of wilderness, one may find himself face to face with the foibles of nature, so it is best to make a thorough study of the conditions you may face and be prepared to combat any that may confront you.

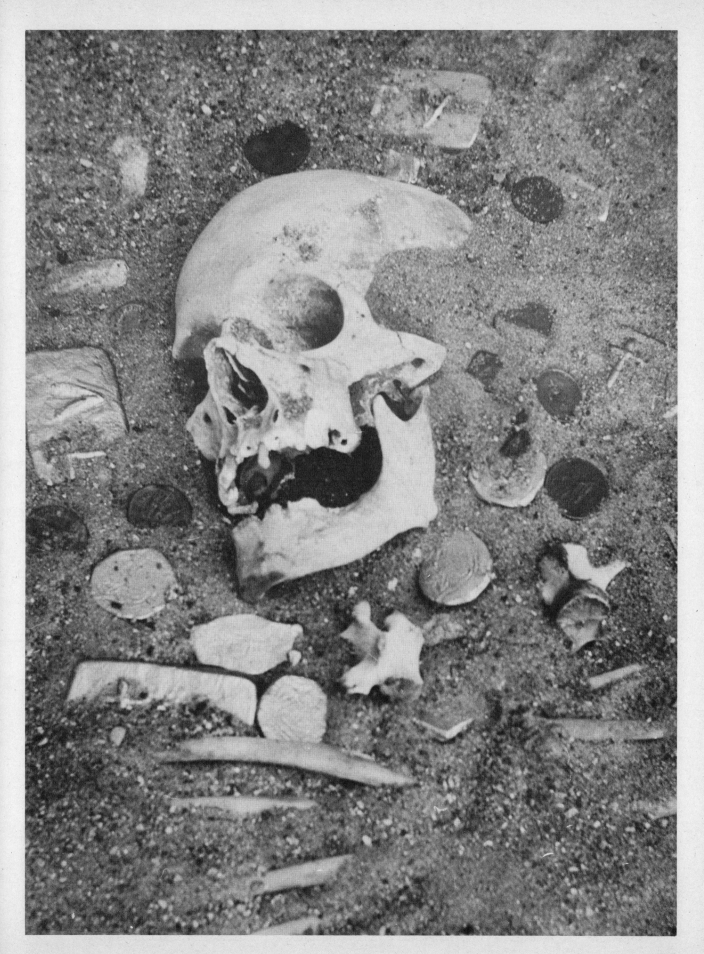

Chapter 24

New Image For Treasure Hunters

As A Means Of Protecting Their Future, The Serious Buffs Are Becoming A Boon To Society!

SERIOUS TREASURE HUNTERS have taken a long look at themselves and at some of the less serious members of their avocation. There are those who don't like what they see and want to do something about it.

One problem, of course, does not involve the treasure hunters as much as it does the destructors and scavengers. Whole ghost towns, for example, are being carted away a board at a time. It may do the ego good to be able to say that a certain board in that new fence around the thirty-foot rancho came out of Bodie, California, but it isn't doing the treasure hunter's image any good. In fact, there are any number of steps being taken to preserve such artifacts of the past and such increasing legal action can only make it more difficult for the treasure hunter.

At the annual Prospectors and Treasure Hunters' Convention held in California City, California, in 1972, a good deal of discussion concerned the future of treasure hunting and what steps could be taken to protect it. The convention, incidentally, is sponsored by the Prospectors Club of Southern California and is the largest event of its kind in the country.

In listening to such treasure hunting veterans as Bill Mahan, Jack Pepper, Charles Garrett and a host of others, it became obvious that the acts of a few irresponsible individuals has done much to bring about criticism by professional archaeologists and historians. The result was a unanimous agreement that the solution had to come from the treasure hunters, themselves, rather than having more legislation forced upon them.

Resolutions are fine, of course, but how does one go about developing a solution to such a threat?

The recently formed Gem and Treasure Hunting Association of San Diego, California, has come up with a partial answer. In fact, one writer has said, "They have made the

Left: An old photo of the original San Diego jail ruins, which will be rebuilt through efforts of treasure hunters. (Below) It is possible that the long lost bell from the San Luis Rey Mission is buried in the local cemetery.

greatest contribution to organized treasure hunting since the invention of the metal detector and, at the same time, have opened up new and exciting areas in which to search.

"Their bright, new image can spread throughout the country, if their lead is followed. In addition to improving the overall picture, their program offers a lot of unique benefits to every individual who participates."

Those are nice words, but the concept that brought them about is based upon the fact that the San Diego association is unlike most other treasure hunting clubs. Members are working closely with historians and archaeological groups in recovering bits of history and, as a result, have gained cooperation and respect from officials where both had been endangered in the past.

"This means that the key has been found which can reverse public opinion about our treasure hunting activities," according to George Mroczkowski, president of the association. "It also acts to assure favorable conditions for treasure hunters in the future and it means that treasure hunters — through cooperation with historians and others — can take their place in contributing to public knowledge and enjoyment through recovery and display of historic artifacts."

Instead of haunting beaches, parks, old mining areas and similar spots frequented by other treasure hunters and members of clubs; sectors that have been picked over many times, the members of the San Diego association have been able to gain access to historic sites where metal detectors never before have been used. The result has been a number of historically important finds in such areas as the famed San Luis Rey Mission at Oceanside, California, one of the original California missions, which is more than two centuries old.

Club members also have been allowed to conduct searches in San Diego's Old Town, site of the original village. In this one-time pueblo are the remains of San Diego's first jail, where Judge Roy Bean once was held prisoner. Other search areas in Old Town have been the site of the original San Diego Union, the town's first newspaper; an old cobbler shop, the old Immaculate Conception Church and a host of other historic ruins.

Mroczkowski is a retired Marine Corps master sergeant, who organized a small treasure hunting club at Camp Pendleton, the Marine's sprawling historic Southern California training base. Among the sites inspected has been an old pioneer site on the grounds of Camp Pendleton. This originally was the Santa Margarita Rancho, dating back to Spanish land grant days and is rich in California history.

"That's how we got started in this operation," the

In searching the grounds of the San Luis Rey Mission, many interesting items such as these bottles were found.

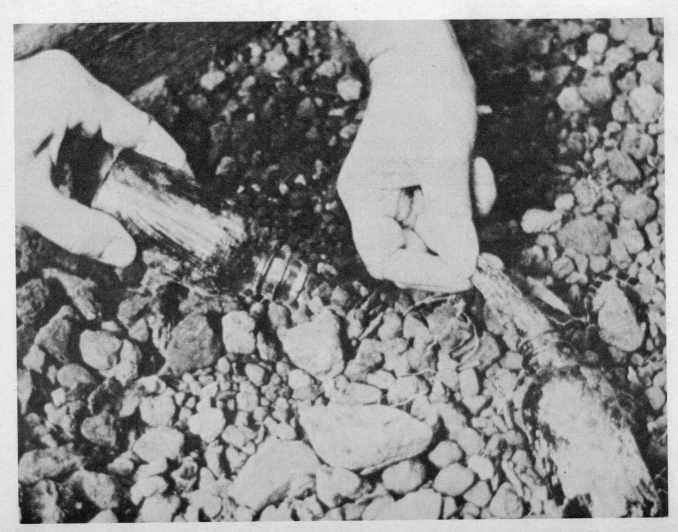

former Marine explains. "We realized that right in our own vicinity were thousands of valuable items and historic artifacts rotting away that would be lost forever, if they weren't recovered soon. We thought that would be a great loss to everyone, so we decided to save as many as we could.

"We selected a few old historic locations and approached officials with our plan. After discussing our mutual interest in preserving historical artifacts, we volunteered to search the premises with metal detectors and agreed to donate all items found either to be displayed there or at a nearby museum. In nearly every case, we met with cooperation. Soon we had expanded our group in order to work all the areas. This was the official beginning of the club." In less than a year, the organization boasted more than a hundred avid members.

At this time several hundred items are on display at the Old Whaley House, an important landmark in Old Town. Most were found in the immediate vicinity by members of the association. Included are coins, weapons, jewelry, buttons, tools, ad infinitum. An elaborate silver cufflink, found on the Whaley House property, is thought to have belonged to Thomas Whaley, original owner of the place. An old Navy uniform insignia was found near a parking meter in the front yard with a metal detector.

Under terms of the agreement, when an item is put on display, it is marked with the name of the finder, after it is researched for age, value, identity, and it also is marked as to where and when it was discovered.

"That's what treasure hunting is all about," George Mroczkowski insists. "The thrill of finding an old, valuable coin or artifact and the enjoyment of showing it to others. Most treasure hunters hardly ever sell anything they find, because they would rather keep it to show.

"In our way, we get to make many exciting finds in areas that otherwise would be closed to us and there is no better way to show a find than in a properly guarded display case, where thousands of people will see it."

Early efforts of the club gained a good deal of publicity and newspaper space — all of it favorable. Armed with these

Above: This elaborate silver cufflink was found on the Whaley House property in Old San Diego. (Below) The members of the Gem and Treasure Hunting Association of San Diego pose at old prospector site on a field trip.

press notices, Mroczkowski is the one who contacts officials at the sites he and members of the club would like to work over. As a result, they have standing invitations for continuing searches in Old Town, the San Luis Rey Mission, Camp Pendleton and other prime search areas. There also are a number of letters of appreciation for their contributions to reconstructing history in the club's files, in spite of the relative youth of the organization.

"It is important, of course, that all searches at historical sites be supervised carefully," Mroczkowski warns, "to make sure that no damage is done and that all holes — if dug — are filled completely. Also, we see to it that all searching is done at a specific time in a predetermined area. No individual members are authorized to search on their own, other than during the specified time.

"The owners or operators of the site always should be notified when the group arrives and when it departs. It is our practice to put all items found in a single container, along with information on their discovery. These are presented to the owners upon departure." Later, however, the club may send several individuals back to the site to photograph the items and do additional research, thus completing the association's files.

In November, 1972, club members made what was considered a major discovery on the grounds of the old Immaculate Conception Church in San Diego's Old Town. Church officials knew that a metal box had been placed somewhere in the church, when it was constructed in 1868. It was important, inasmuch as it contained papers relative to the church's history and ownership of the land.

Two members of the club volunteered their services. Mike Jacobs and Mark Criswell were searching beneath the floor of the parish with a metal detector when they got a reading behind an old brick wall. The pair carefully dug out two of the bricks and found the remains of a tin box — its bottom rusted out — on a marble slab. Apparently there had been access to the box since the church had been built, as there were a 1911 penny, an 1878 silver dollar and an 1860 two-cent piece among the coins in the rusted box. Some of the papers in the box had been damaged by the action of the rust, but they are being pieced together and have offered important history on the church's past.

The club members were allowed to search a site where two old houses had been torn down to make way for a new museum. Elton Cox, got a signal on his detector and began digging with Richard Flores. At the four-foot level, they discovered a small brass medallion, which is formed in the shape of a heart. It was presented, according to the inscription, to Mrs. Mildred H. Lewis, Los Angeles La Fiesta Queen, in 1896. Other than a mention of it in an old magazine, club members have been able to find out little about the medallion and still are puzzled as to how it ended up under four feet of dirt, more than a hundred miles from where it was presented originally. But the solution still is being pursued through research. Meantime, the medallion is on display in the Whaley House.

Members of the San Diego group also received permission to excavate the site of San Diego's first jail, which is located in Old Town. The site was gridded off with string markers, then using metal detectors and sifters, the club

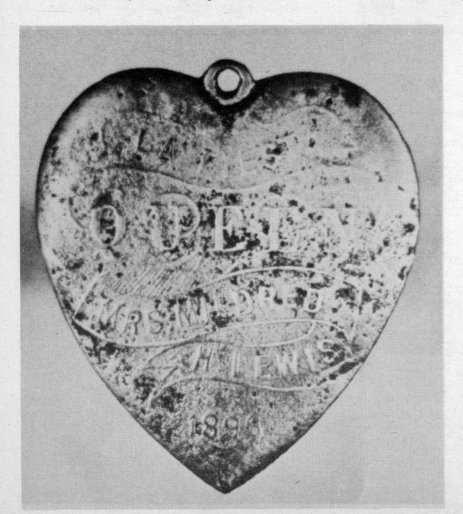

This brass medallion belonged to the 1896 Los Angeles Fiesta queen, but was found buried under four feet of earth in San Diego Old Town. How it got there is a mystery.

These items, even including an old dog license, are artifacts found by treasure hunters in the ruins of Old Town, relate to the early history.

members began searching the ruins. It was not long before most of the cobblestone foundation had been uncovered, with archaeologists from as far away as San Francisco arriving to gather information during the digging. Among the items found were a rusted old gun and several window bars. One legend connected with the jail involves the famous — or infamous, depending upon viewpoint — Roy Bean, the incident taking place long before he moved to Texas and set himself up with a lawbook and a Bible as the Law West of the Pecos. According to legend, Bean had fought a duel in San Diego. He made the mistake of winning and was locked up in the jail. However, he managed to escape by digging his way out beneath the foundations with an ordinary table spoon, which is supposed to have been slipped to him by a girlfriend.

At present, according to George Mroczkowski, the club plans on restoring the old jail and seeks to have it designated by the state as an historical landmark.

Searches of the original site of the San Diego Union have yielded old coins, rings and jewelry, including two gold pieces. One was a 1769 pillar dollar of Mexican origin.

The project that probably has brought Mroczkowski and the Gem and Treasure Hunting Association the most reknown — not to mention instant respect — has been their work with the old Spanish missions. This affiliation began as long ago as 1958, when Mroczkowski was passing the San Luis Rey Mission.

"I noticed the Franciscan brothers excavating in the mission's sunken gardens with pick and shovel. We parked our jeep, introduced ourselves and offered our help and metal detectors to locate valuable relics that might have been buried over the years," the club organizer recalls.

This array of unlikely items was located by treasure hunters on the original site of the San Diego Union.

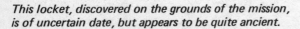
This locket, discovered on the grounds of the mission, is of uncertain date, but appears to be quite ancient.

According to Mroczkowski, their cooperation was accepted and the relationship still continues.

Mission San Luis Rey was founded in June, 1798, but was not completed until 1830, according to church records. It was built of adobe and had walls 6½ feet thick and more than thirty feet high. It became the largest of the chain of California missions and more baptisms, marriages and funerals were performed there than at any of the others in the chain.

In 1834, however, the Mexican Government signed a law that took the missions from the padres and turned them over to the Indians. The Franciscan brothers left and the missions immediately began to fall into ruin, vandals stripping the once stately structures of tiles, timbers and almost anything that could be carried away.

On March 18, 1865, shortly before his death at the hands of John Wilkes Booth, President Abraham Lincoln signed a new bill returning the San Luis Rey Mission to the church. Restoration began and, to this day, work still goes on.

There was one mystery, however, that plagued Mroczkowski and his group. "I had heard stories about one of the mission bells that had been buried for safe keeping by the padres during the secularization. The location was unknown."

With nothing more than a rumor, Mroczkowski and five of his group decided to make a concentrated search for the bell.

"About one o'clock on a Sunday afternoon, we were

This is the type of mission bell that is supposed to be buried in the grounds of the San Luis Rey Mission and for which the search is being continued by club members.

checking the orange groves behind the mission," he recalls. "The rest of the group had broken for lunch, while I continued searching.

"As I reached the end of the row of trees and started back on another row, I got an odd feeling. A couple of steps farther on, my Fisher Gemini detector picked up a solid reading, which I checked from four different directions before I called the rest of the crew. I was certain I had found the bell."

The group began digging and it took a total of nine hours before they struck metal. "When we finally could see the object, there was a good deal of excitement. It was a bright bronze color and we thought sure it was the missing bell.

"The padres brought in their back hoe and hooked a cable to the object and lifted. We all felt a degree of disappointment, when we discovered it wasn't the bell."

What had been uncovered instead was an "alambique," a Spanish brandy still. Research revealed this example to be something over 160 years old. In spite of the fact that the bell had not been recovered, this was considered an equally rare find, as there was only one other such still in the United States.

Inasmuch as there has been a great deal of flooding in

Above: The new and old intertwine in this collection taken during a day's search of San Diego's Old Town. (Below) A huge square spike of the type used in old wooden ships and ship's clock were found at the mission.

the area over the past two centuries, causing the movement of a great deal of topsoil, Mroczkowski feels that there is an entire brandy cellar buried somewhere in the immediate area.

Meanwhile, the brandy still has been cleaned up and is on display in the mission museum.

The San Diego club members have been involved in other projects as well, one including restoration of a gargoyle to the sunken garden. It had been moved into the mission's inner court for safekeeping at one point, but was moved back to the area, where the mission Indians once bathed and washed their clothing.

Because of their help, club members were allowed to search the sunken garden, even checking out an old tile kiln, where the roof tiles for the original mission were baked.

A number of aritfacts were turned up, including an old ship's clock, a button from an old Spanish uniform, a locket fashioned from gold and mother of pearl; a large, square iron spike of the type used in affixing Spanish ship's deck planking, as well as numerous bits of pottery.

But the missing bell has not been forgotten. "We plan to continue our cooperative programs with the missions and other organizations," Mroczkowski says. "We all enjoy the work, because there is so much history to be uncovered." The artifacts found on the mission grounds are turned over to the padres for inclusion in their museum, incidentally, in keeping with the policies of the club.

Treasure hunters also have done something to clean up their image in Arizona, specifically Tombstone, where each Spring the annual Tombstone Mining Fair is held.

The event features the famed Tombstone National Treasure Hunt wherein prizes and tokens are buried over the town. The hunt, beginning in the middle of the town's football field, opens when an antique gun fires the signal. At that moment, treasure hunters with metal detectors are off to see what they can find. The winner who comes in with the most goodies has his named engraved on the White's Electronic Perpetual Trophy, which is on continual display at the Tombstone Chamber of Commerce.

There also are plenty of side trips that treasure seekers can make. For example, one searcher found an old knife and a corroded .44 cartridge on the site of the Last Chance Saloon, some two miles from the center of town.

One entire Arizona treasure hunting club showed up one year and, after the contest, adjourned to the nearby Clanton Ranch, where the Clanton gang of Wyatt Earp and O.K. Corral infamy lived. There is alleged to be $50,000 in gold hidden on the ranch. This is reputed to be the loot from a train hold up conducted by the father of Ike and Billy Clanton.

According to local legend, the father of the Clanton boys did not get along with his sons and is supposed to have told a nephew the location of the gold. The last of the tribe, known as Pop Clanton, was a familiar figure in Arizona until his death at age 90-plus during the Depression years.

The question as to why he never recovered the treasure himself remains. However, it is a fact that he did approach one James West, a respected Phoenix businessman and an authority on Arizona forts of the frontier era, offering to let him in on the treasure.

At the time, West says, he paid little attention, feeling the old man was senile. However, more recently, he has come across newspaper accounts of the $50,000 robbery and has come to realize that there is fact as the basis of the legend.

The Tombstone National Treasure Hunt is unique, but already is being copied in other locations, where planned metal detector tests can be conducted. As a fun event, the sponsors say it allows even the neophyte an opportunity to find a prize. It also is giving the public a better understanding of what treasure hunting is all about.

In several areas of the Southwest, treasure hunting clubs have invited the travel editors of local newspaper to accompany them on such outings. In each case, of course, the theme has been "search but don't destroy," especially when seeking artifacts in old ghost towns. In short, when a hole is dug, it also is filled up. When buildings are searched, they are not damaged. If a board is removed, it is replaced.

Such efforts have done a good deal in these communities to improve the image of today's treasure hunter, whether pro or amateur.

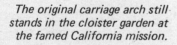

The original carriage arch still stands in the cloister garden at the famed California mission.

Ed Bartholomew (left) and Charles Garrett display awards presented them during Oklahoma City International Treasure Show in November, 1974. Both authors — Bartholomew has written 55 books on treasure hunting and Western history — Garrett also is a manufacturer of metal detectors.

As an adjunct to public relations, a number of individuals and companies dealing in treasure equipment have started museums to help explain to the public precisely what the business is all about. One of those who has invested his own time and money in such an effort is Charles Garrett.

The Garrett Electronics Treasure Museum was opened officially in April, 1971, when the electronics firm moved into its new 10,000-square-foot building in Garland, Texas. In reality, the collection of artifacts and relics was started back in the Fifties, when Charles Garrett began using his first metal detector. As do most treasure hunters, he saved every relic and collectable no matter how valuable, storing them away in cardboard boxes.

"In 1969 orders for the Garrett metal detector forces us to consider a new building and the treasure museum was an integral part of the planning from the beginning. This was not because we wanted to impress people with what had been found, but to give beginning treasure hunters an idea of how interesting and varied the hobby can be for a person who enjoys being outdoors and following the trails of history," Garrett says.

Almost from the day they opened the museum, it was full of interesting relics found by Garrett himself, employees of Garrett Electronics or purchased from the professional treasure hunters who stop by when they are in town. Within the next few months, Garrett plans to expand the museum even further, knocking out a few walls to more than double the exhibit area. "We are completing a photograph collection which will show professional treasure hunters and their finds from all over the world to complement our collection of artifacts and relics."

Unlike other museums on well-traveled highways, this museum is designed only for the treasure hunter. A visitor can take a leisurely tour of the display area without being rushed and there are several interesting stories to be heard about the recovery of some of the items.

"Since there are several distinct fields of treasure hunting, such as coinshooting, Civil War relic hunting, ghost towning, cache hunting, prospecting, Indian relic collecting and general collectable and primitive collecting, we have structured our displays accordingly," Garrett says. "We have a good collection of arrow points and other Indian relics, as well as a display case of old rings that have been found with metal detectors. Many of the old guns in our collection have historical importance such as the bent gun barrel located at the site of a great battle involving the U.S. Army and the Nez Perce Indians in Idaho."

One of the highlights of this treasure museum is a display of Wells Fargo relics. This includes a strongbox believed to have been buried in Oklahoma by Grat Dalton, just before the Dalton gang was wiped out at Coffeyville, Kansas, October 5, 1892.

Along with the strongbox are several canvas bags and seals, found in the box when it was uncovered by a Garrett customer. Also in the Wells Fargo collection are several handguns used by W. F. & Co. guards, a set of handcuffs, a badge and a sawed-off shotgun used to protect some of the larger money shipments during the years Wells Fargo operated as an overland express company. The strongbox had a hole in the bottom, which has been welded shut. Speculation on the past contents of the heavy iron safe never fails to spark a conversation among visitors.

The treasure museum also contains an interesting collection of old bottles and primitive tools, as well as Civil War relics. During working hours, employees are on hand to answer questions and provide information on treasure hunting, collecting and the proper use of metal detectors. The museum is located at 2814 National Drive in Garland, near the intersection of Interstate Highway 635 and Kingsley Road.

MANUFACTURERS & DISTRIBUTORS

The below-listed manufacturers and distributors cover the entire range of needs for treasure hunting in its many forms. Virtually all of them offer catalogs that can be obtained upon request, enclosing a stamped, self-addressed envelope.

A.H. Electronics, P.O. Box 45, Wheeling, Illinois 60090

Jim Alexander Enterprises, 616 Arkansas, South Houston, Texas 77587

Amateur Treasure Hunters Association, P.O. Box 475, Oscoda, Michigan 48750

Carl Anderson, P.O. Box 13441L, Tampa, Florida 33611

Apollo Sales, P.O. Box 248, Osceola, Indiana 46561

The Association, 300 State Street, Oscoda, Michigan 48750

Aurora, 6296 Beach Boulevard, Buena Park, California 90620

J.S. Burbridge, 713 S. Meridan, San Bernardino, California 90302

Canadian Frontier, P.O. Box 2071, Vancouver, B.C., Canada

Carter Manufacturing Company, Lost Hills, California 93249

Cleveland Supply, 320 Main Street, San Angelo, Texas 76901

Coe Prospector Supply, 9264 Katella Avenue, Anaheim, California 92804

Collector, 7471 Melrose Avenue, Los Angeles, California 90046

Compass Electronics Corporation, 3700 24th Avenue, Forrest Grove, Oregon 97116

Compton Rock Shop, 1405 S. Long Beach Boulevard, Compton, California 90221

The Coulter Company, P.O. Box 842, Temple City, California 91780

D&K Detector Sales, 13809 S.E. Division, Portland, Oregon 97236

Jim Davis, P.O. Box 1002, Burbank, California 91505

Detectron, P.O. Box 243, San Gabriel, California 91778

Delos Toole, 1722 Craighton, Hacienda Heights, California 91745

Dillon, 32738 Kentucky Street, Yucaipa, California 92399

Don's Treasure Hunting Supply, P.O. Box 177, Menomonee Falls, Wisconsin 53051

D-Tex Electronics, 614 Easy Street, P.O. Box 451, Garland, Texas 74040

Eight States Associates, Incorporated, 1918 Pearl Street, P.O. Box 1438, Boulder, Colorado 80302

Engineered Things, P.O. Box 10022, Portland, Oregon 97210

Excelsior Electronics Company, 7448 Deering Avenue, Canoga Park, California 91303

Exstone Company, Box 90717, Worldway Postal Center, Los Angeles, California 90009

Feather River Treasure Hunter's Supply, 2094 E. Main Street, East Quincy, California 95971

George Finder Company, Box 37, Lakewood, California 92614

Fireball Electronic Metal Detector Company, 1807 E. Eighth Street, Odessa, Texas 79760

Fisher Research Laboratory, P.O. Box 490, Belmont, California 94002

Robert E. Forbes, 1008 N. Atlanta Street, Metairie, Louisiana 70003

Gardiner Electronics, 4729 N. Seventh Avenue, Phoenix, Arizona 85013

Garrett Electronics, 2814 National Drive, Garland, Texas 75041

J.A. Gasiewicz, 249 Beale Avenue, Cheektowaga, New York 14225

General Electronic Detection Company, 16238 Lakewood Boulevard, Bellflower, California 90706

J.K. Gilbert Company, 111 W. Lowden Street, Fort Worth, Texas 76110

The Goldak Company, Incorporated, 1101-A Air Way, Glendale, California 91201

Gold Diver's, 3534 W. Rosecrans Avenue, Hawthorne, California 90250

Growco Enterprises, P.O. Box 1202, Canoga Park, California 91304

Heath Company, Benton Harbor, Michigan 49022

Indian Territory Supply Company, P.O. Box 2336, Tulsa, Oklahoma 74101

Jacobsen Suppliers, 9322 California Avenue, South Gate, California 90280

Ray Jefferson, Main & Cotton Sts., Philadelphia, Pennsylvania 19127

Jeranco, P.O. Box 1207, Canoga Park, California 91304

Jetco Electronic Industries, Incorporated, P.O. Box 26669, El Paso, Texas 79926

Keene Engineering, 11483 Vanowen Street, North Hollywood, California 91605

Kem's, 14039 Don Julian Road, La Puente, California 91746

Grace Kendrick, 485 W. Fourth Street, Fallon, Nevada 89406

Ken's Detector Service, Shidler, Oklahoma 74652

Knight Engineering Service Company, 820 W. Hyde Park Boulevard, Inglewood, California 90302

Metal Detector Sales & Rentals Company, 1582 Carmen Drive, Simi Valley, California 93065

Mineral of the Month Club, Box 487, Yucaipa, California 92399

Mother Lode Diving Shop, 2001 Capitol Avenue, Sacramento, California 95814

The Murphy Company, 17071 Ventura Boulevard, Suite 211C, Encino, California 91316

National Treasure Hunters Association, P.O. Box 110, Pocatello, Idaho 83201

National Treasure Hunters League, P.O. Box 53, Mesquite, Texas 75149

Oklahoma Treasure Hunters Supply, 1122 N. Robinson, Oklahoma City, Oklahoma 73103

The Old Prospector's Shack, 5077 Elkin Road, Union Lake, Michigan 48085

Pacific Northwest Instruments, 3104 Johns Avenue, Klamath Falls, Oregon 97601

Pan-O-Matic Corporation, 9907 S.E. 82nd Avenue, Portland, Oregon 97266

Pan Your Own Gold, Box 431, Midway City, California 92655

Planalysis, 2427 Daily Street, Los Angeles, California 90031

Petro Electronics, P.O. Box 255, Bowanda, New York 14070

Relco, P.O. Box 10839, Houston, Texas 77018

Research Products, P.O. Box 13441, Tampa, Florida 33611

Research Search & Salvage, 6140 S.W. 79 Court, Miami, Florida 33143

Rocky Mountain Detectors, P.O. Box 5366, Postal Station A, Calgary, Alberta, Canada

Roth Industries, Box 90993, Worldway, Los Angeles, California 90009

Sage Christian Enterprises, Box 326, 321 W. First Street, Park Rapids, Minnesota 56470

Sherando, P.O. Box 563, 101 Kings Highway East, Haddonfield, New Jersey 08033

Sierra Diving Center, 723 W. Fourth Street, Reno, Nevada 89503

Solco, Tennent, New Jersey 07763

Sports Alliance, Incorporated, 12016 Wilshire Boulevard, Los Angeles, California 90025

Tanner Electronic Systems Technology, Incorporated, 19428 Londelius Street, Northridge, California 91324

Tayscope Co., P.O. Box 715, North Hollywood, California 91603

Telka Enterprises, P.O. Box 82, Grafton, Wisconsin 53024

Tinker & Rasor, 417 Agostino Road, San Gabriel, California 91778

Treasure Electronics, Route 1, Box 56, Benton, Louisiana 71006

Treasure Enterprises, P.O. Box 10947, Houston, Texas 77018

Treasure Land, 38554 Groesbeck Highway, Mount Clemons, Michigan 40043

Treasure House, Tennent, New Jersey 07763

Treasure Hunting, Unlimited, 406 Broadway, Truth or Consequences, New Mexico 87901

The Treasure Shack, 8500 E. Eleventh Street, U.S. Highway 66, Tulsa, Oklahoma 74112

Treasure Sport Specialty Company, Box 345, Anoka, Minnesota 55303

Tribal Hall, Apache Junction, Arizona 85220

Kitty and Russell Umbraco, 6019 Arlington Boulevard, Richmond, California 94805

Untapped Treasures, P.O. Box 4286, Pocatello, Idaho 83201

Venn's Custom Plastics, P.O. Box 4263, Amarillo, Texas 79105

Viking Detectors, P.O. Box 10880, Houston, Texas 77018

Larry Violette, P.O. Box 74, Rehoboth, Massachusetts 02769

J.M. Warnick, 426 Stockbridge Avenue, Buffalo, New York 14215

Westbury Sales Company, P.O. Box 434, Westbury, New York 11590

Western Sports, 3030 E. Fifteenth, Spokane, Washington 99203

White's Electronics, Incorporated, 1011 Pleasant Valley Road, Sweet Home, Oregon 97386

White's Electronics, Limited, 33784 Hazel Street, Abbotsford, British Columbia, Canada

William Williams, 836 S. Bundy Drive, West Los Angeles, California 90049

WPS Enterprises, 619 California Avenue, Long Beach, California 90805

Xyzyx Information Corporation, 21116 Vanowen Street, Canoga Park, California 91303

BOOKS, DIRECTORS & PUBLISHERS

H. Glenn Carson Enterprises, 801 Juniper Avenue, Boulder, Colorado 80302

Dynamic Publications, P.O. Box 1762, San Angelo, Texas 76901

Frontier Book Company, P.O. Box 805, Fort Davis, Texas 79734

Eureka Press, P.O. Box 1215, Odessa, Texas 79670

Info Books, P.O. Box 5001, San Angelo, Texas 76901

Krause Publications, Iola, Wisconsin 54945

Northern Map Company, 2252 N. Kildare Avenue, Chicago, Illinois 60639

Old Bottle Collecting Publications, P.O. Box 276, Ashland, Oregon 97520

Old Settlers' Publishing Company, P.O. Box 4132, Panorama City, California 91412

Old Time Bottle Publishing Company, 611 Lancaster Drive, N.E., Salem, Oregon 97301

People's Publishing Company, 1440 W. Walnut Street, Compton, California 90220

Phoenix Books, 18531 Ventura Boulevard, Tarzana, California 91356

Silver Manual, P.O. Box 548, Woodville, Texas 75979

Varna Enterprises, P.O. Box 216, Van Nuys, California 91404

Western Heritage Press, 1530 Bonnie Brae, Houston, Texas 77006

PERIODICALS & MAGAZINES

The Epitaph, P.O. Box 1880, Tombstone, Arizona 85638

National Prospector's Gazette, Segundo, Colorado 81070

Treasure, 7950 Deering Avenue, Canoga Park, California 91304

Treasure Search, 7950 Deering Avenue, Canoga Park, California 91304

Treasure World, P.O. Box Drawer L, Conroe, Texas 77301

Western Treasure, 1440 W. Walnut Street, Compton, California 90220